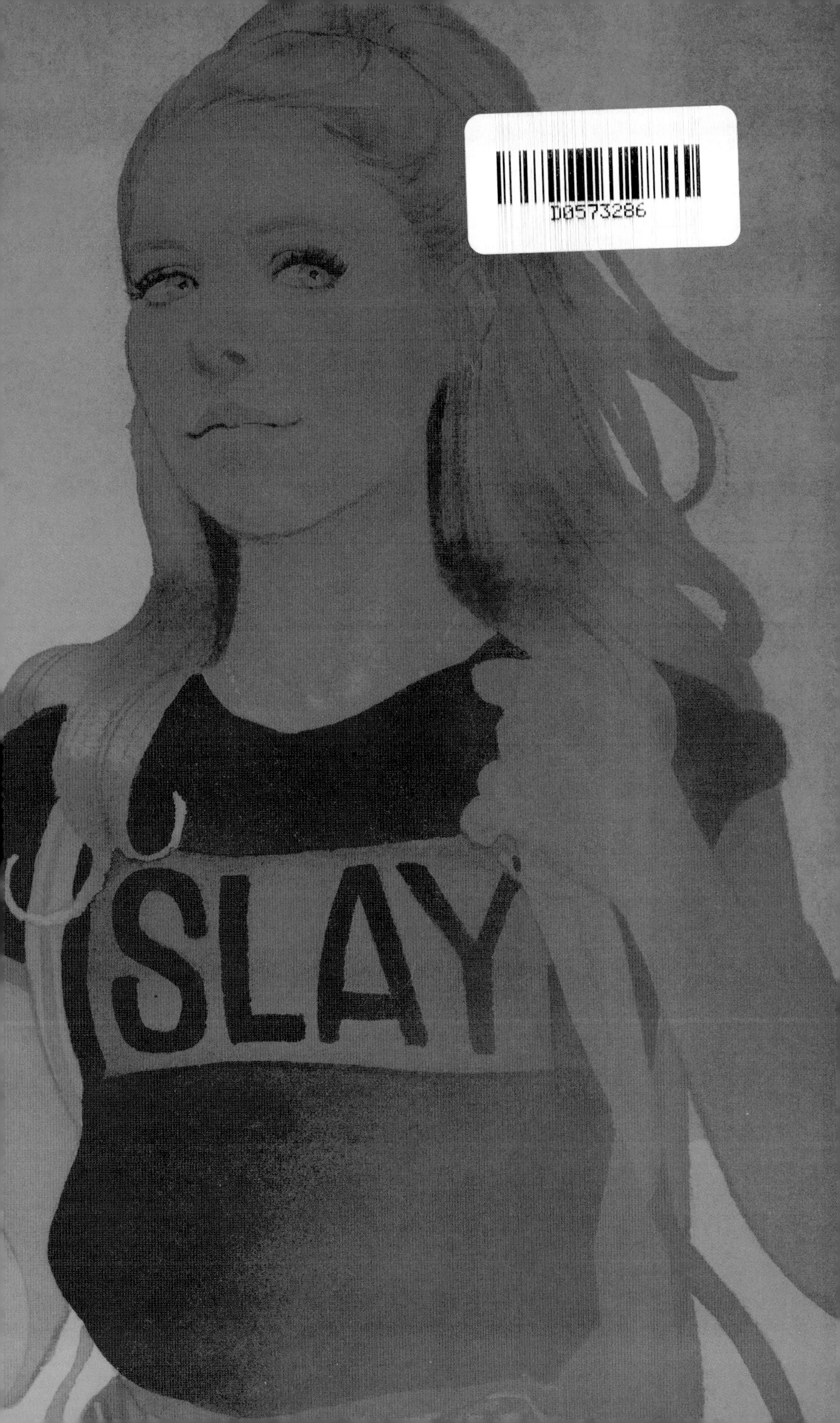
SLAY

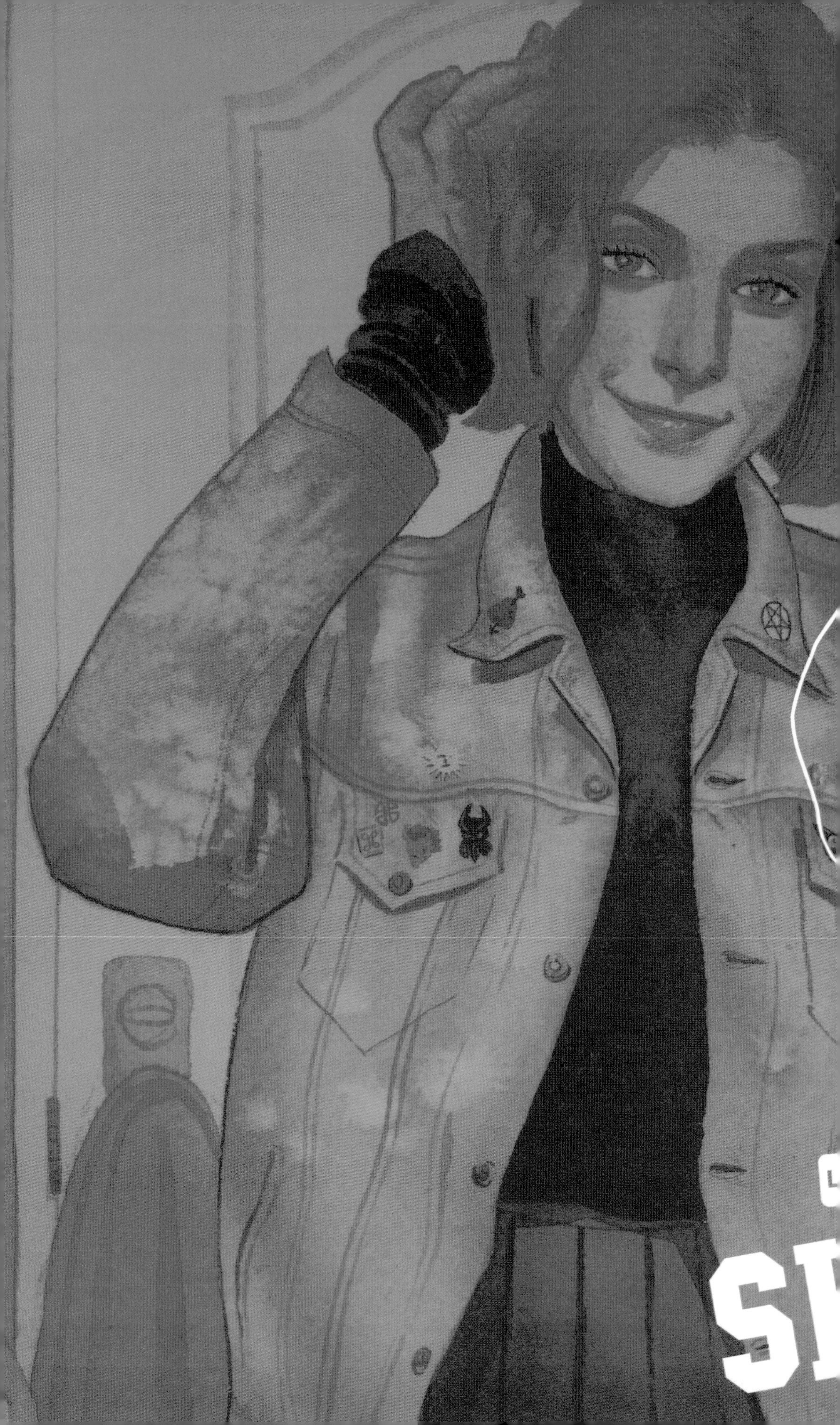

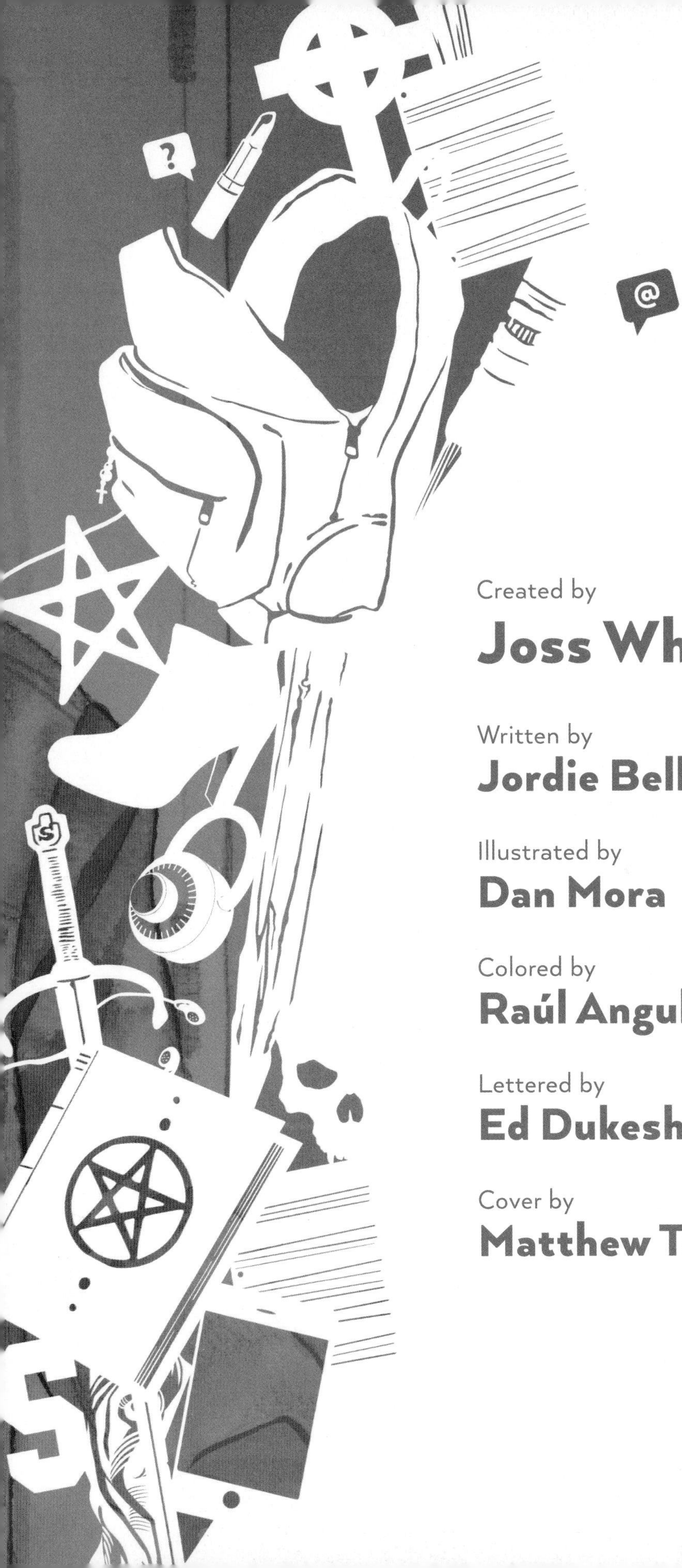

Created by
Joss Whedon

Written by
Jordie Bellaire

Illustrated by
Dan Mora

Colored by
Raúl Angulo

Lettered by
Ed Dukeshire

Cover by
Matthew Taylor

CHAPTER ONE

Issue One Cover by **Matthew Taylor**

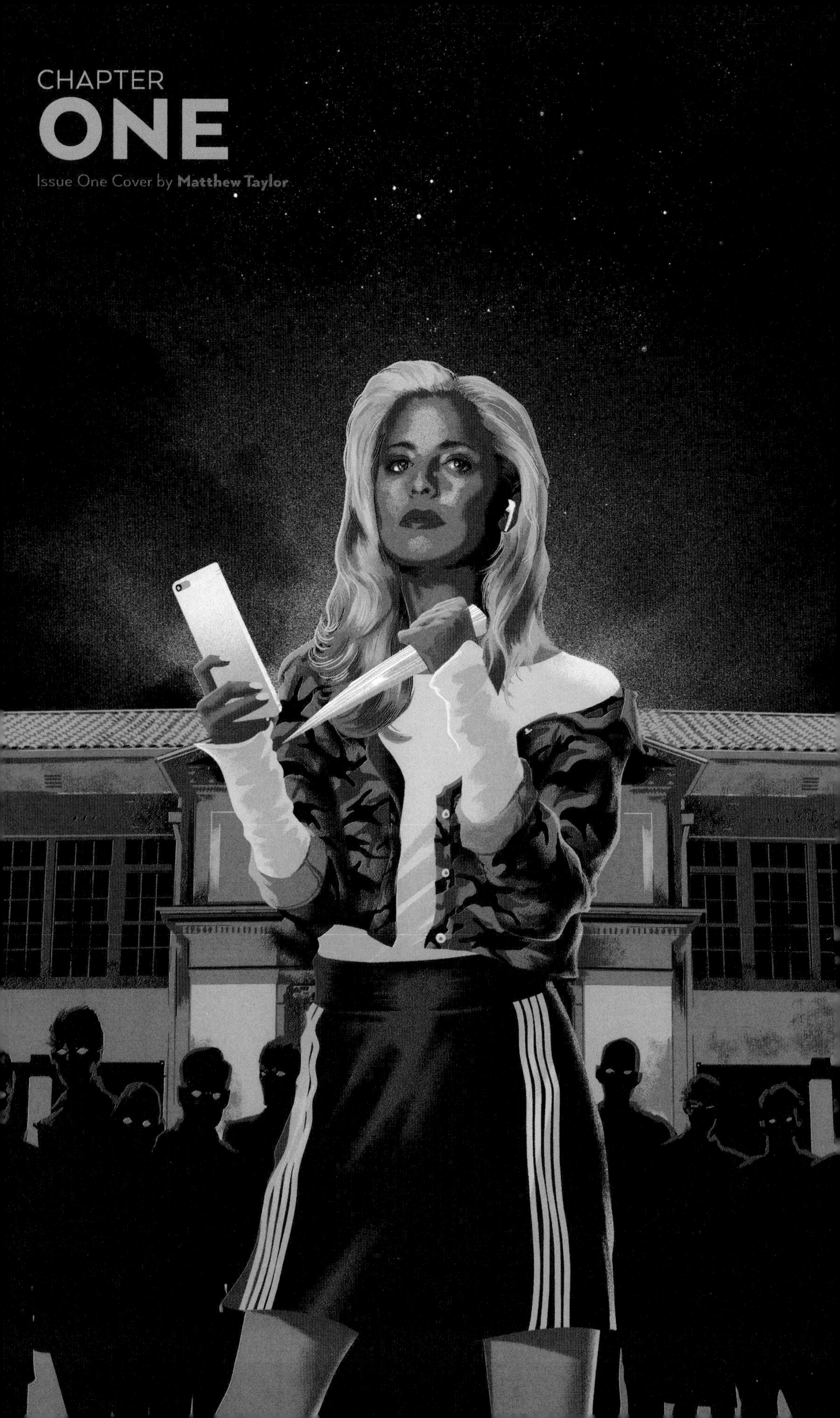

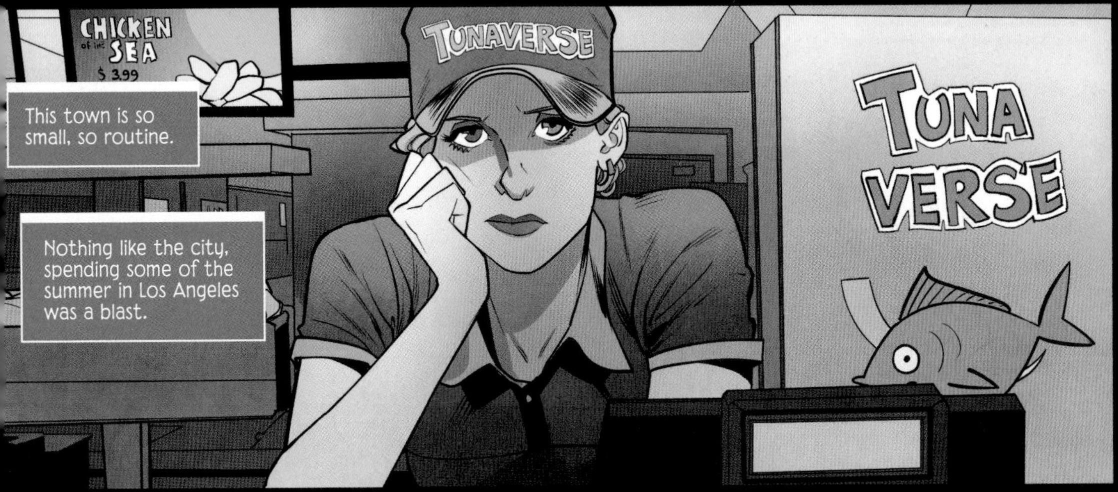
CHICKEN OF THE SEA $3.99
TUNAVERSE
This town is so small, so routine.
Nothing like the city, spending some of the summer in Los Angeles was a blast.
TUNA VERSE

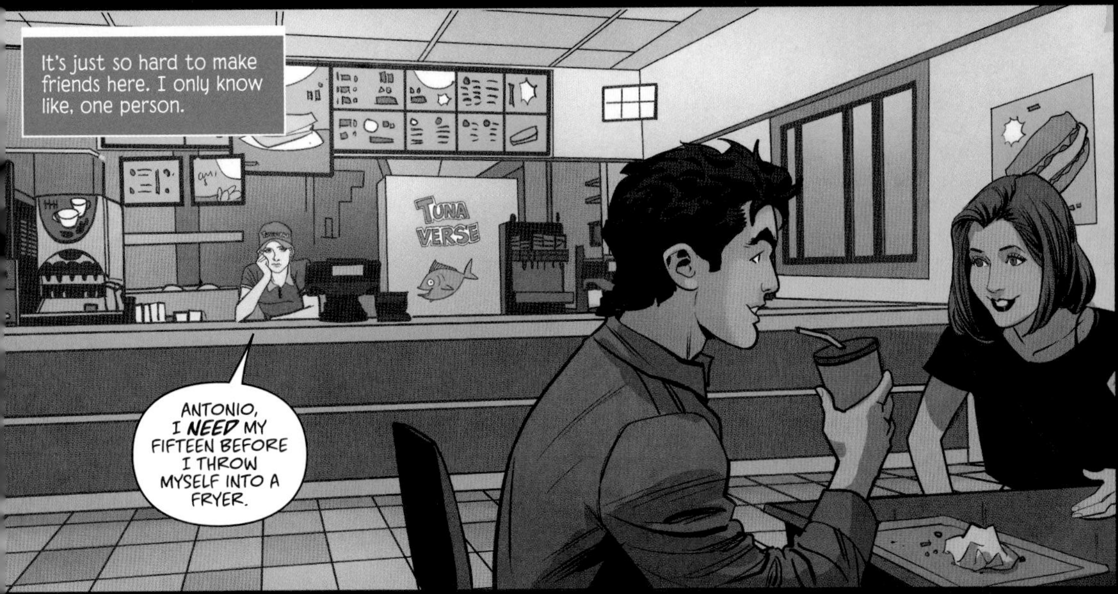
It's just so hard to make friends here. I only know like, one person.
TUNA VERSE
ANTONIO, I NEED MY FIFTEEN BEFORE I THROW MYSELF INTO A FRYER.

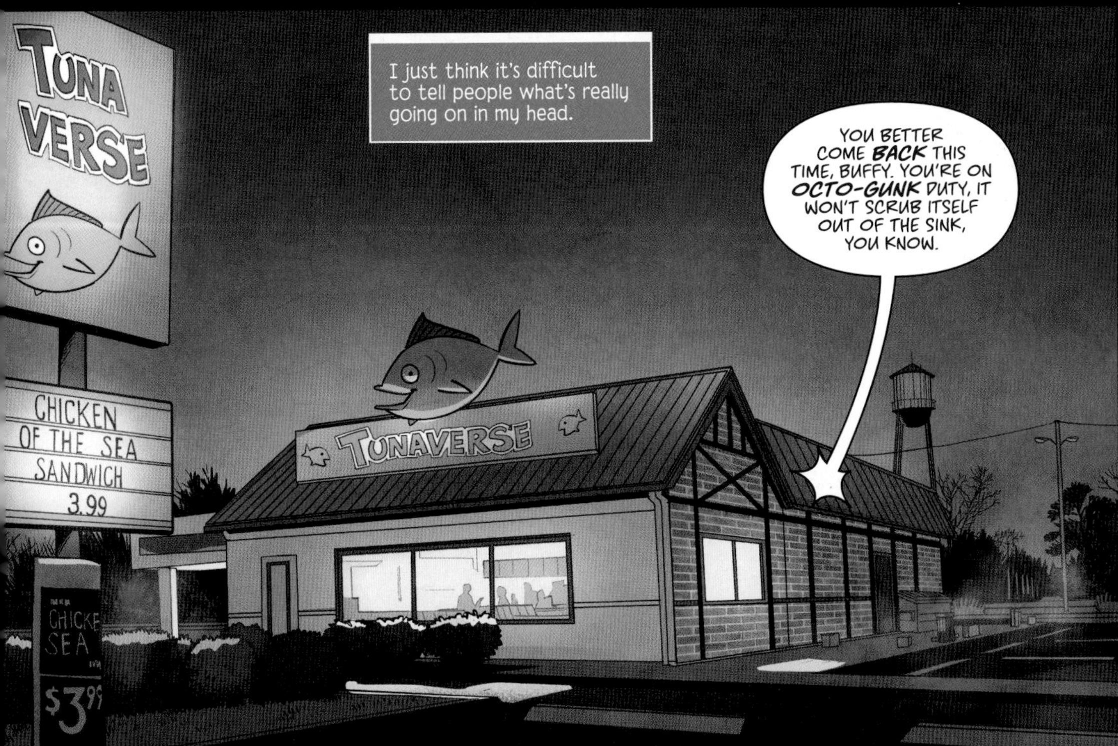
TUNA VERSE
I just think it's difficult to tell people what's really going on in my head.
YOU BETTER COME BACK THIS TIME, BUFFY. YOU'RE ON OCTO-GUNK DUTY, IT WON'T SCRUB ITSELF OUT OF THE SINK, YOU KNOW.
CHICKEN OF THE SEA SANDWICH 3.99
TUNAVERSE
$3.99

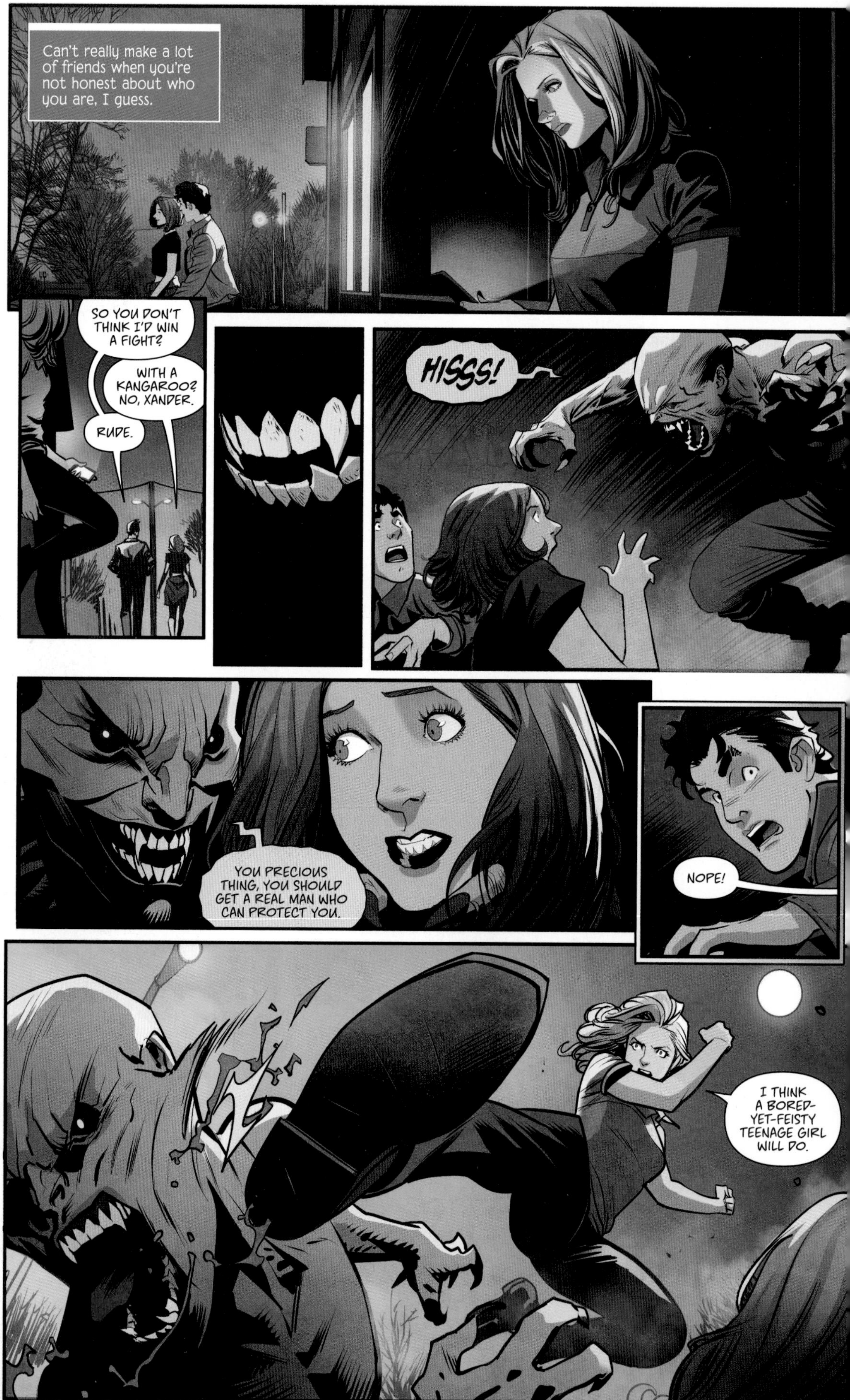
Can't really make a lot of friends when you're not honest about who you are, I guess.
SO YOU DON'T THINK I'D WIN A FIGHT?
WITH A KANGAROO? NO, XANDER.
RUDE.
HISSS!
YOU PRECIOUS THING, YOU SHOULD GET A REAL MAN WHO CAN PROTECT YOU.
NOPE!
I THINK A BORED-YET-FEISTY TEENAGE GIRL WILL DO.

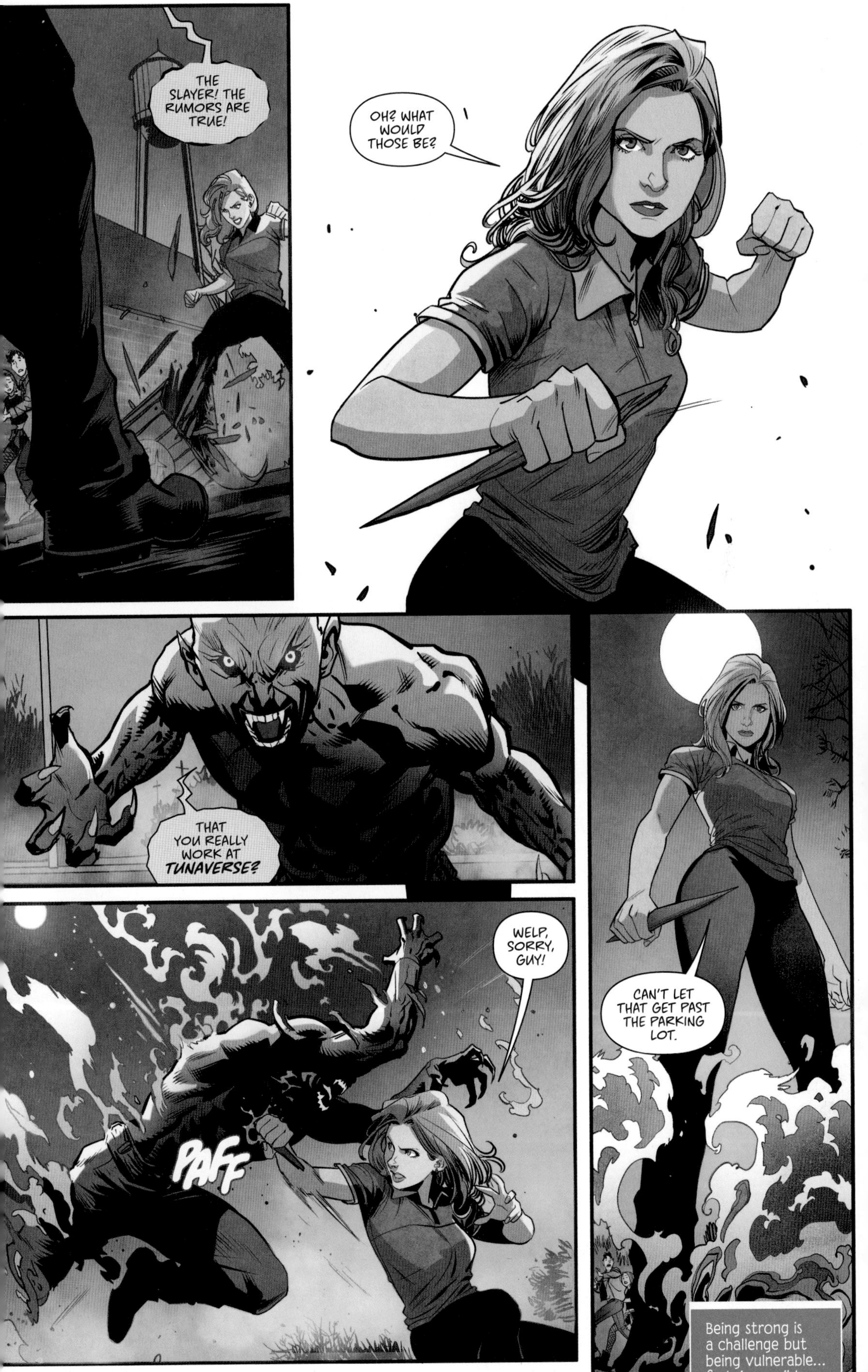

THE SLAYER! THE RUMORS ARE TRUE!
OH? WHAT WOULD THOSE BE?
THAT YOU REALLY WORK AT *TUNAVERSE?*
WELP, SORRY, GUY!
PAFF
CAN'T LET THAT GET PAST THE PARKING LOT.
Being strong is a challenge but being vulnerable... feels impossible.

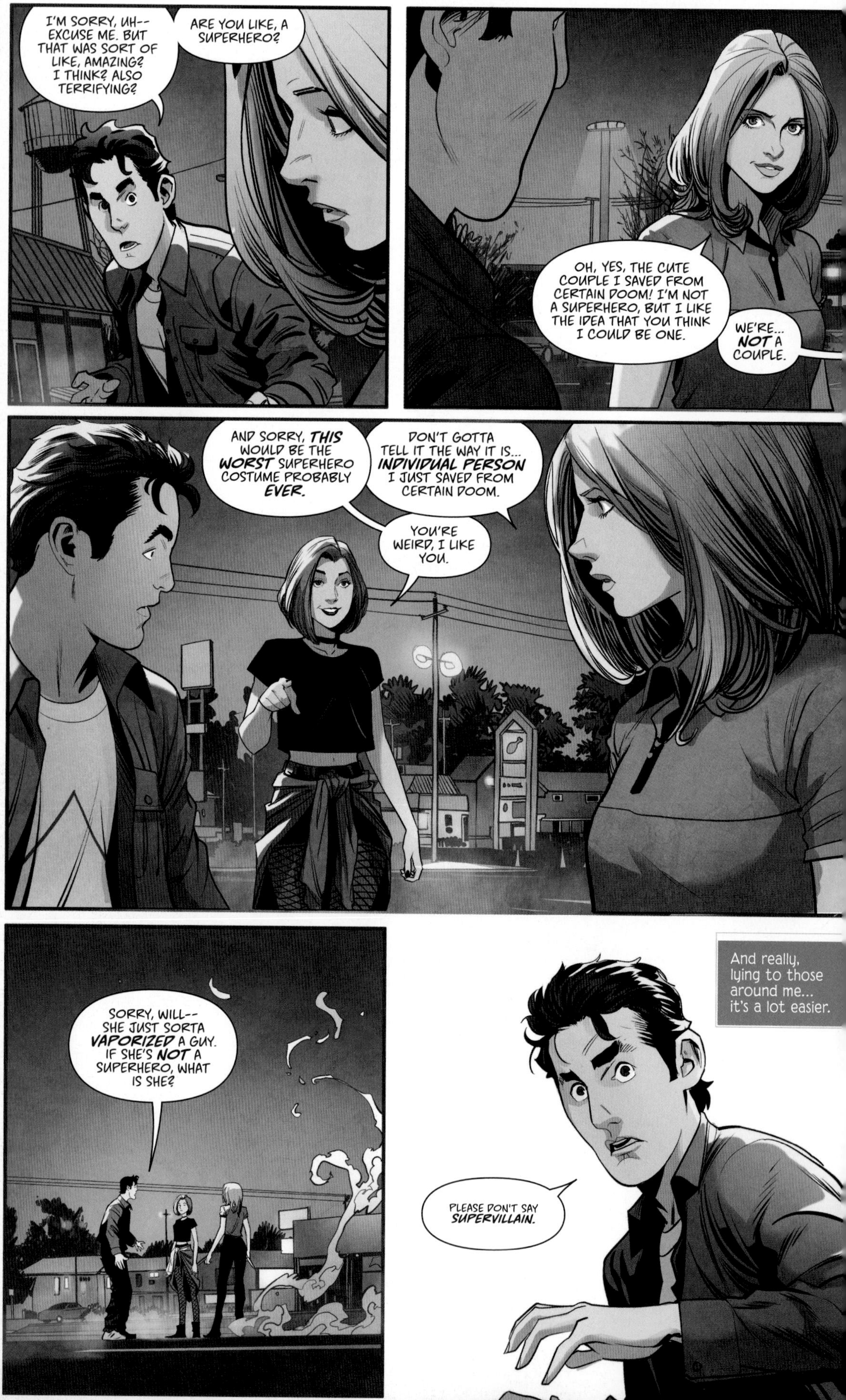
I'M SORRY, UH-- EXCUSE ME. BUT THAT WAS SORT OF LIKE, AMAZING? I THINK? ALSO TERRIFYING?
ARE YOU LIKE, A SUPERHERO?
OH, YES, THE CUTE COUPLE I SAVED FROM CERTAIN DOOM! I'M NOT A SUPERHERO, BUT I LIKE THE IDEA THAT YOU THINK I COULD BE ONE.
WE'RE... NOT A COUPLE.
AND SORRY, THIS WOULD BE THE WORST SUPERHERO COSTUME PROBABLY EVER.
DON'T GOTTA TELL IT THE WAY IT IS... INDIVIDUAL PERSON I JUST SAVED FROM CERTAIN DOOM.
YOU'RE WEIRD, I LIKE YOU.
SORRY, WILL-- SHE JUST SORTA VAPORIZED A GUY. IF SHE'S NOT A SUPERHERO, WHAT IS SHE?
And really, lying to those around me... it's a lot easier.
PLEASE DON'T SAY SUPERVILLAIN.

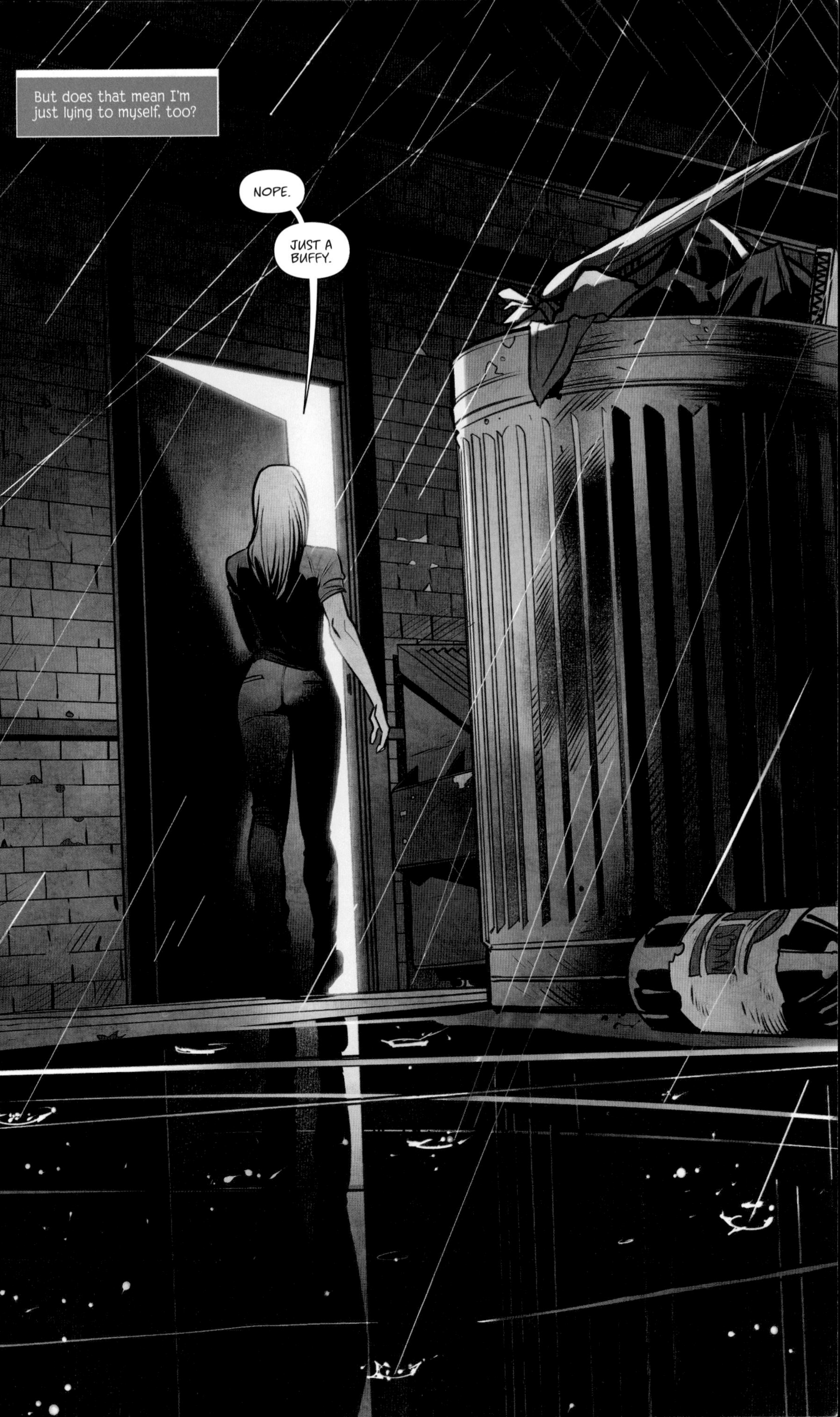
But does that mean I'm just lying to myself, too?
NOPE.
JUST A BUFFY.

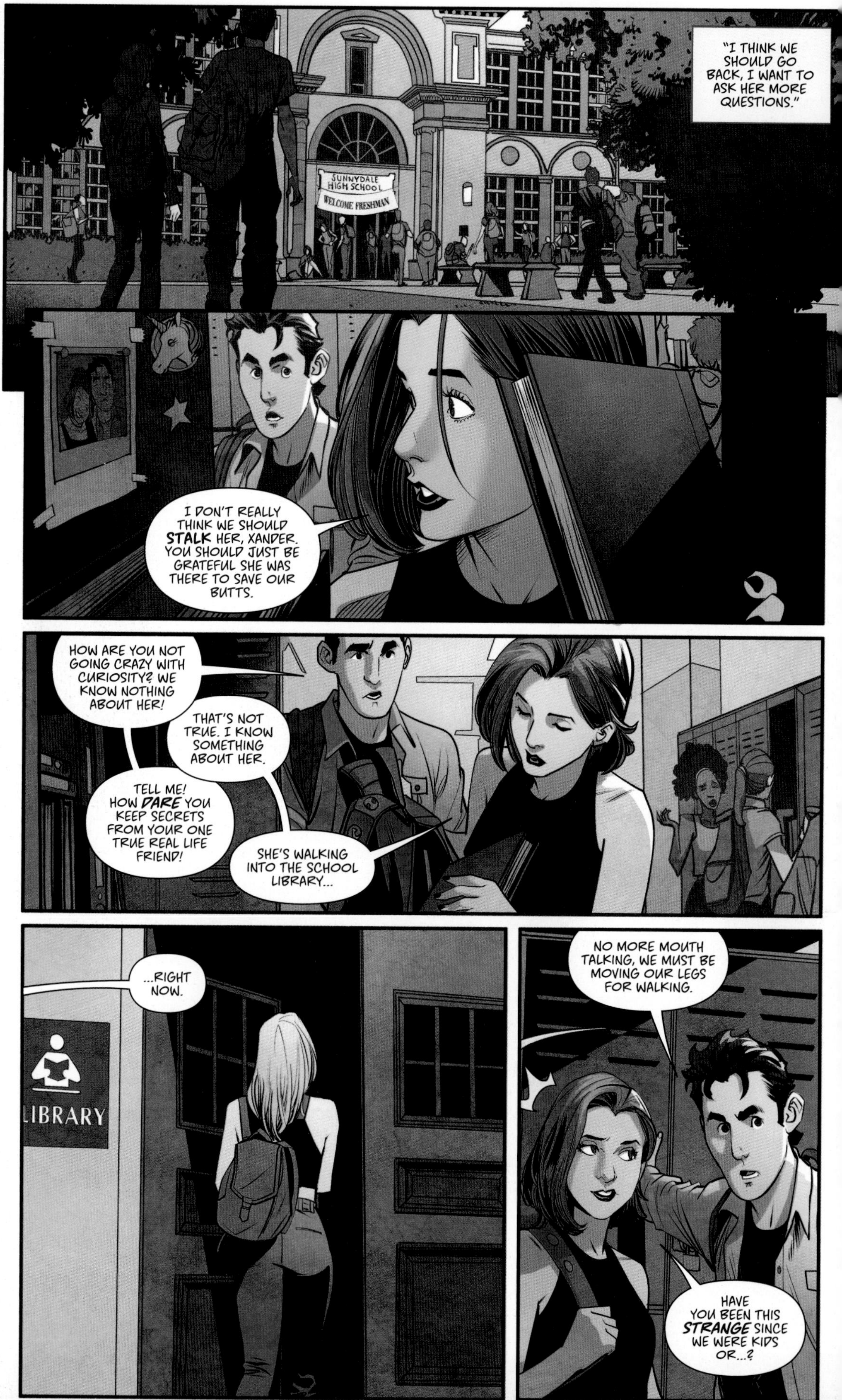
"I THINK WE SHOULD GO BACK, I WANT TO ASK HER MORE QUESTIONS."
SUNNYDALE HIGH SCHOOL
WELCOME FRESHMAN
I DON'T REALLY THINK WE SHOULD STALK HER, XANDER. YOU SHOULD JUST BE GRATEFUL SHE WAS THERE TO SAVE OUR BUTTS.
HOW ARE YOU NOT GOING CRAZY WITH CURIOSITY? WE KNOW NOTHING ABOUT HER!
THAT'S NOT TRUE. I KNOW SOMETHING ABOUT HER.
TELL ME! HOW DARE YOU KEEP SECRETS FROM YOUR ONE TRUE REAL LIFE FRIEND!
SHE'S WALKING INTO THE SCHOOL LIBRARY...
...RIGHT NOW.
LIBRARY
NO MORE MOUTH TALKING, WE MUST BE MOVING OUR LEGS FOR WALKING.
HAVE YOU BEEN THIS STRANGE SINCE WE WERE KIDS OR...?

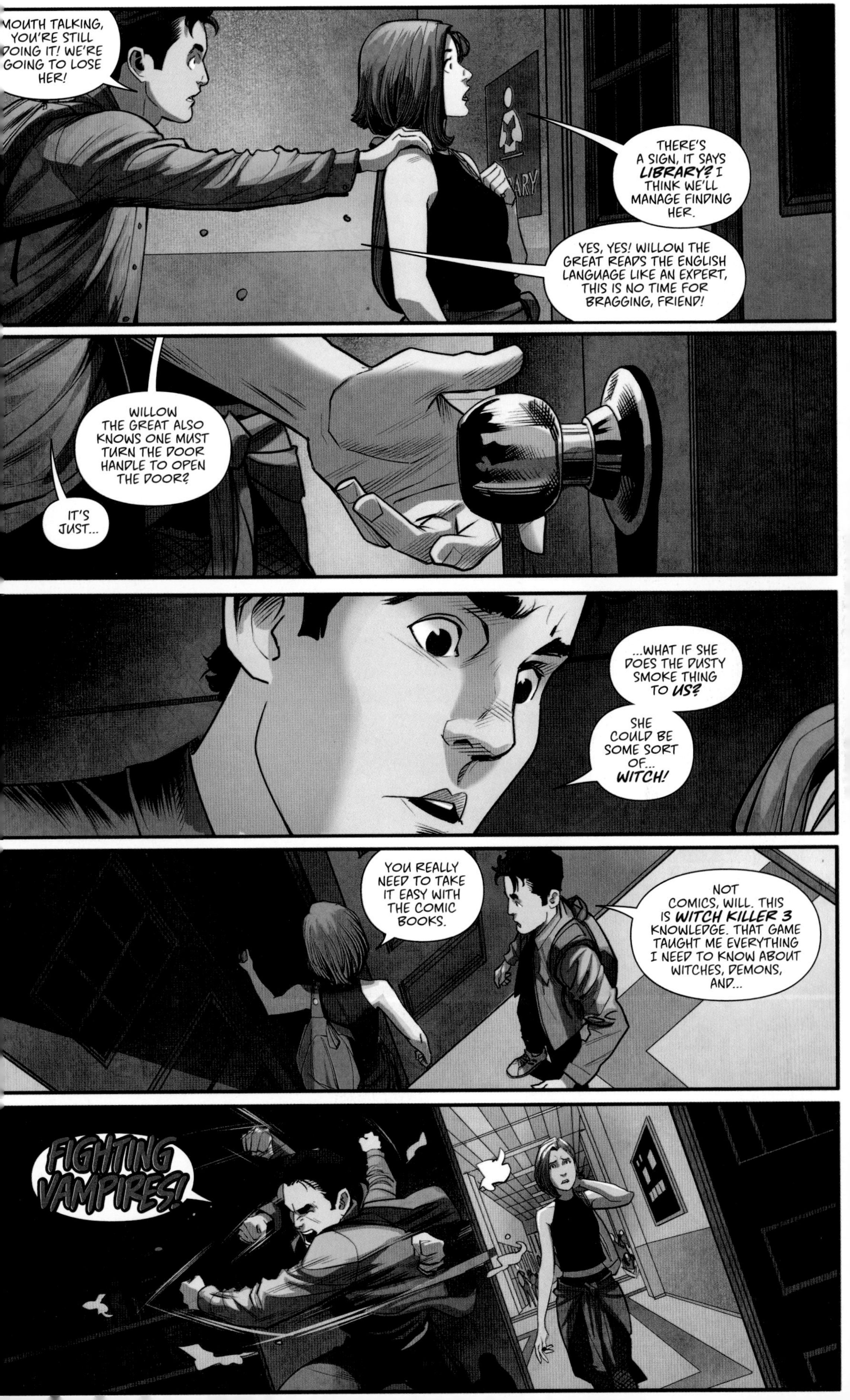
MOUTH TALKING, YOU'RE STILL DOING IT! WE'RE GOING TO LOSE HER!
THERE'S A SIGN, IT SAYS LIBRARY? I THINK WE'LL MANAGE FINDING HER.
YES, YES! WILLOW THE GREAT READS THE ENGLISH LANGUAGE LIKE AN EXPERT, THIS IS NO TIME FOR BRAGGING, FRIEND!
WILLOW THE GREAT ALSO KNOWS ONE MUST TURN THE DOOR HANDLE TO OPEN THE DOOR?
IT'S JUST...
...WHAT IF SHE DOES THE DUSTY SMOKE THING TO US?
SHE COULD BE SOME SORT OF... WITCH!
YOU REALLY NEED TO TAKE IT EASY WITH THE COMIC BOOKS.
NOT COMICS, WILL. THIS IS WITCH KILLER 3 KNOWLEDGE. THAT GAME TAUGHT ME EVERYTHING I NEED TO KNOW ABOUT WITCHES, DEMONS, AND...
FIGHTING VAMPIRES!

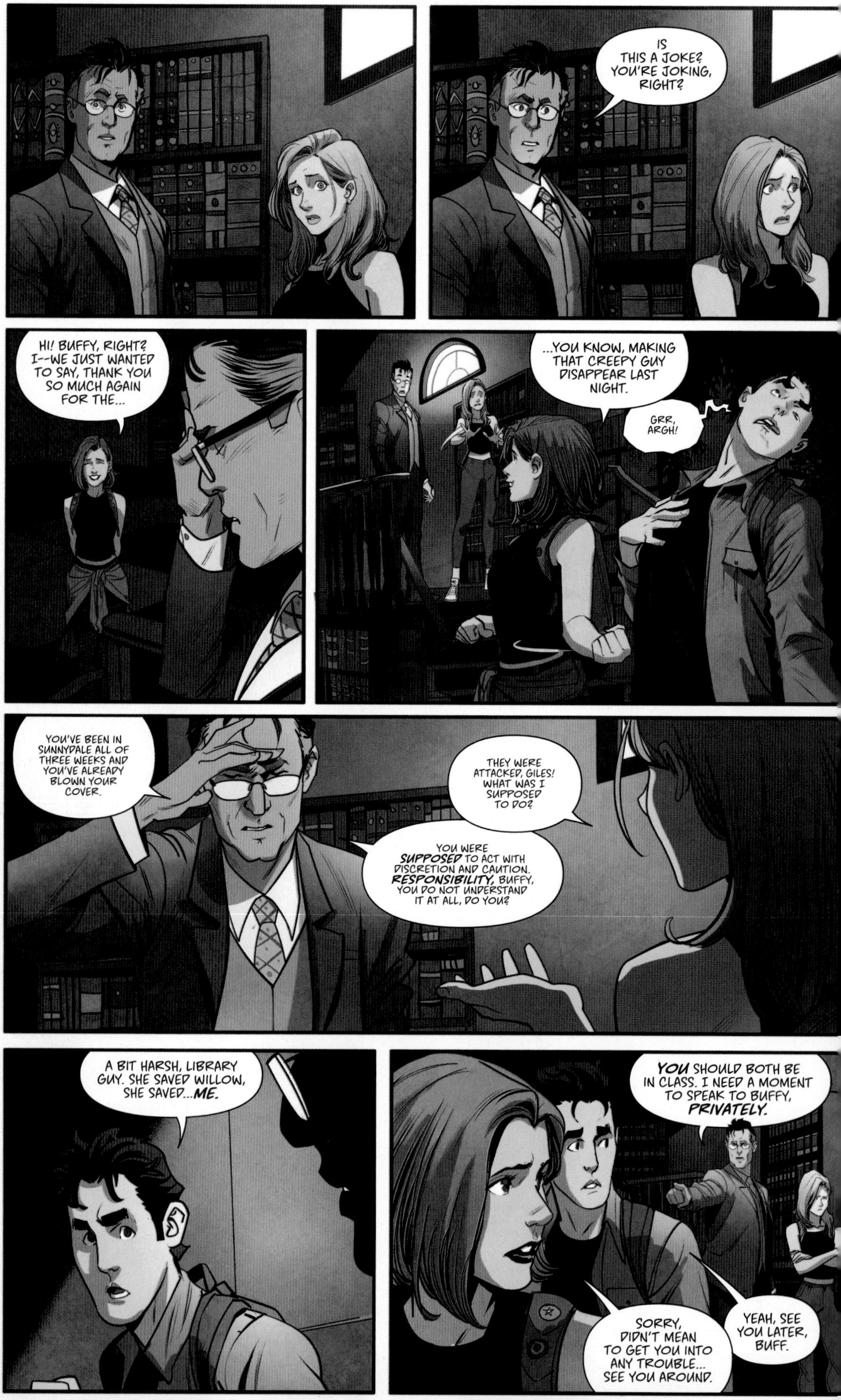
IS THIS A JOKE? YOU'RE JOKING, RIGHT?
HI! BUFFY, RIGHT? I--WE JUST WANTED TO SAY, THANK YOU SO MUCH AGAIN FOR THE...
...YOU KNOW, MAKING THAT CREEPY GUY DISAPPEAR LAST NIGHT.
GRR, ARGH!
YOU'VE BEEN IN SUNNYDALE ALL OF THREE WEEKS AND YOU'VE ALREADY BLOWN YOUR COVER.
THEY WERE ATTACKED, GILES! WHAT WAS I SUPPOSED TO DO?
YOU WERE SUPPOSED TO ACT WITH DISCRETION AND CAUTION. RESPONSIBILITY, BUFFY, YOU DO NOT UNDERSTAND IT AT ALL, DO YOU?
A BIT HARSH, LIBRARY GUY. SHE SAVED WILLOW, SHE SAVED...ME.
YOU SHOULD BOTH BE IN CLASS. I NEED A MOMENT TO SPEAK TO BUFFY, PRIVATELY.
SORRY, DIDN'T MEAN TO GET YOU INTO ANY TROUBLE... SEE YOU AROUND.
YEAH, SEE YOU LATER, BUFF.

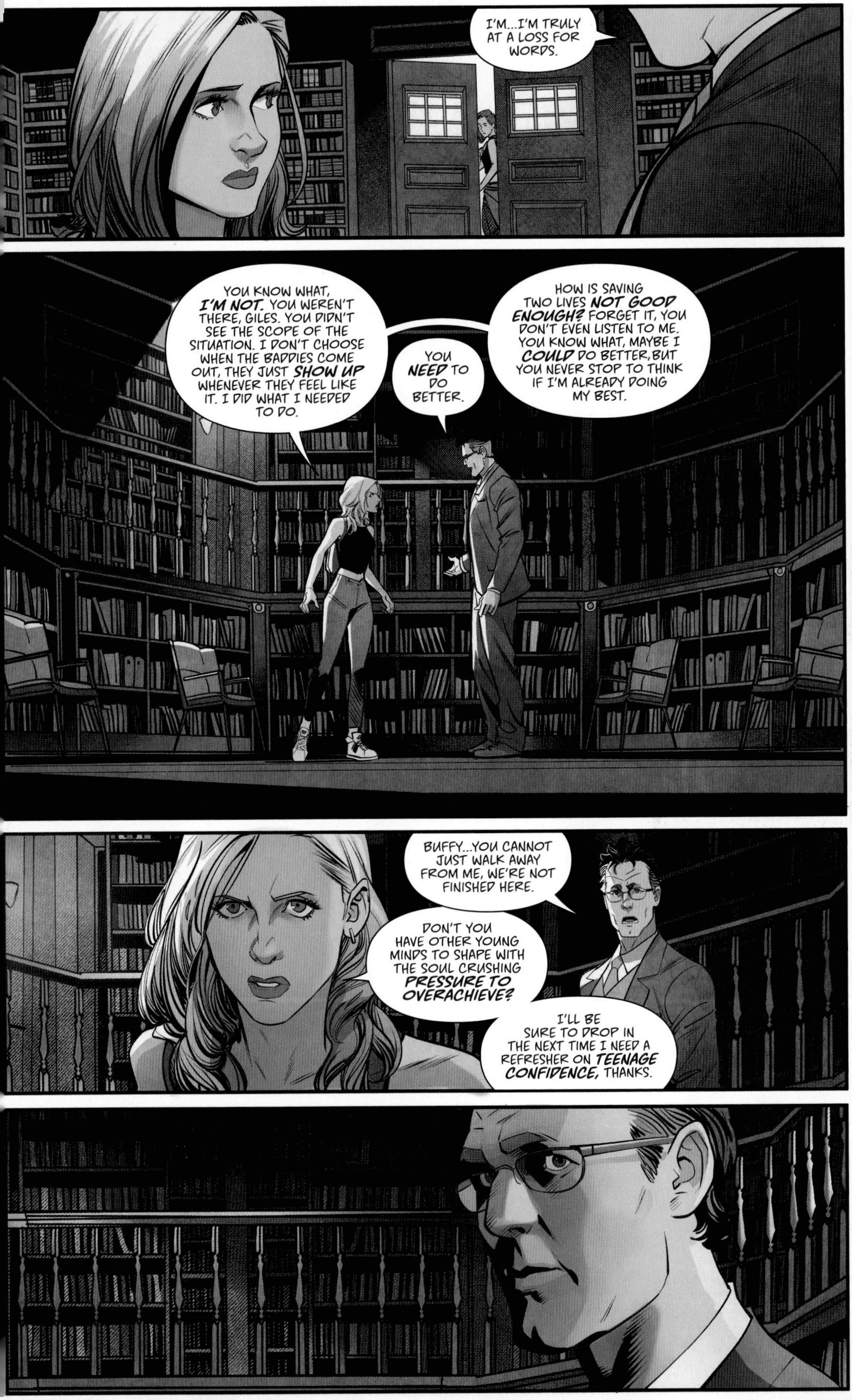
I'M...I'M TRULY AT A LOSS FOR WORDS.
YOU KNOW WHAT, I'M NOT. YOU WEREN'T THERE, GILES. YOU DIDN'T SEE THE SCOPE OF THE SITUATION. I DON'T CHOOSE WHEN THE BADDIES COME OUT, THEY JUST SHOW UP WHENEVER THEY FEEL LIKE IT. I DID WHAT I NEEDED TO DO.
YOU NEED TO DO BETTER.
HOW IS SAVING TWO LIVES NOT GOOD ENOUGH? FORGET IT, YOU DON'T EVEN LISTEN TO ME. YOU KNOW WHAT, MAYBE I COULD DO BETTER, BUT YOU NEVER STOP TO THINK IF I'M ALREADY DOING MY BEST.
BUFFY...YOU CANNOT JUST WALK AWAY FROM ME, WE'RE NOT FINISHED HERE.
DON'T YOU HAVE OTHER YOUNG MINDS TO SHAPE WITH THE SOUL CRUSHING PRESSURE TO OVERACHIEVE?
I'LL BE SURE TO DROP IN THE NEXT TIME I NEED A REFRESHER ON TEENAGE CONFIDENCE, THANKS.

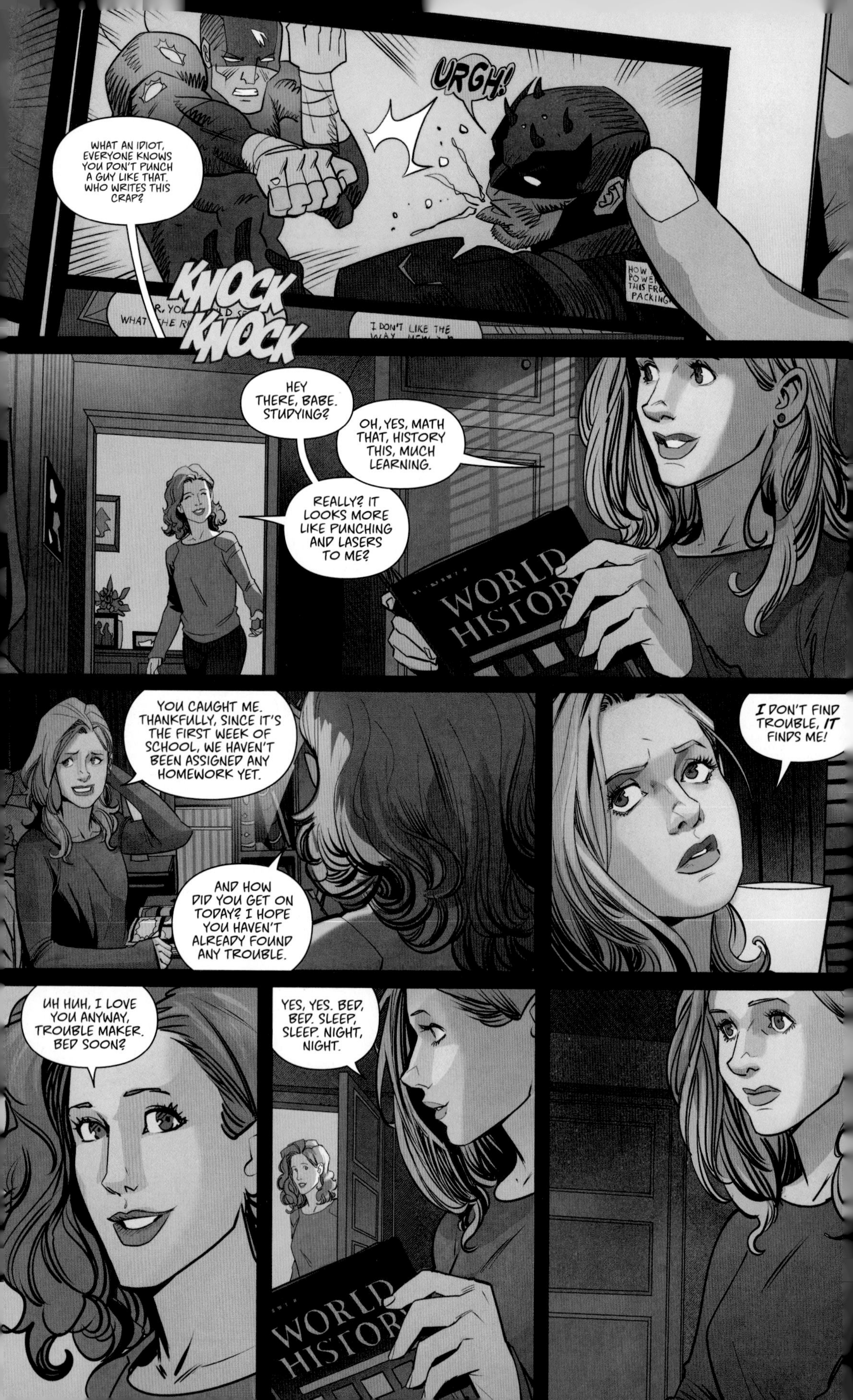
URGH!
WHAT AN IDIOT, EVERYONE KNOWS YOU DON'T PUNCH A GUY LIKE THAT. WHO WRITES THIS CRAP?
KNOCK KNOCK
HEY THERE, BABE. STUDYING?
OH, YES, MATH THAT, HISTORY THIS, MUCH LEARNING.
REALLY? IT LOOKS MORE LIKE PUNCHING AND LASERS TO ME?
WORLD HISTORY
YOU CAUGHT ME. THANKFULLY, SINCE IT'S THE FIRST WEEK OF SCHOOL, WE HAVEN'T BEEN ASSIGNED ANY HOMEWORK YET.
AND HOW DID YOU GET ON TODAY? I HOPE YOU HAVEN'T ALREADY FOUND ANY TROUBLE.
I DON'T FIND TROUBLE, IT FINDS ME!
UH HUH, I LOVE YOU ANYWAY, TROUBLE MAKER. BED SOON?
YES, YES. BED, BED. SLEEP, SLEEP. NIGHT, NIGHT.
WORLD HISTORY

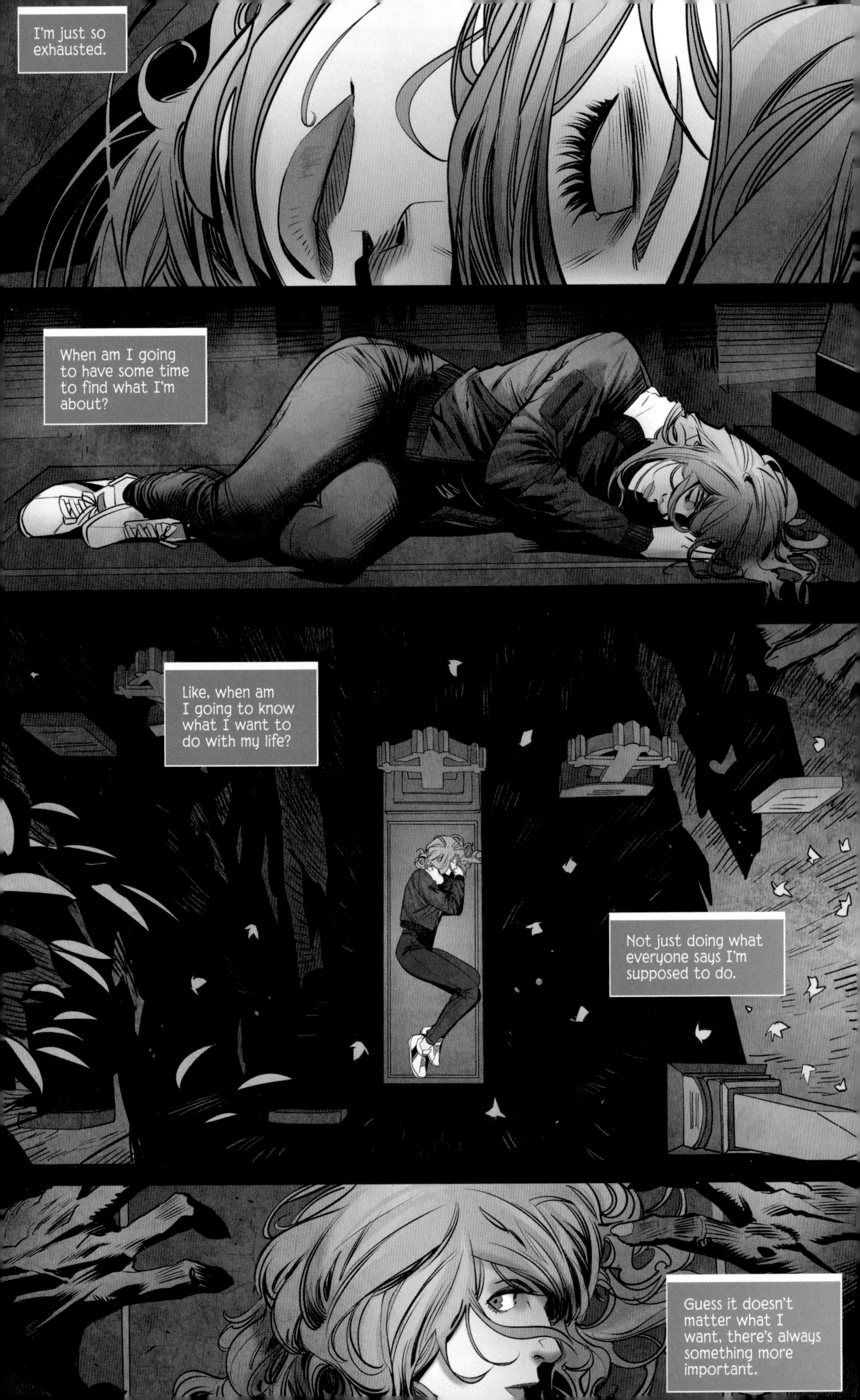
I'm just so exhausted.
When am I going to have some time to find what I'm about?
Like, when am I going to know what I want to do with my life?
Not just doing what everyone says I'm supposed to do.
Guess it doesn't matter what I want, there's always something more important.

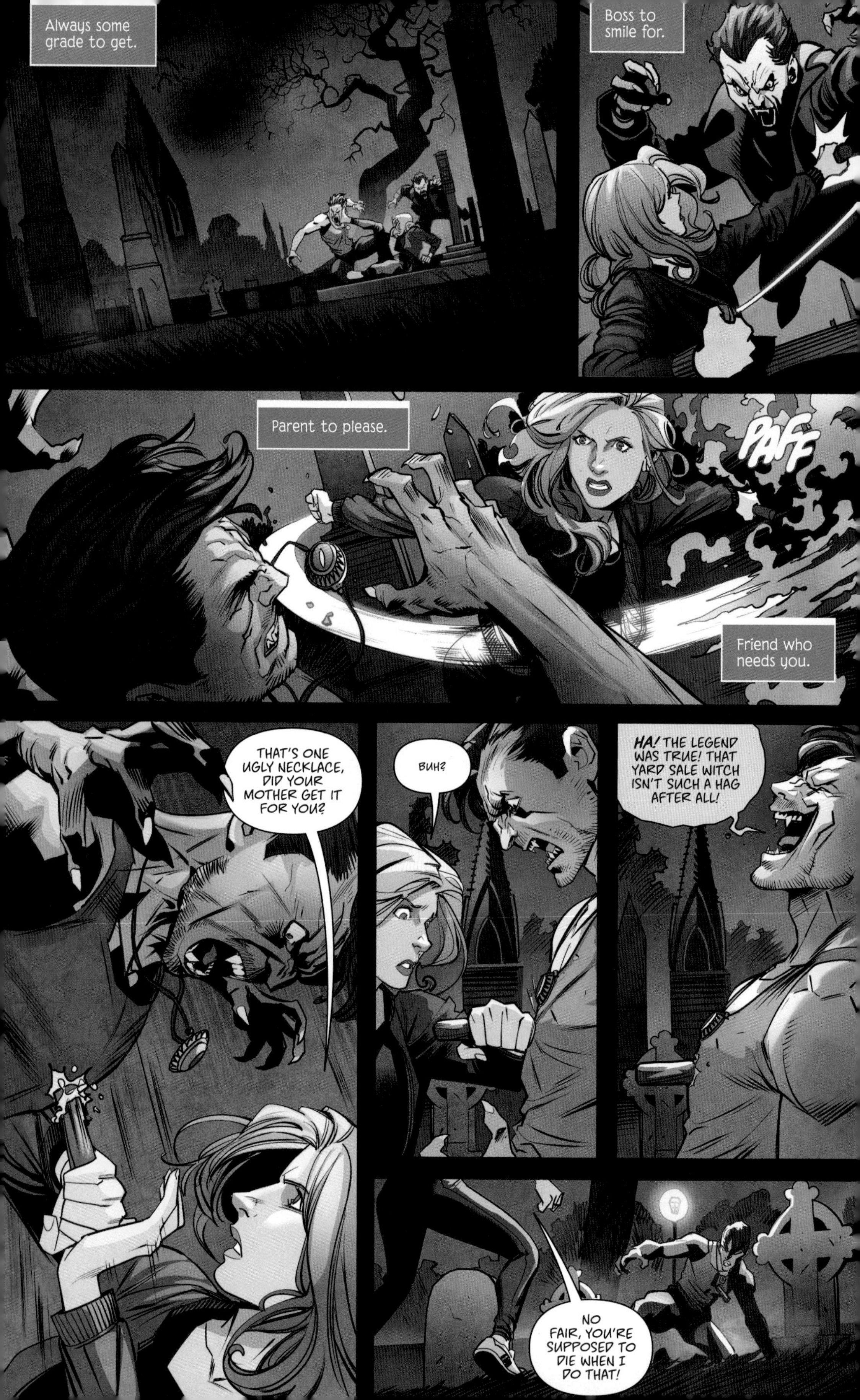
Always some grade to get.
Boss to smile for.
Parent to please.
PAFF
Friend who needs you.
THAT'S ONE UGLY NECKLACE, DID YOUR MOTHER GET IT FOR YOU?
BUH?
HA! THE LEGEND WAS TRUE! THAT YARD SALE WITCH ISN'T SUCH A HAG AFTER ALL!
NO FAIR, YOU'RE SUPPOSED TO DIE WHEN I DO THAT!

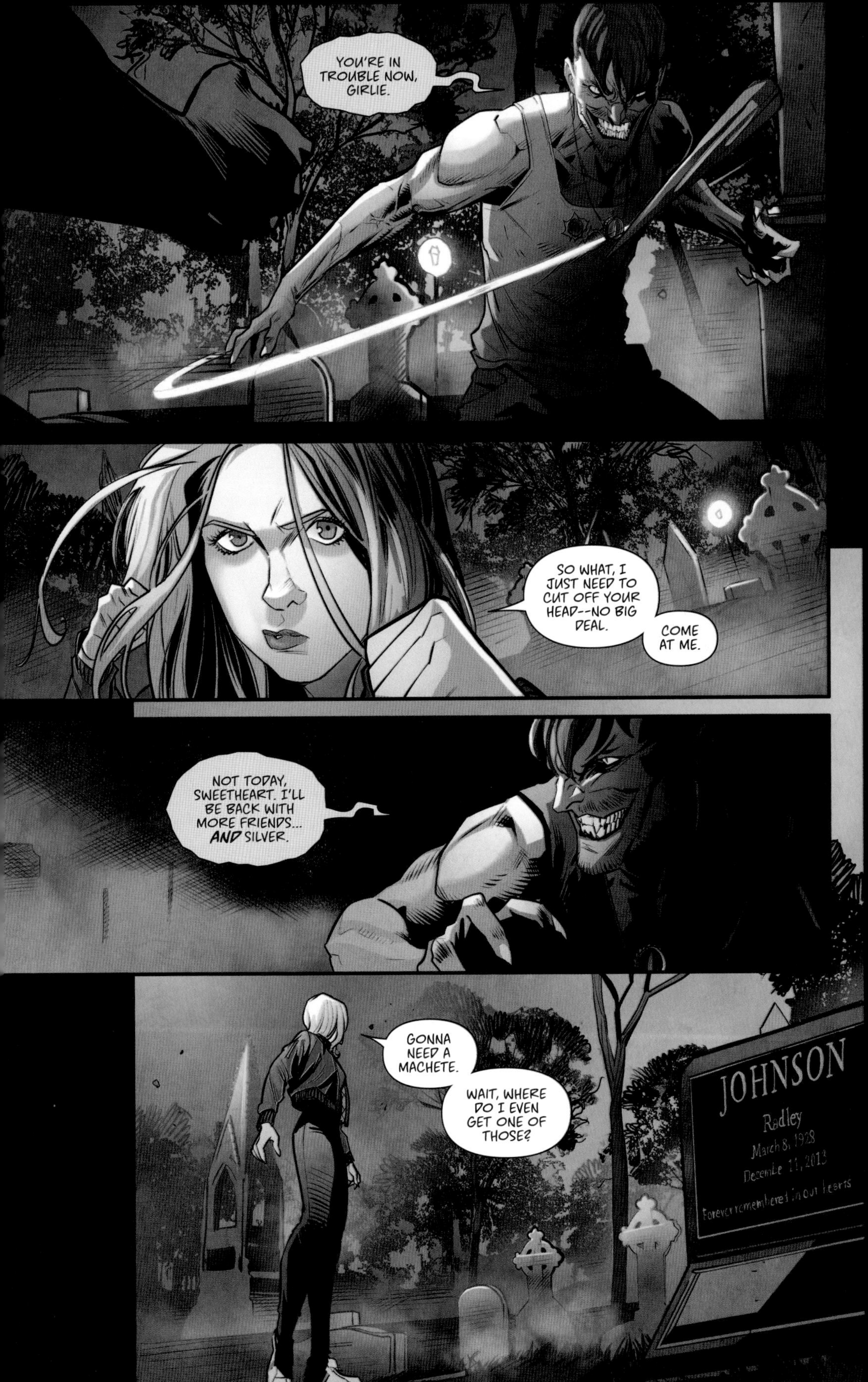
YOU'RE IN TROUBLE NOW, GIRLIE.
SO WHAT, I JUST NEED TO CUT OFF YOUR HEAD--NO BIG DEAL.
COME AT ME.
NOT TODAY, SWEETHEART. I'LL BE BACK WITH MORE FRIENDS... ***AND*** SILVER.
GONNA NEED A MACHETE.
WAIT, WHERE DO I EVEN GET ONE OF THOSE?
JOHNSON
Radley
March 8, 1928
Decembe 11, 2013
Forever remembered in our hearts

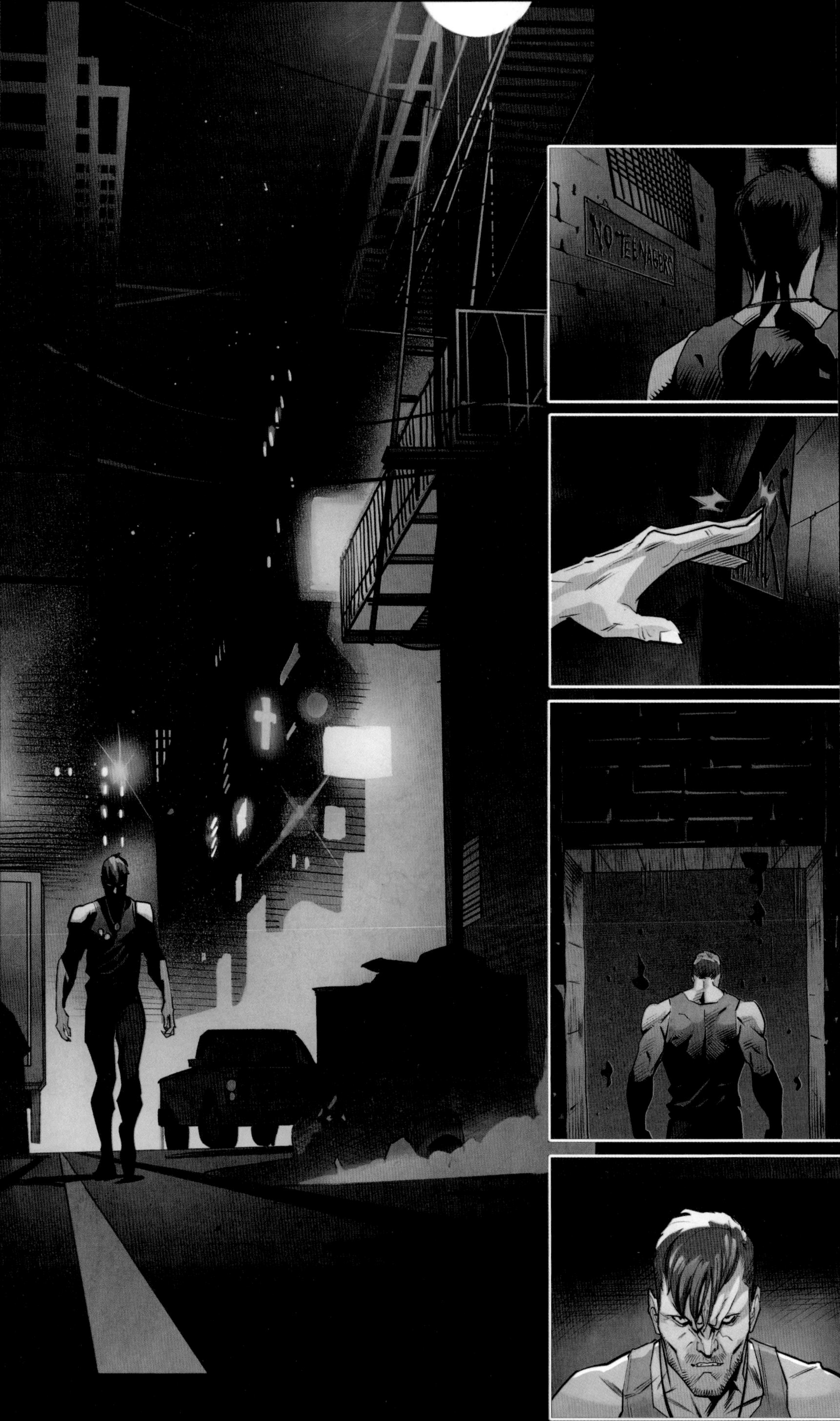
NO TEENAGERS

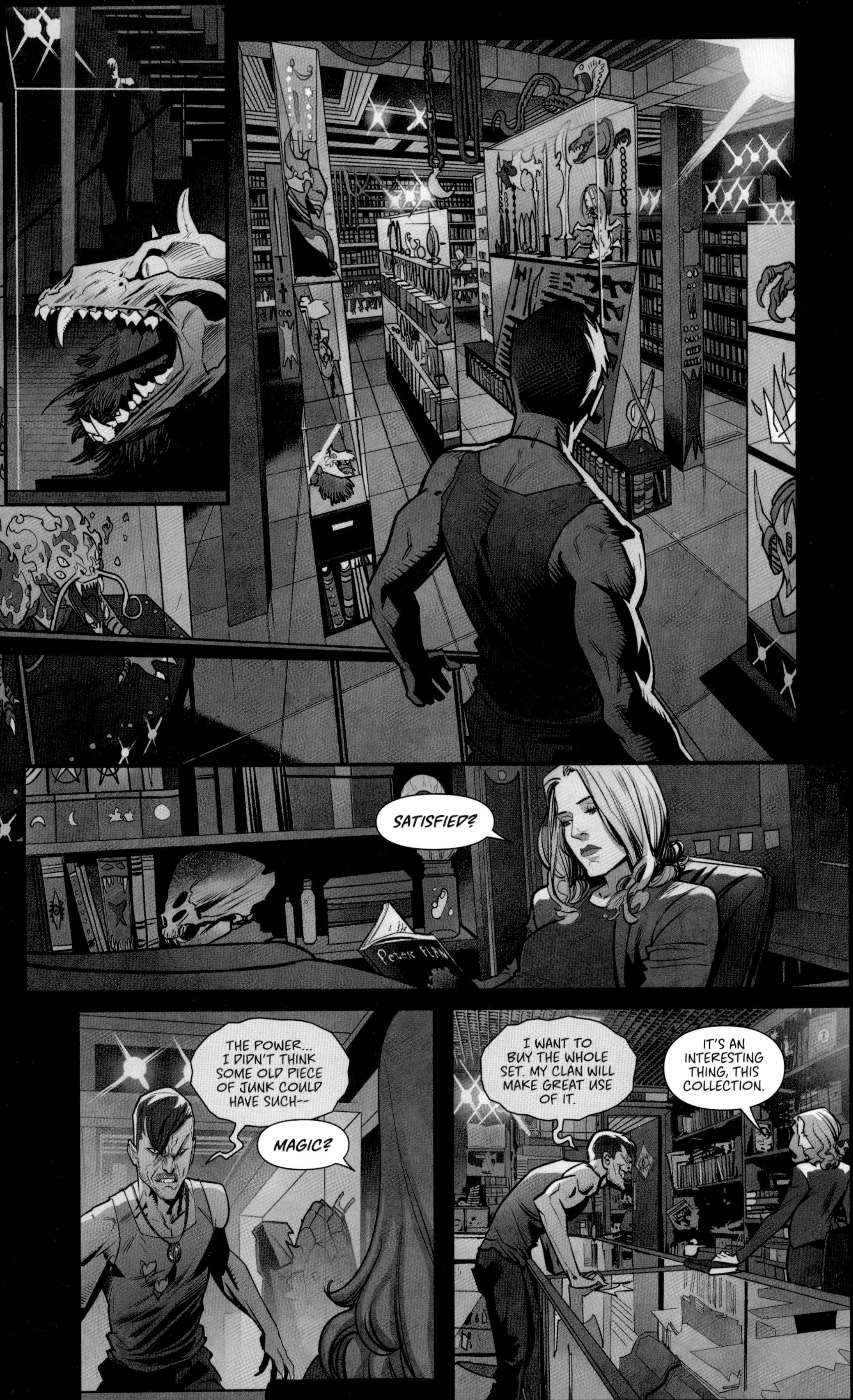
SATISFIED?
Peter FLAN
THE POWER... I DIDN'T THINK SOME OLD PIECE OF JUNK COULD HAVE SUCH--
MAGIC?
I WANT TO BUY THE WHOLE SET. MY CLAN WILL MAKE GREAT USE OF IT.
IT'S AN INTERESTING THING, THIS COLLECTION.

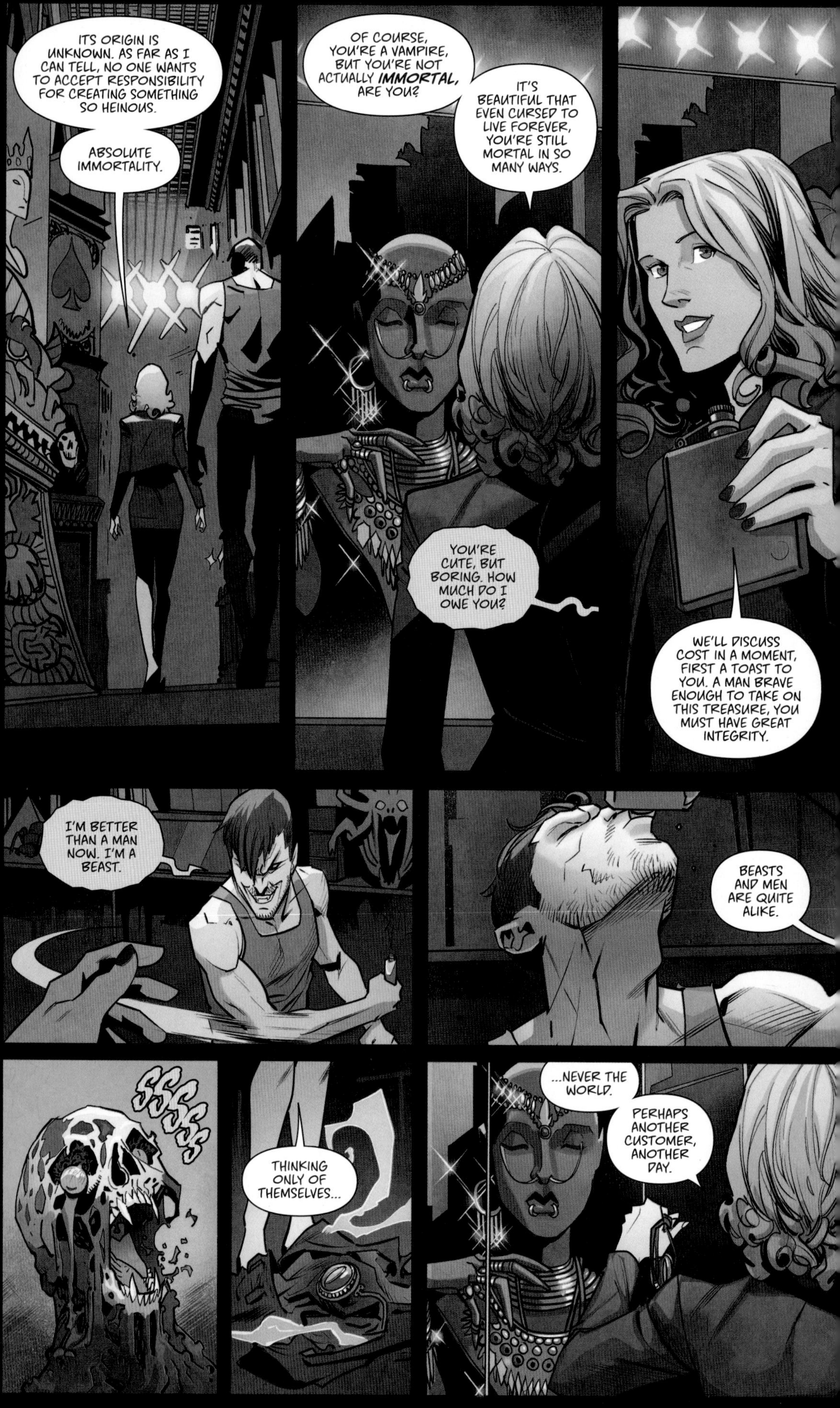
ITS ORIGIN IS UNKNOWN. AS FAR AS I CAN TELL, NO ONE WANTS TO ACCEPT RESPONSIBILITY FOR CREATING SOMETHING SO HEINOUS.
ABSOLUTE IMMORTALITY.
OF COURSE, YOU'RE A VAMPIRE, BUT YOU'RE NOT ACTUALLY IMMORTAL, ARE YOU?
IT'S BEAUTIFUL THAT EVEN CURSED TO LIVE FOREVER, YOU'RE STILL MORTAL IN SO MANY WAYS.
YOU'RE CUTE, BUT BORING. HOW MUCH DO I OWE YOU?
WE'LL DISCUSS COST IN A MOMENT, FIRST A TOAST TO YOU. A MAN BRAVE ENOUGH TO TAKE ON THIS TREASURE, YOU MUST HAVE GREAT INTEGRITY.
I'M BETTER THAN A MAN NOW. I'M A BEAST.
BEASTS AND MEN ARE QUITE ALIKE.
SSSSS
THINKING ONLY OF THEMSELVES...
...NEVER THE WORLD.
PERHAPS ANOTHER CUSTOMER, ANOTHER DAY.

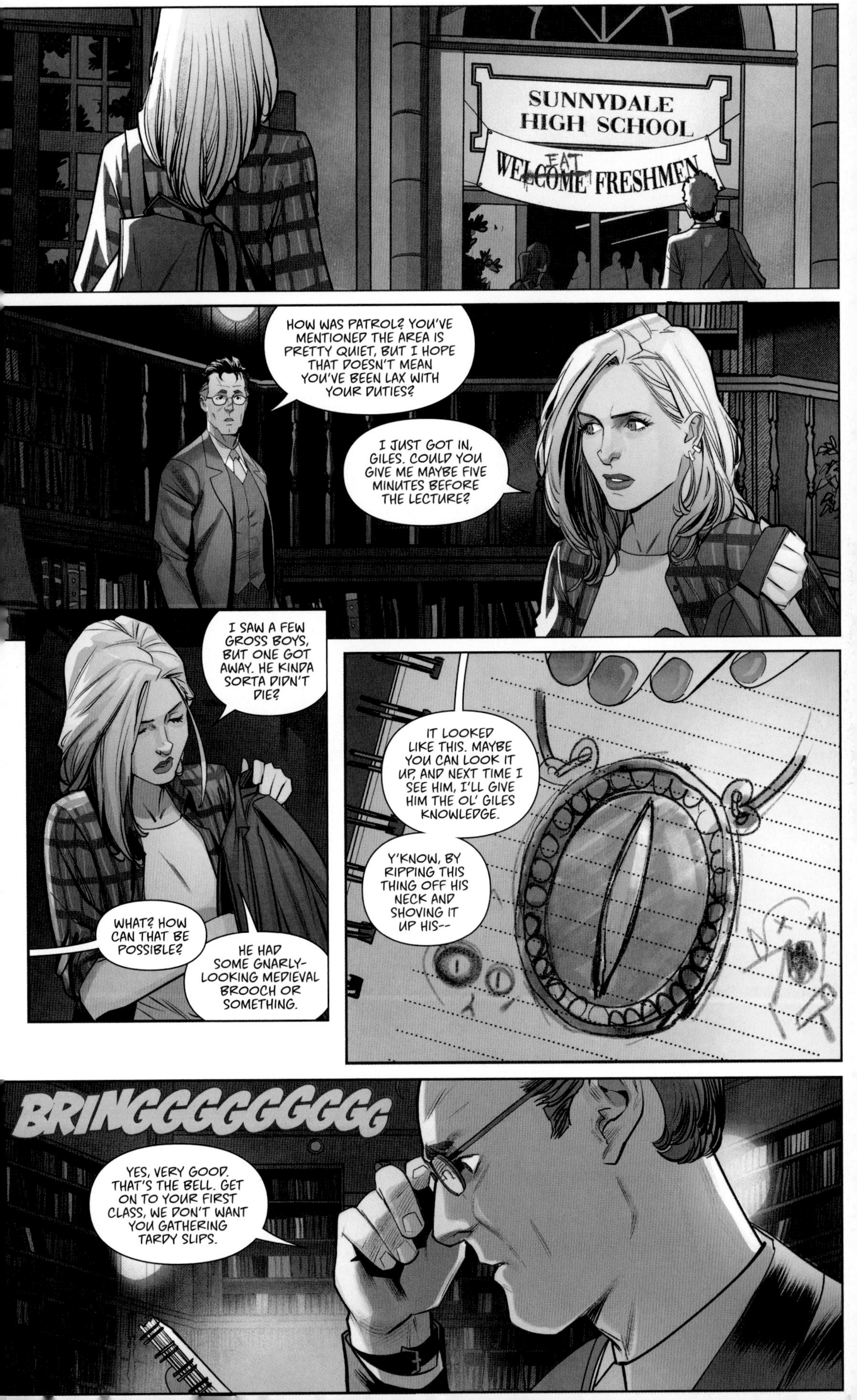
SUNNYDALE HIGH SCHOOL
WELCOME EAT FRESHMEN
HOW WAS PATROL? YOU'VE MENTIONED THE AREA IS PRETTY QUIET, BUT I HOPE THAT DOESN'T MEAN YOU'VE BEEN LAX WITH YOUR DUTIES?
I JUST GOT IN, GILES. COULD YOU GIVE ME MAYBE FIVE MINUTES BEFORE THE LECTURE?
I SAW A FEW GROSS BOYS, BUT ONE GOT AWAY. HE KINDA SORTA DIDN'T DIE?
WHAT? HOW CAN THAT BE POSSIBLE?
HE HAD SOME GNARLY-LOOKING MEDIEVAL BROOCH OR SOMETHING.
IT LOOKED LIKE THIS. MAYBE YOU CAN LOOK IT UP, AND NEXT TIME I SEE HIM, I'LL GIVE HIM THE OL' GILES KNOWLEDGE.
Y'KNOW, BY RIPPING THIS THING OFF HIS NECK AND SHOVING IT UP HIS--
BRINGGGGGGGGG
YES, VERY GOOD. THAT'S THE BELL. GET ON TO YOUR FIRST CLASS, WE DON'T WANT YOU GATHERING TARDY SLIPS.

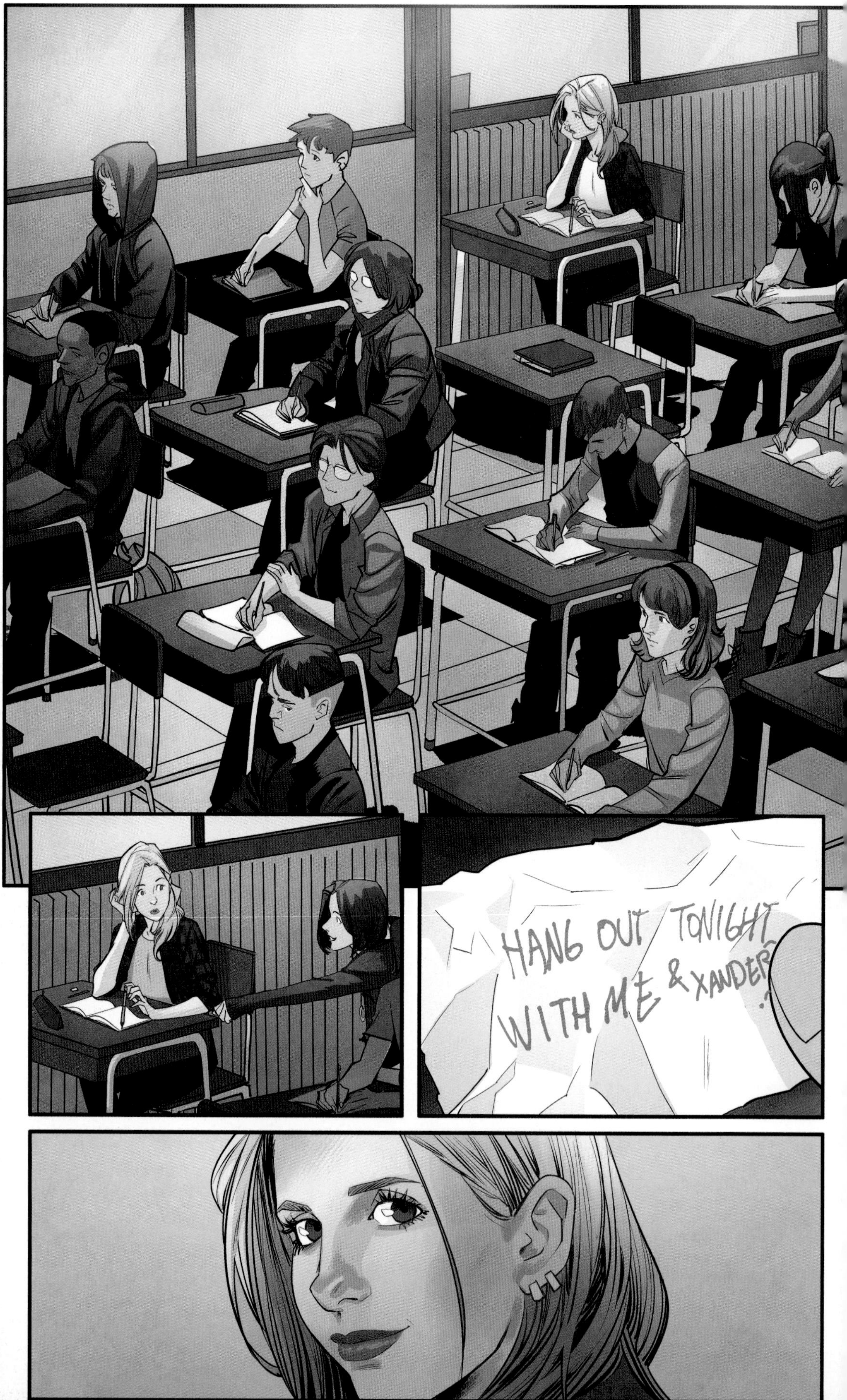
HANG OUT TONIGHT WITH ME & XANDER?

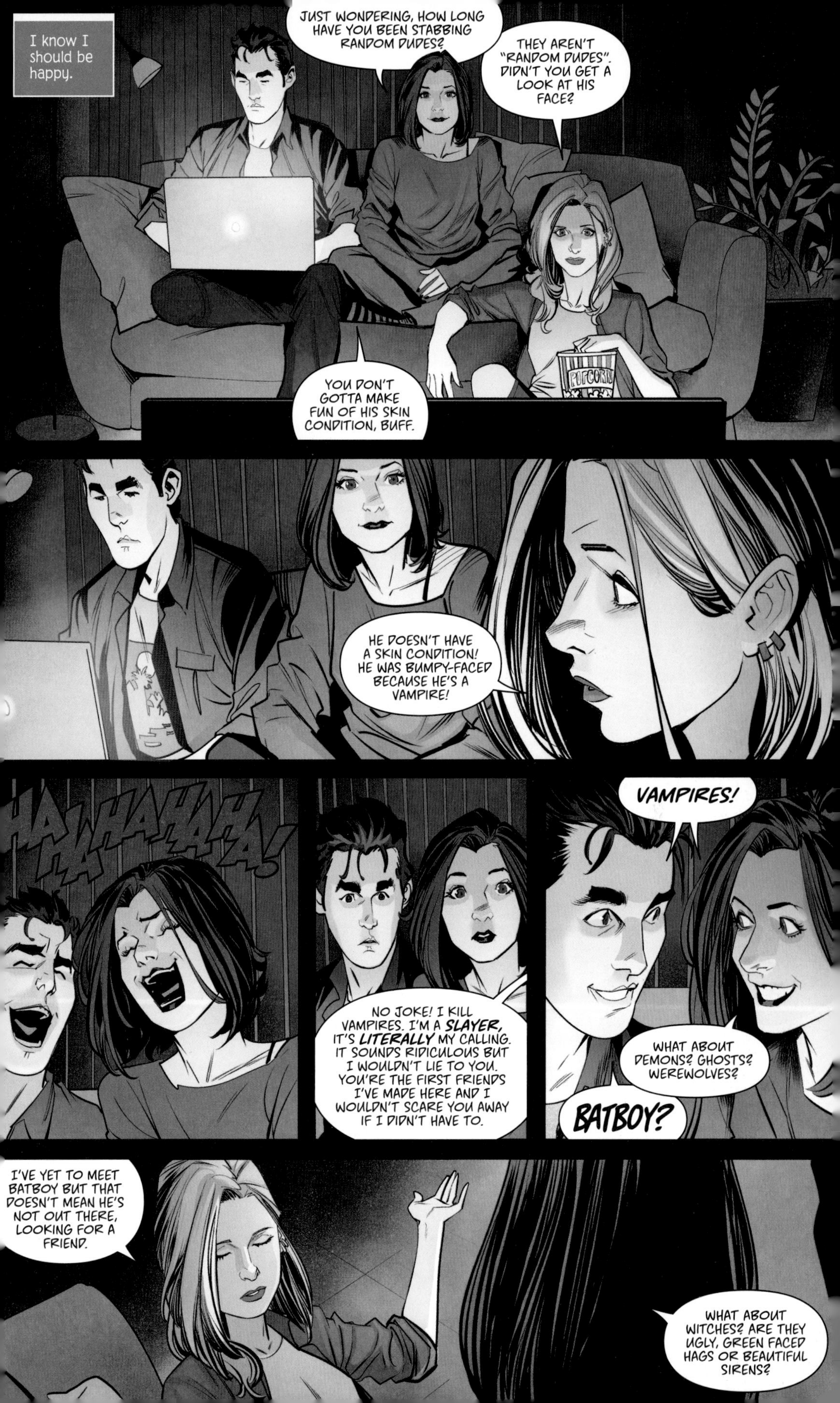
I know I should be happy.
JUST WONDERING, HOW LONG HAVE YOU BEEN STABBING RANDOM DUDES?
THEY AREN'T "RANDOM DUDES". DIDN'T YOU GET A LOOK AT HIS FACE?
POPCORN
YOU DON'T GOTTA MAKE FUN OF HIS SKIN CONDITION, BUFF.
HE DOESN'T HAVE A SKIN CONDITION! HE WAS BUMPY-FACED BECAUSE HE'S A VAMPIRE!
HAHAHAHAHAHA!
NO JOKE! I KILL VAMPIRES. I'M A SLAYER, IT'S LITERALLY MY CALLING. IT SOUNDS RIDICULOUS BUT I WOULDN'T LIE TO YOU. YOU'RE THE FIRST FRIENDS I'VE MADE HERE AND I WOULDN'T SCARE YOU AWAY IF I DIDN'T HAVE TO.
VAMPIRES!
WHAT ABOUT DEMONS? GHOSTS? WEREWOLVES?
BATBOY?
I'VE YET TO MEET BATBOY BUT THAT DOESN'T MEAN HE'S NOT OUT THERE, LOOKING FOR A FRIEND.
WHAT ABOUT WITCHES? ARE THEY UGLY, GREEN FACED HAGS OR BEAUTIFUL SIRENS?

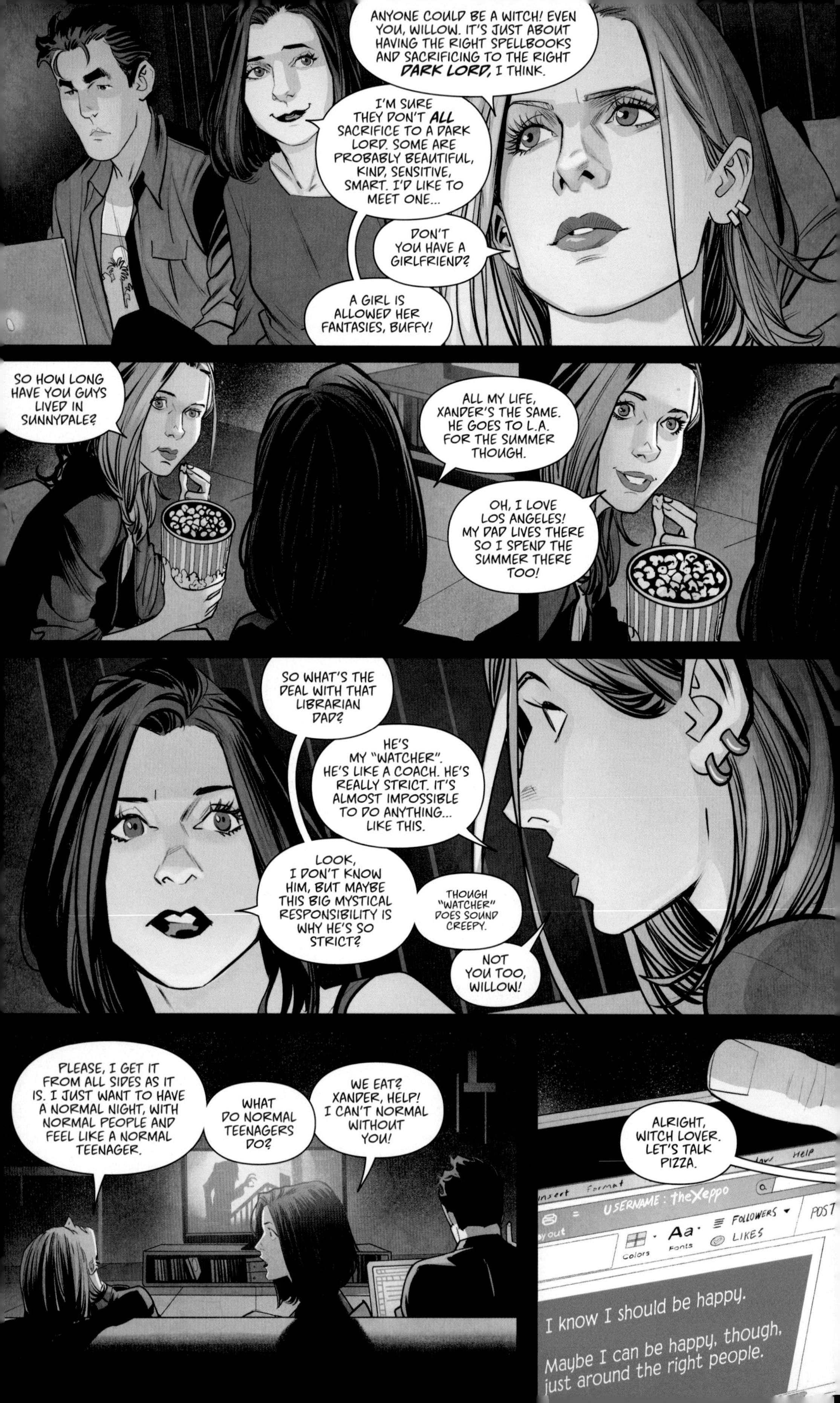
ANYONE COULD BE A WITCH! EVEN YOU, WILLOW. IT'S JUST ABOUT HAVING THE RIGHT SPELLBOOKS AND SACRIFICING TO THE RIGHT DARK LORD, I THINK.
I'M SURE THEY DON'T ALL SACRIFICE TO A DARK LORD. SOME ARE PROBABLY BEAUTIFUL, KIND, SENSITIVE, SMART. I'D LIKE TO MEET ONE...
DON'T YOU HAVE A GIRLFRIEND?
A GIRL IS ALLOWED HER FANTASIES, BUFFY!
SO HOW LONG HAVE YOU GUYS LIVED IN SUNNYDALE?
ALL MY LIFE, XANDER'S THE SAME. HE GOES TO L.A. FOR THE SUMMER THOUGH.
OH, I LOVE LOS ANGELES! MY DAD LIVES THERE SO I SPEND THE SUMMER THERE TOO!
SO WHAT'S THE DEAL WITH THAT LIBRARIAN DAD?
HE'S MY "WATCHER". HE'S LIKE A COACH. HE'S REALLY STRICT. IT'S ALMOST IMPOSSIBLE TO DO ANYTHING... LIKE THIS.
LOOK, I DON'T KNOW HIM, BUT MAYBE THIS BIG MYSTICAL RESPONSIBILITY IS WHY HE'S SO STRICT?
THOUGH "WATCHER" DOES SOUND CREEPY.
NOT YOU TOO, WILLOW!
PLEASE, I GET IT FROM ALL SIDES AS IT IS. I JUST WANT TO HAVE A NORMAL NIGHT, WITH NORMAL PEOPLE AND FEEL LIKE A NORMAL TEENAGER.
WHAT DO NORMAL TEENAGERS DO?
WE EAT? XANDER, HELP! I CAN'T NORMAL WITHOUT YOU!
ALRIGHT, WITCH LOVER. LET'S TALK PIZZA.
Insert Format
Help
USERNAME : theXeppo
FOLLOWERS
LIKES
POST
Colors
Fonts
I know I should be happy.
Maybe I can be happy, though, just around the right people.

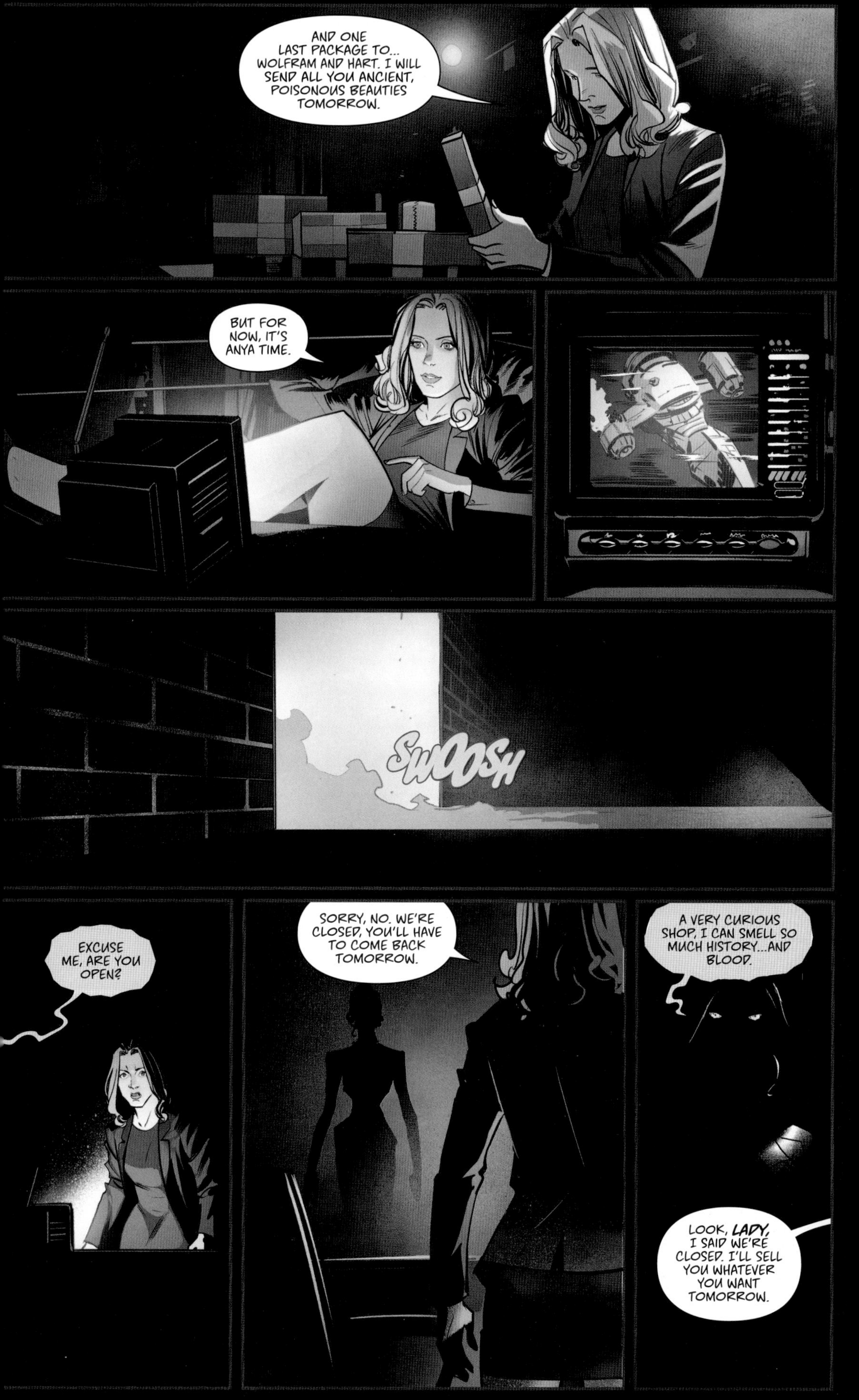
AND ONE LAST PACKAGE TO... WOLFRAM AND HART. I WILL SEND ALL YOU ANCIENT, POISONOUS BEAUTIES TOMORROW.
BUT FOR NOW, IT'S ANYA TIME.
SWOOSH
EXCUSE ME, ARE YOU OPEN?
SORRY, NO. WE'RE CLOSED, YOU'LL HAVE TO COME BACK TOMORROW.
A VERY CURIOUS SHOP, I CAN SMELL SO MUCH HISTORY...AND BLOOD.
LOOK, LADY, I SAID WE'RE CLOSED. I'LL SELL YOU WHATEVER YOU WANT TOMORROW.

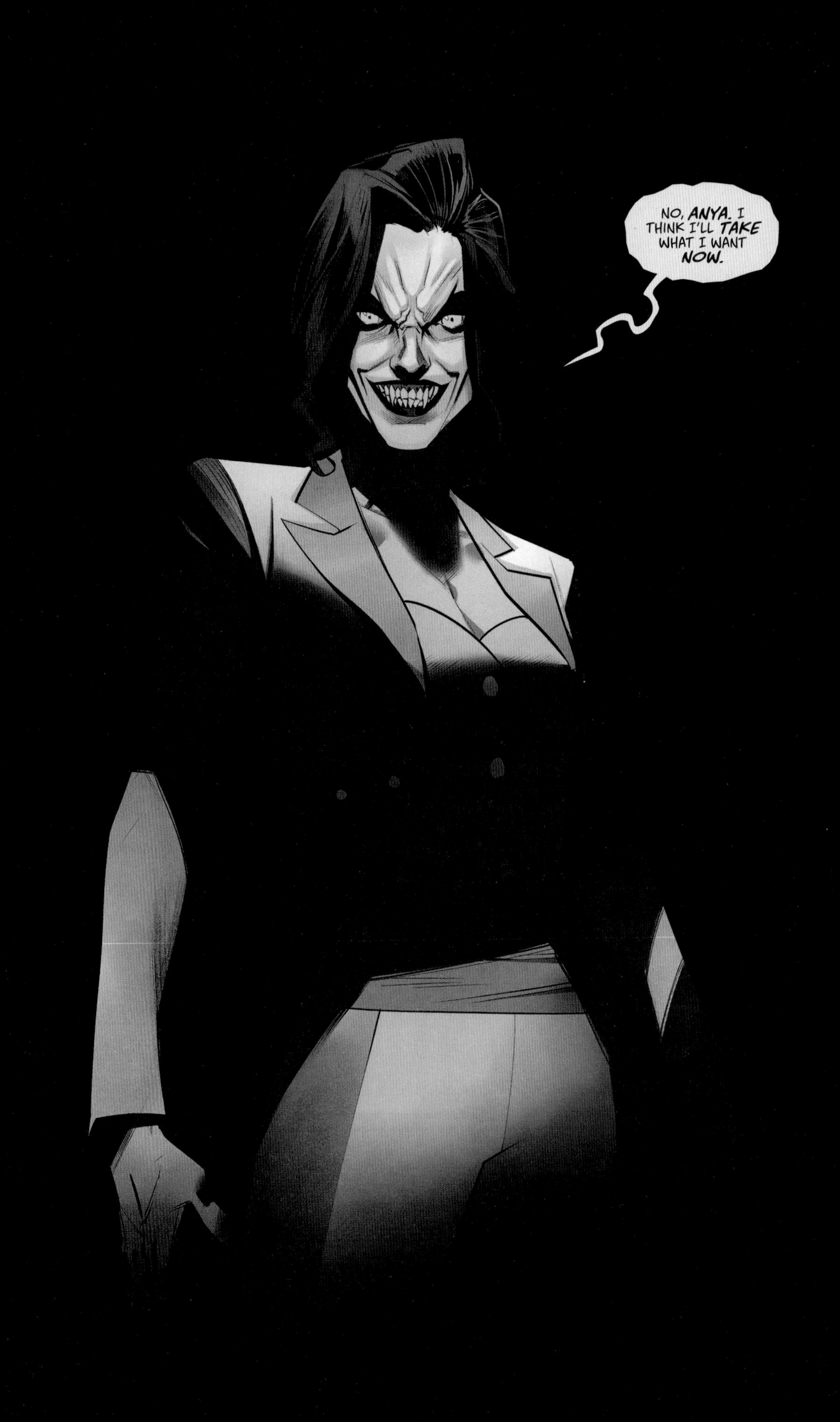
NO, ANYA. I THINK I'LL TAKE WHAT I WANT NOW.

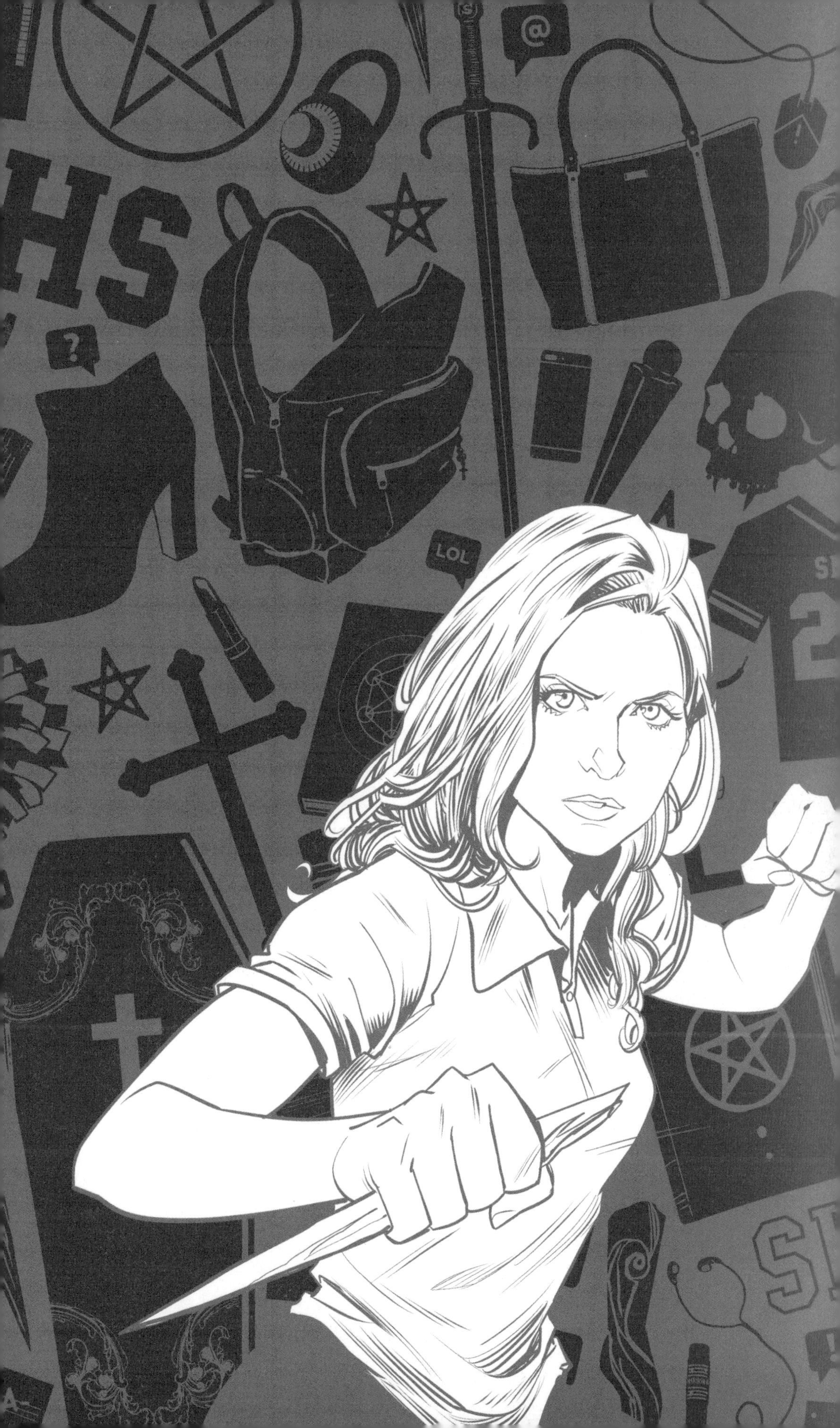
HS
LOL

CHAPTER TWO

Issue Two Cover by **Matthew Taylor**

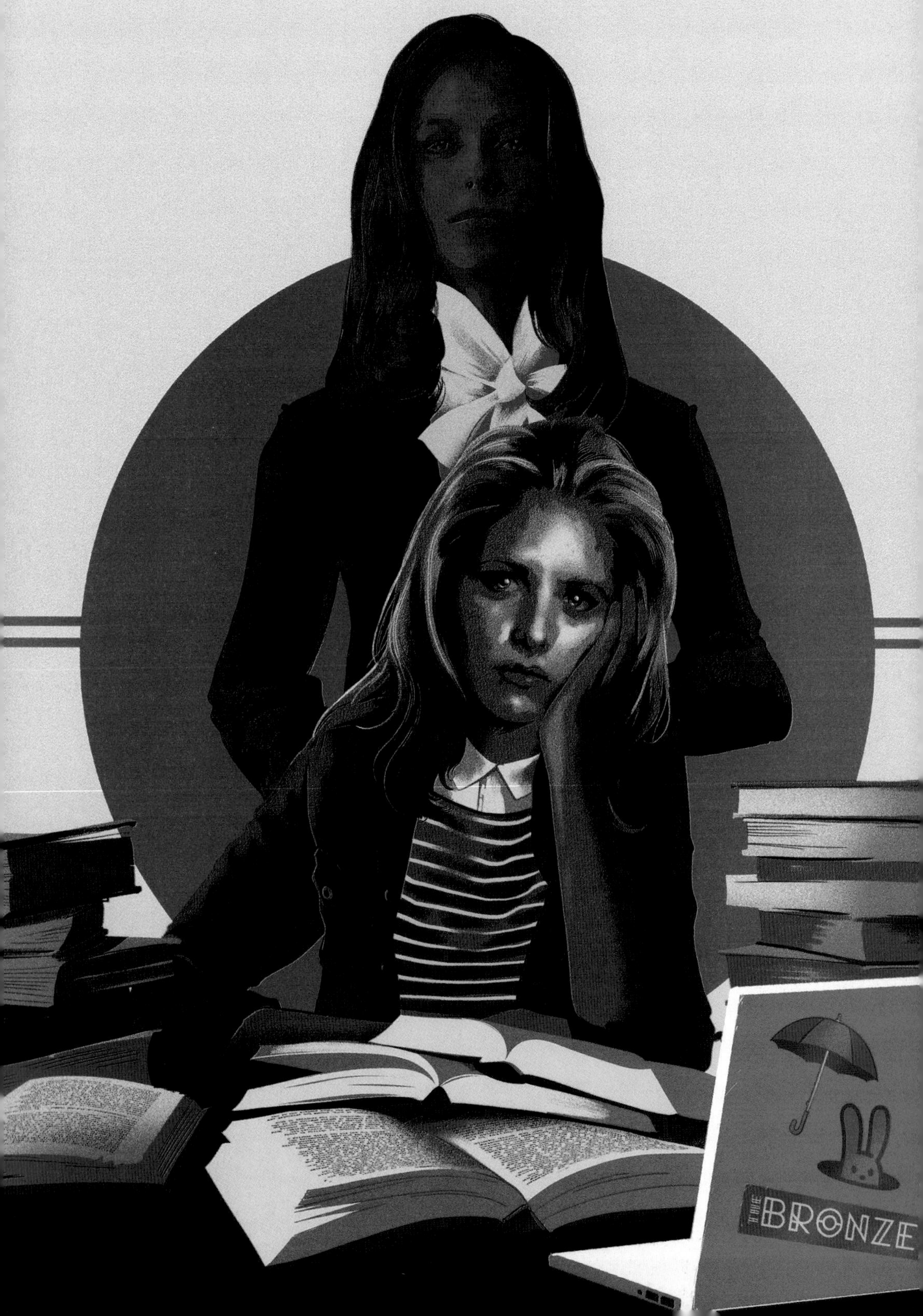

BRONZE

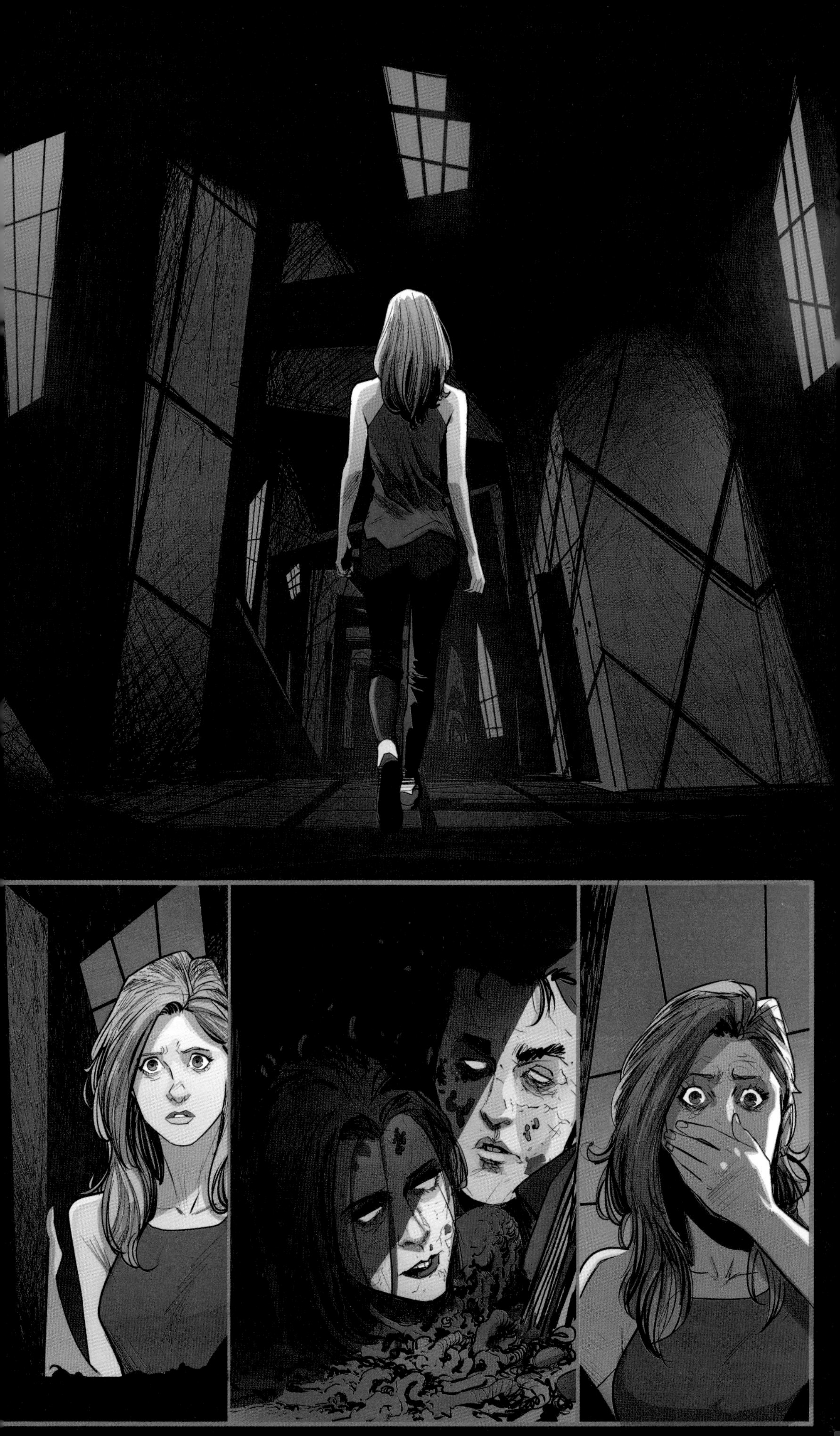

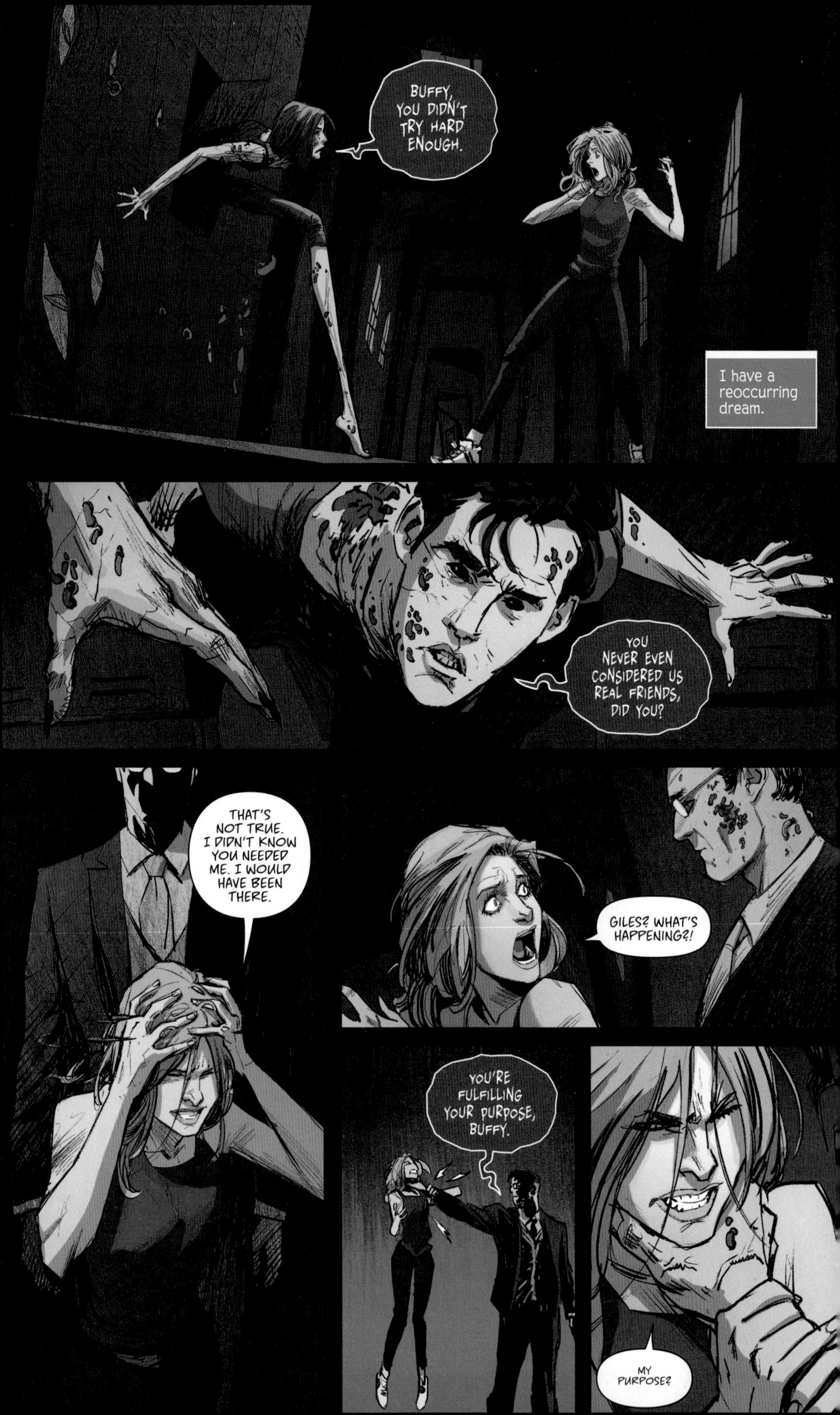
BUFFY, YOU DIDN'T TRY HARD ENOUGH.
I have a reoccurring dream.
YOU NEVER EVEN CONSIDERED US REAL FRIENDS, DID YOU?
THAT'S NOT TRUE. I DIDN'T KNOW YOU NEEDED ME. I WOULD HAVE BEEN THERE.
GILES? WHAT'S HAPPENING?!
YOU'RE FULFILLING YOUR PURPOSE, BUFFY.
MY PURPOSE?

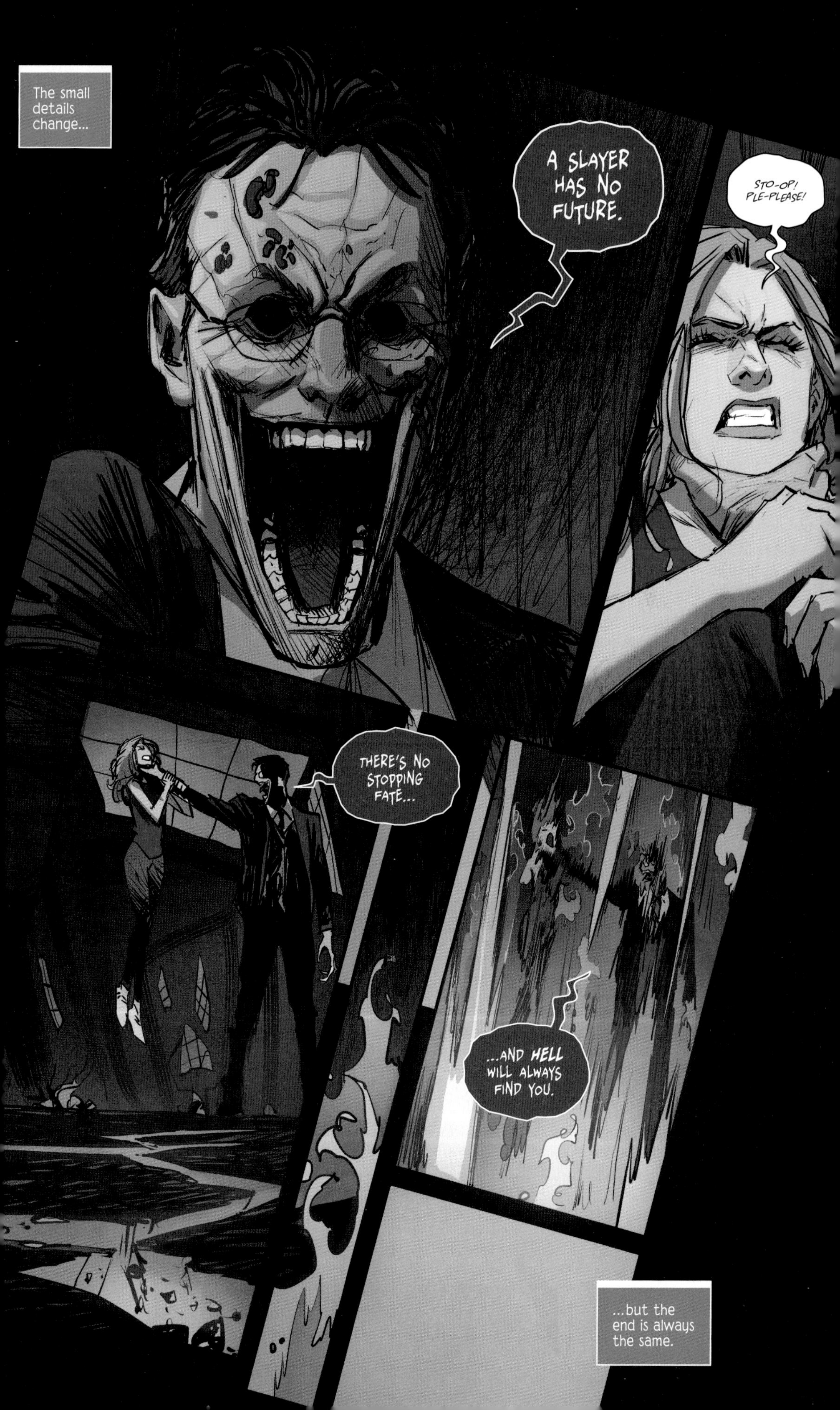
The small details change...
A SLAYER HAS NO FUTURE.
STO-OP! PLE-PLEASE!
THERE'S NO STOPPING FATE...
...AND HELL WILL ALWAYS FIND YOU.
...but the end is always the same.

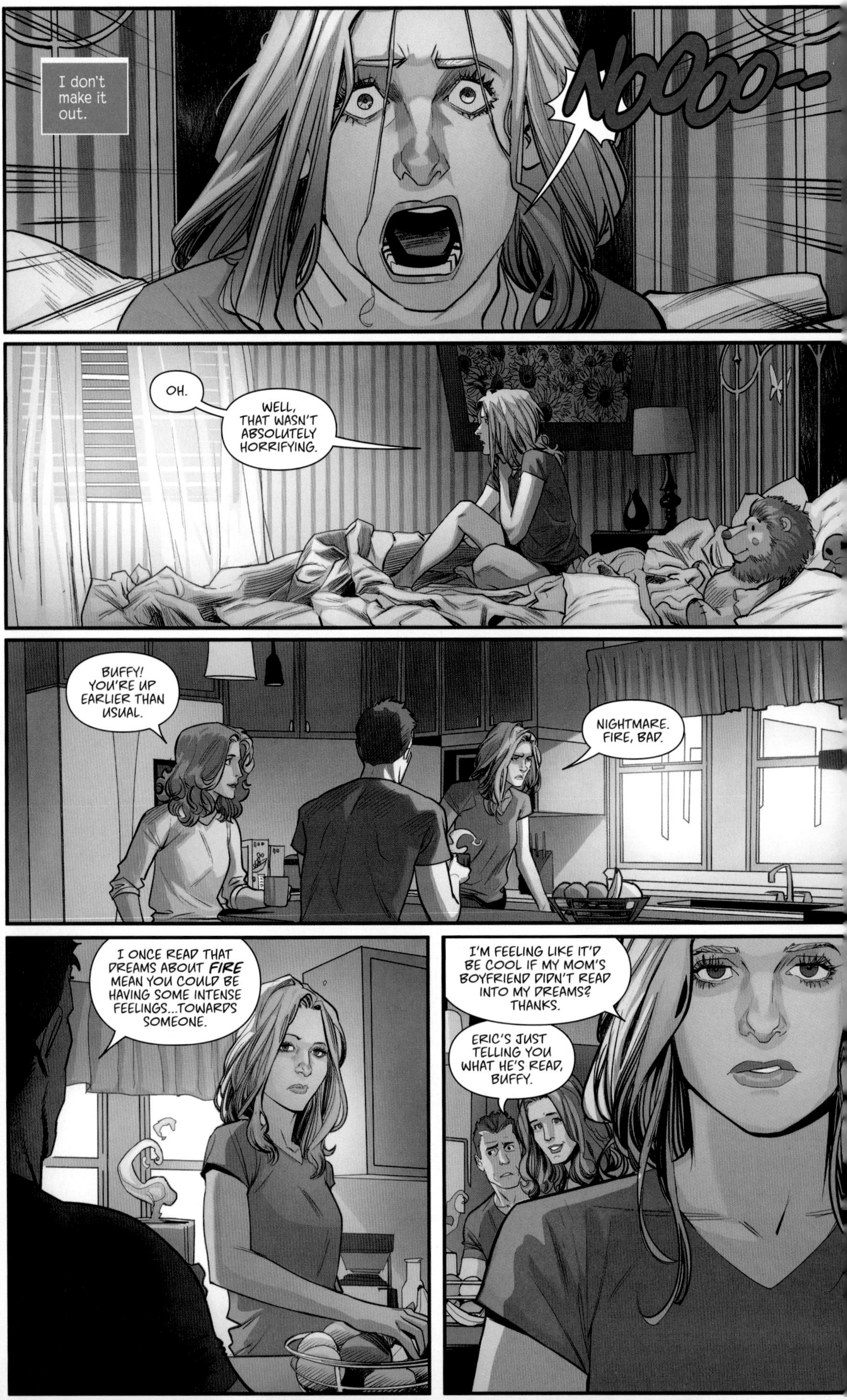
I don't make it out.
NOOOOO--
OH.
WELL, THAT WASN'T ABSOLUTELY HORRIFYING.
BUFFY! YOU'RE UP EARLIER THAN USUAL.
NIGHTMARE. FIRE, BAD.
I ONCE READ THAT DREAMS ABOUT FIRE MEAN YOU COULD BE HAVING SOME INTENSE FEELINGS...TOWARDS SOMEONE.
I'M FEELING LIKE IT'D BE COOL IF MY MOM'S BOYFRIEND DIDN'T READ INTO MY DREAMS? THANKS.
ERIC'S JUST TELLING YOU WHAT HE'S READ, BUFFY.

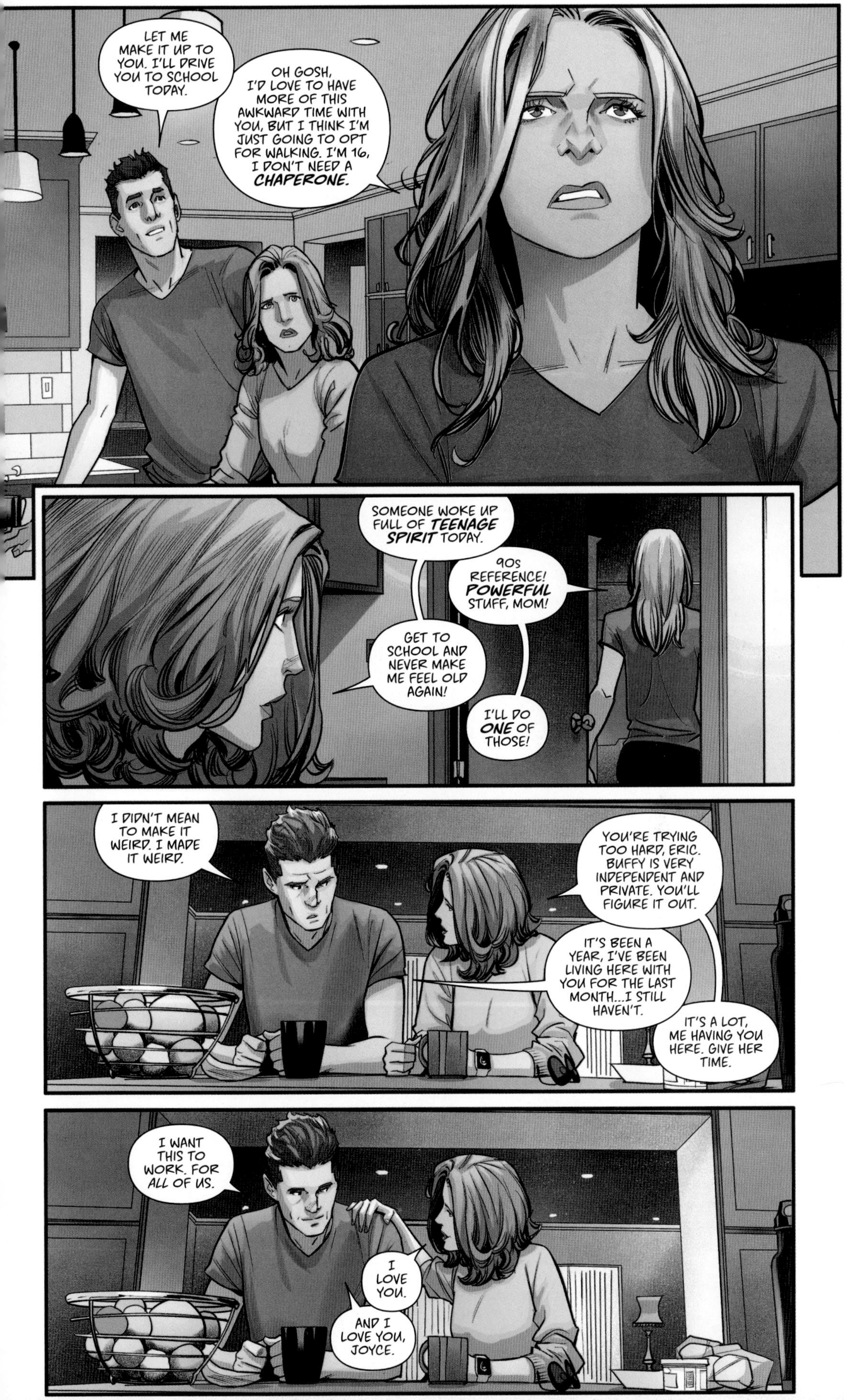
LET ME MAKE IT UP TO YOU. I'LL DRIVE YOU TO SCHOOL TODAY.
OH GOSH, I'D LOVE TO HAVE MORE OF THIS AWKWARD TIME WITH YOU, BUT I THINK I'M JUST GOING TO OPT FOR WALKING. I'M 16, I DON'T NEED A CHAPERONE.
SOMEONE WOKE UP FULL OF TEENAGE SPIRIT TODAY.
90s REFERENCE! POWERFUL STUFF, MOM!
GET TO SCHOOL AND NEVER MAKE ME FEEL OLD AGAIN!
I'LL DO ONE OF THOSE!
I DIDN'T MEAN TO MAKE IT WEIRD. I MADE IT WEIRD.
YOU'RE TRYING TOO HARD, ERIC. BUFFY IS VERY INDEPENDENT AND PRIVATE. YOU'LL FIGURE IT OUT.
IT'S BEEN A YEAR, I'VE BEEN LIVING HERE WITH YOU FOR THE LAST MONTH...I STILL HAVEN'T.
IT'S A LOT, ME HAVING YOU HERE. GIVE HER TIME.
I WANT THIS TO WORK. FOR ALL OF US.
I LOVE YOU.
AND I LOVE YOU, JOYCE.

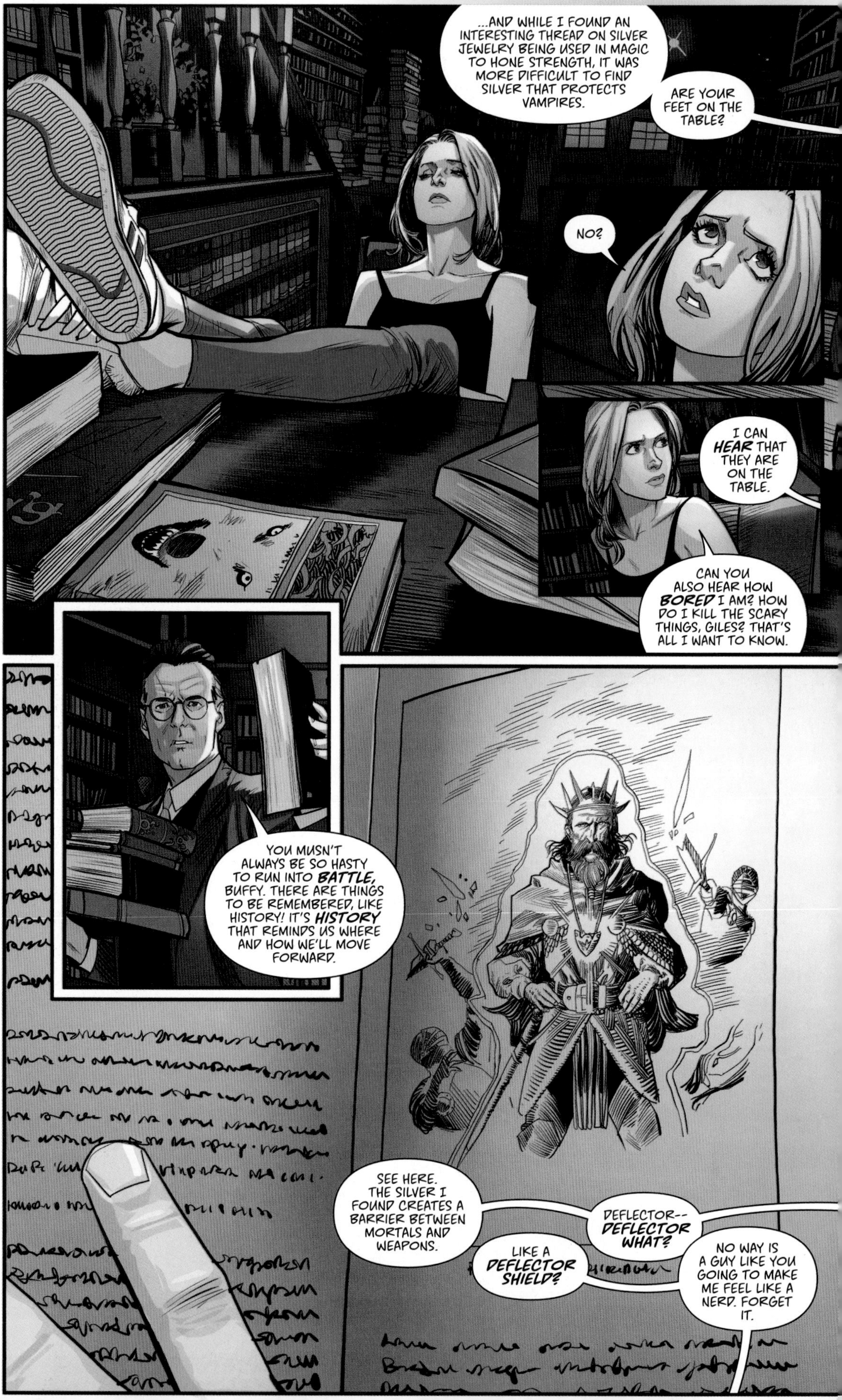
...AND WHILE I FOUND AN INTERESTING THREAD ON SILVER JEWELRY BEING USED IN MAGIC TO HONE STRENGTH, IT WAS MORE DIFFICULT TO FIND SILVER THAT PROTECTS VAMPIRES.
ARE YOUR FEET ON THE TABLE?
NO?
I CAN HEAR THAT THEY ARE ON THE TABLE.
CAN YOU ALSO HEAR HOW BORED I AM? HOW DO I KILL THE SCARY THINGS, GILES? THAT'S ALL I WANT TO KNOW.
YOU MUSN'T ALWAYS BE SO HASTY TO RUN INTO BATTLE, BUFFY. THERE ARE THINGS TO BE REMEMBERED, LIKE HISTORY! IT'S HISTORY THAT REMINDS US WHERE AND HOW WE'LL MOVE FORWARD.
SEE HERE. THE SILVER I FOUND CREATES A BARRIER BETWEEN MORTALS AND WEAPONS.
LIKE A DEFLECTOR SHIELD?
DEFLECTOR-- DEFLECTOR WHAT?
NO WAY IS A GUY LIKE YOU GOING TO MAKE ME FEEL LIKE A NERD. FORGET IT.

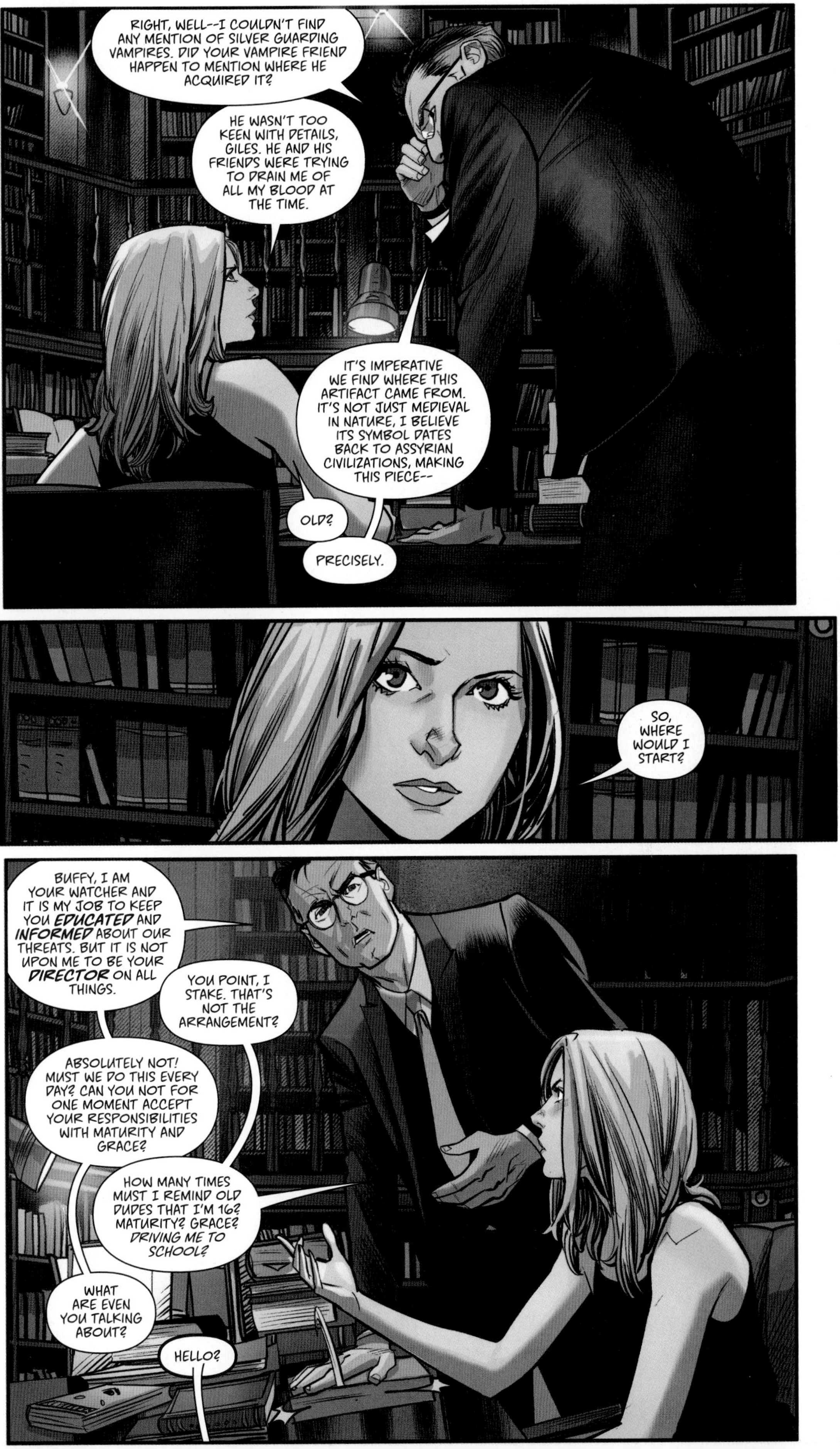
RIGHT, WELL--I COULDN'T FIND ANY MENTION OF SILVER GUARDING VAMPIRES. DID YOUR VAMPIRE FRIEND HAPPEN TO MENTION WHERE HE ACQUIRED IT?
HE WASN'T TOO KEEN WITH DETAILS, GILES. HE AND HIS FRIENDS WERE TRYING TO DRAIN ME OF ALL MY BLOOD AT THE TIME.
IT'S IMPERATIVE WE FIND WHERE THIS ARTIFACT CAME FROM. IT'S NOT JUST MEDIEVAL IN NATURE, I BELIEVE ITS SYMBOL DATES BACK TO ASSYRIAN CIVILIZATIONS, MAKING THIS PIECE--
OLD?
PRECISELY.
SO, WHERE WOULD I START?
BUFFY, I AM YOUR WATCHER AND IT IS MY JOB TO KEEP YOU ***EDUCATED*** AND ***INFORMED*** ABOUT OUR THREATS. BUT IT IS NOT UPON ME TO BE YOUR ***DIRECTOR*** ON ALL THINGS.
YOU POINT, I STAKE. THAT'S NOT THE ARRANGEMENT?
ABSOLUTELY NOT! MUST WE DO THIS EVERY DAY? CAN YOU NOT FOR ONE MOMENT ACCEPT YOUR RESPONSIBILITIES WITH MATURITY AND GRACE?
HOW MANY TIMES MUST I REMIND OLD DUDES THAT I'M 16? MATURITY? GRACE? *DRIVING ME TO SCHOOL?*
WHAT ARE EVEN YOU TALKING ABOUT?
HELLO?

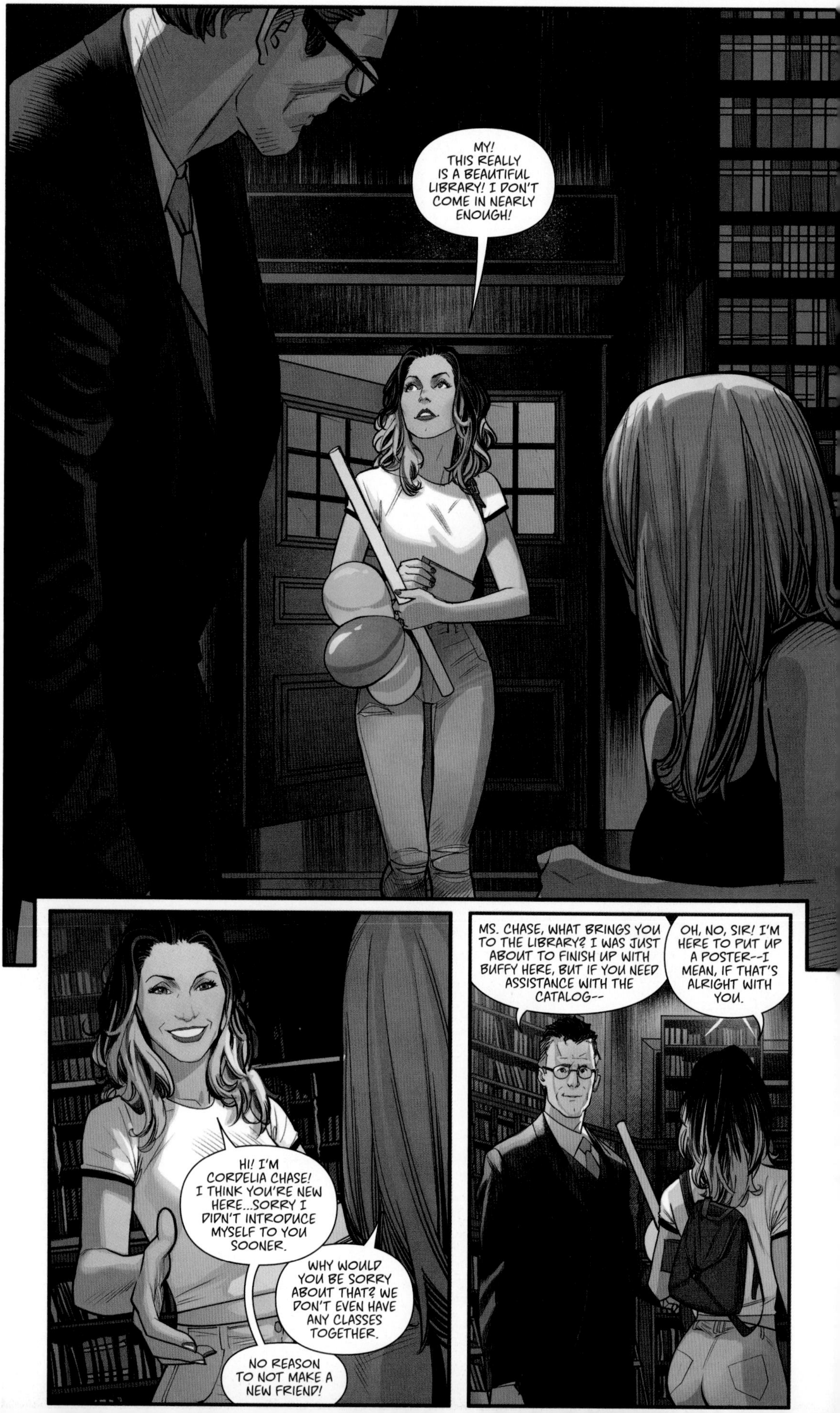
MY! THIS REALLY IS A BEAUTIFUL LIBRARY! I DON'T COME IN NEARLY ENOUGH!
HI! I'M CORDELIA CHASE! I THINK YOU'RE NEW HERE...SORRY I DIDN'T INTRODUCE MYSELF TO YOU SOONER.
WHY WOULD YOU BE SORRY ABOUT THAT? WE DON'T EVEN HAVE ANY CLASSES TOGETHER.
NO REASON TO NOT MAKE A NEW FRIEND!
MS. CHASE, WHAT BRINGS YOU TO THE LIBRARY? I WAS JUST ABOUT TO FINISH UP WITH BUFFY HERE, BUT IF YOU NEED ASSISTANCE WITH THE CATALOG--
OH, NO, SIR! I'M HERE TO PUT UP A POSTER--I MEAN, IF THAT'S ALRIGHT WITH YOU.

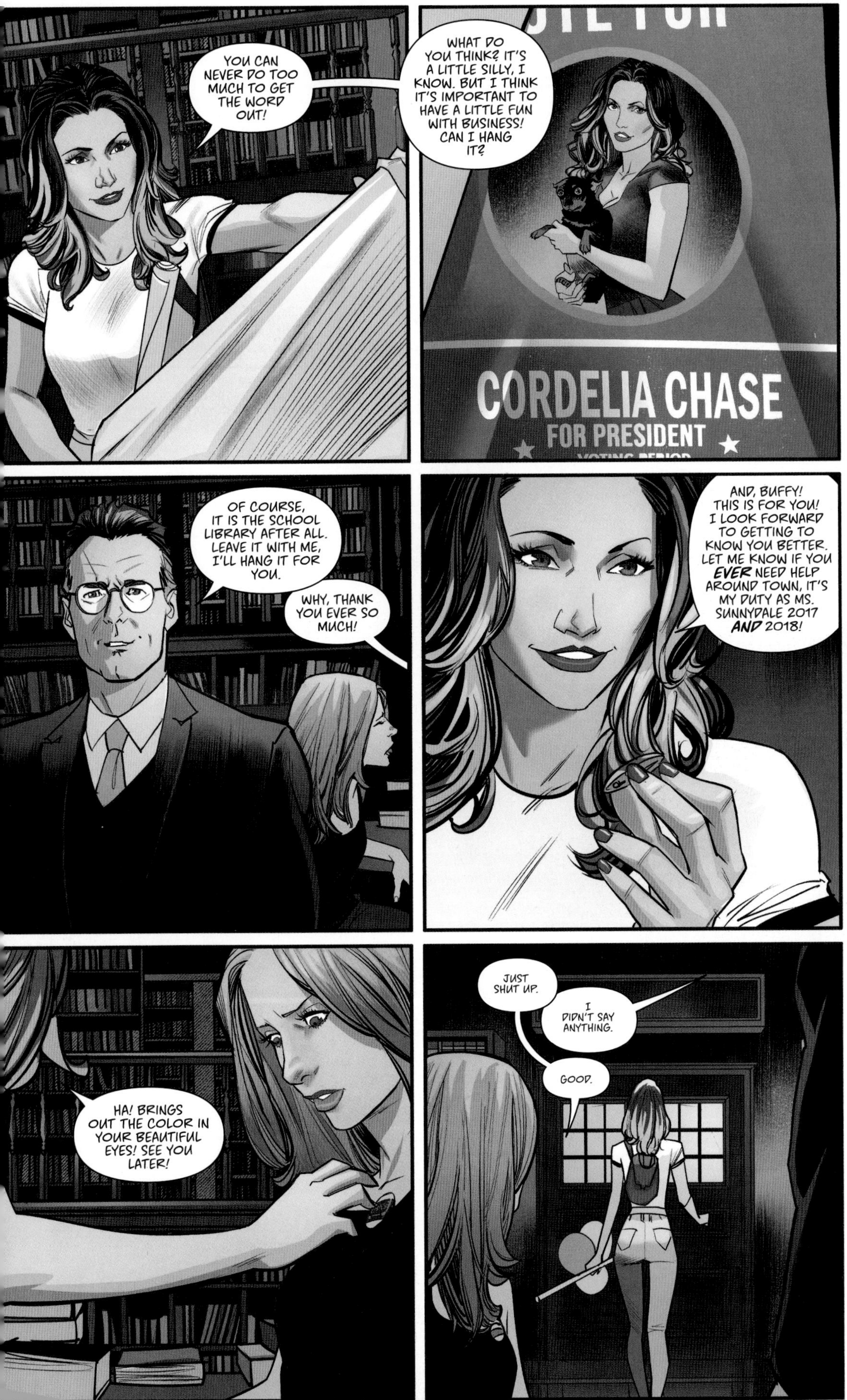
YOU CAN NEVER DO TOO MUCH TO GET THE WORD OUT!
WHAT DO YOU THINK? IT'S A LITTLE SILLY, I KNOW. BUT I THINK IT'S IMPORTANT TO HAVE A LITTLE FUN WITH BUSINESS! CAN I HANG IT?
CORDELIA CHASE
FOR PRESIDENT
OF COURSE, IT IS THE SCHOOL LIBRARY AFTER ALL. LEAVE IT WITH ME, I'LL HANG IT FOR YOU.
WHY, THANK YOU EVER SO MUCH!
AND, BUFFY! THIS IS FOR YOU! I LOOK FORWARD TO GETTING TO KNOW YOU BETTER. LET ME KNOW IF YOU EVER NEED HELP AROUND TOWN, IT'S MY DUTY AS MS. SUNNYDALE 2017 AND 2018!
HA! BRINGS OUT THE COLOR IN YOUR BEAUTIFUL EYES! SEE YOU LATER!
JUST SHUT UP.
I DIDN'T SAY ANYTHING.
GOOD.

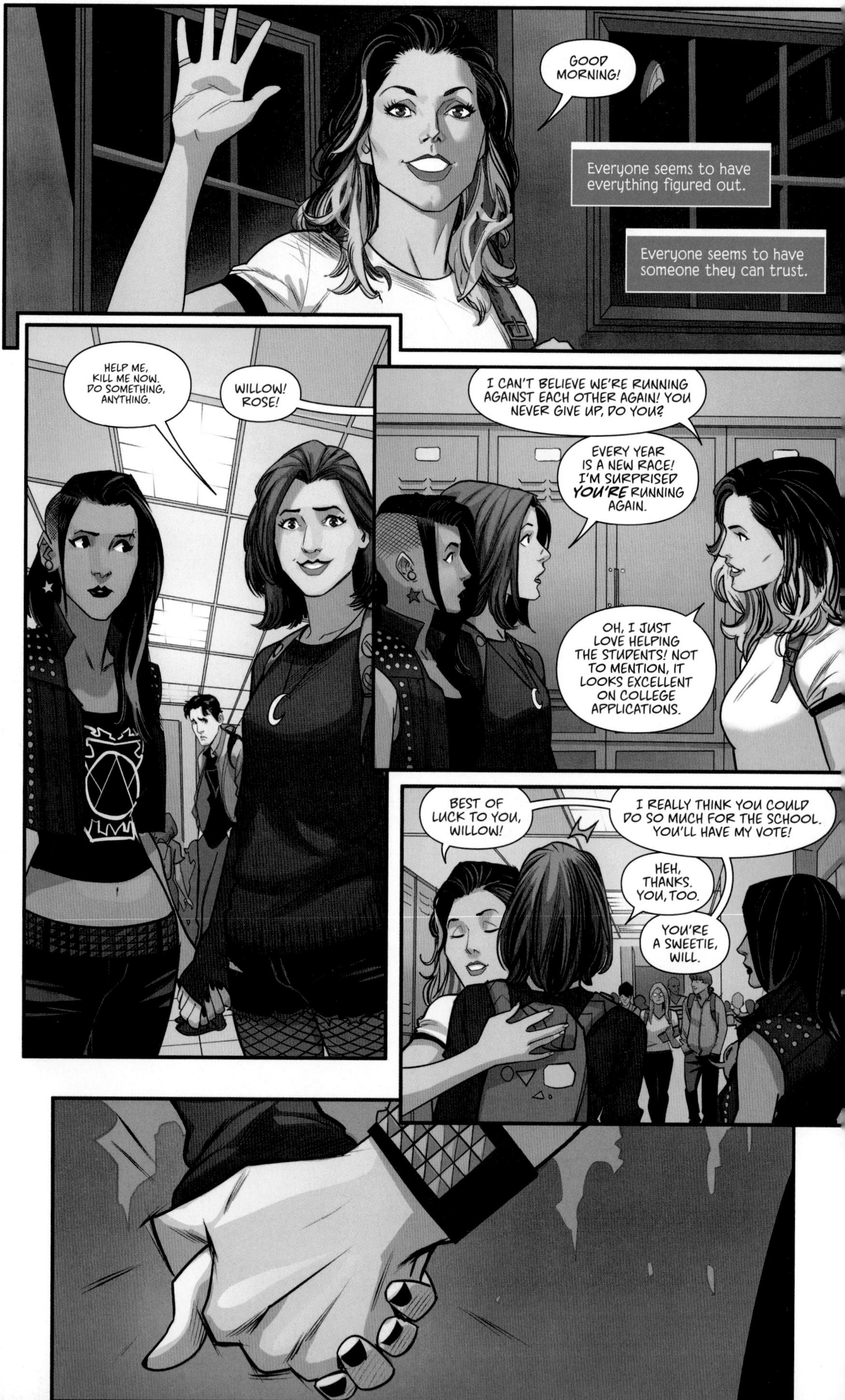
GOOD MORNING!
Everyone seems to have everything figured out.
Everyone seems to have someone they can trust.
HELP ME, KILL ME NOW. DO SOMETHING, ANYTHING.
WILLOW! ROSE!
I CAN'T BELIEVE WE'RE RUNNING AGAINST EACH OTHER AGAIN! YOU NEVER GIVE UP, DO YOU?
EVERY YEAR IS A NEW RACE! I'M SURPRISED YOU'RE RUNNING AGAIN.
OH, I JUST LOVE HELPING THE STUDENTS! NOT TO MENTION, IT LOOKS EXCELLENT ON COLLEGE APPLICATIONS.
BEST OF LUCK TO YOU, WILLOW!
I REALLY THINK YOU COULD DO SO MUCH FOR THE SCHOOL. YOU'LL HAVE MY VOTE!
HEH, THANKS. YOU, TOO.
YOU'RE A SWEETIE, WILL.

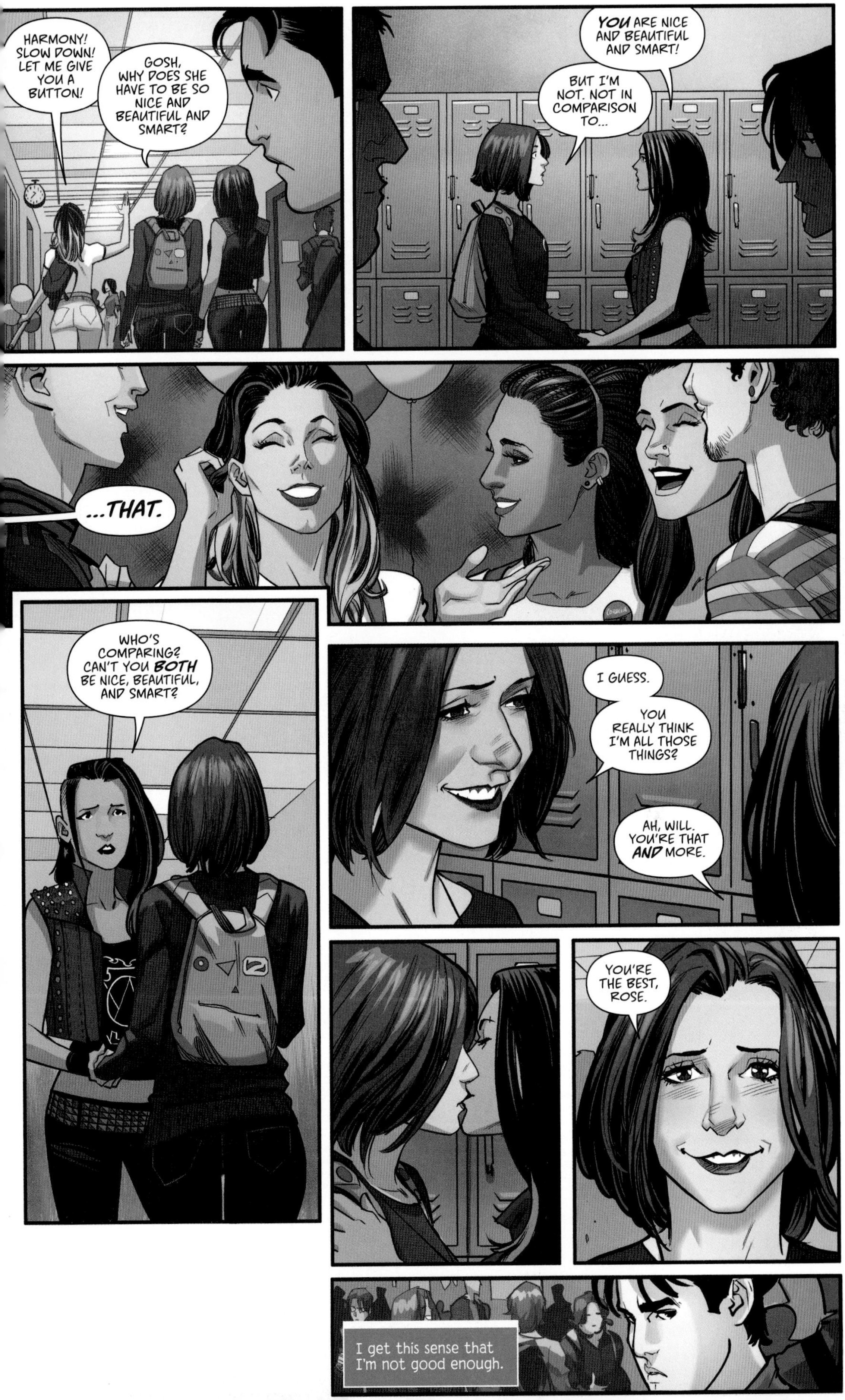

HARMONY! SLOW DOWN! LET ME GIVE YOU A BUTTON!
GOSH, WHY DOES SHE HAVE TO BE SO NICE AND BEAUTIFUL AND SMART?
BUT I'M NOT. NOT IN COMPARISON TO...
YOU ARE NICE AND BEAUTIFUL AND SMART!
...THAT.
WHO'S COMPARING? CAN'T YOU BOTH BE NICE, BEAUTIFUL, AND SMART?
I GUESS.
YOU REALLY THINK I'M ALL THOSE THINGS?
AH, WILL. YOU'RE THAT AND MORE.
YOU'RE THE BEST, ROSE.
I get this sense that I'm not good enough.

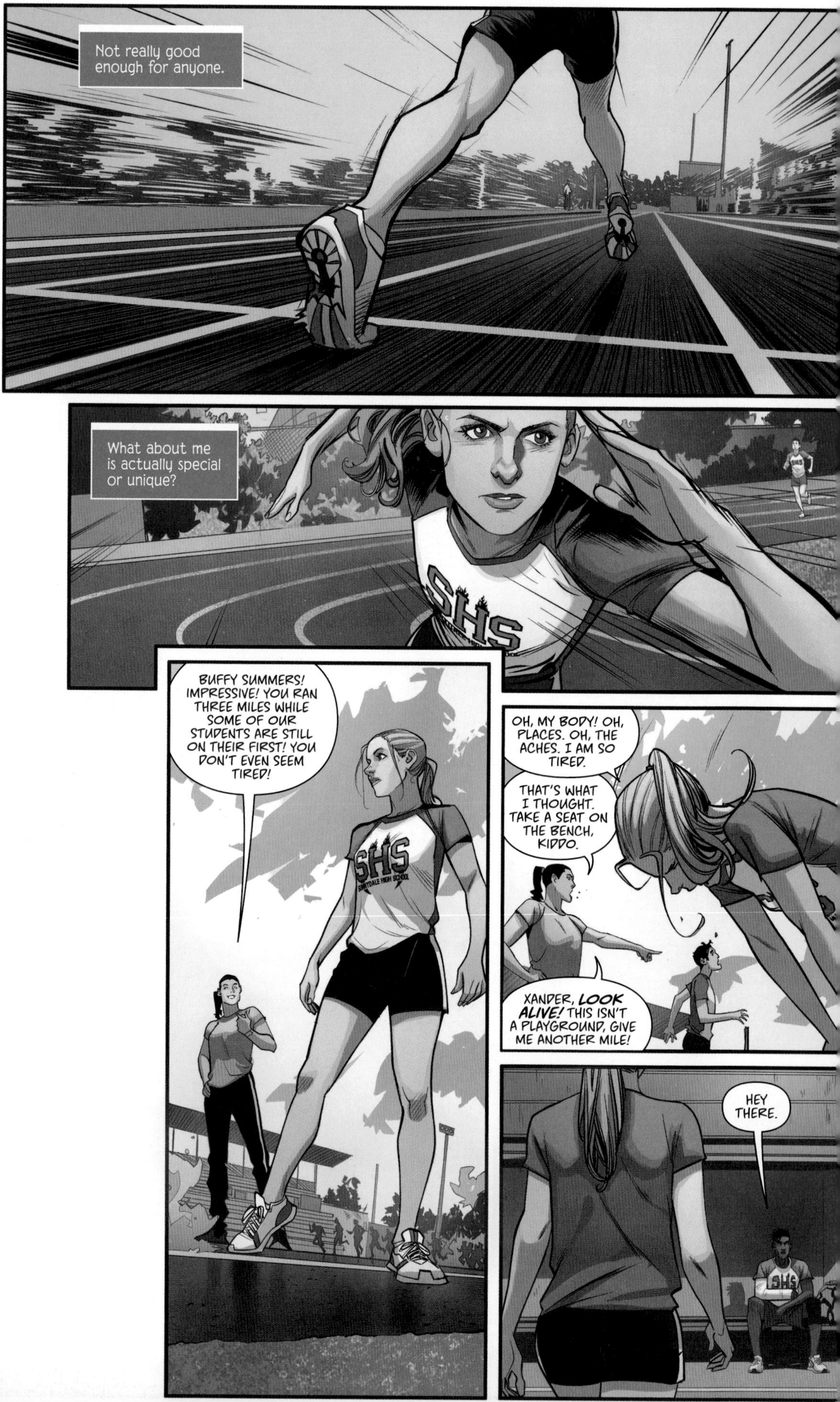
Not really good enough for anyone.
What about me is actually special or unique?
SHS
BUFFY SUMMERS! IMPRESSIVE! YOU RAN THREE MILES WHILE SOME OF OUR STUDENTS ARE STILL ON THEIR FIRST! YOU DON'T EVEN SEEM TIRED!
SHS
SUNNYDALE HIGH SCHOOL
OH, MY BODY! OH, PLACES. OH, THE ACHES. I AM SO TIRED.
THAT'S WHAT I THOUGHT. TAKE A SEAT ON THE BENCH, KIDDO.
XANDER, **LOOK ALIVE!** THIS ISN'T A PLAYGROUND, GIVE ME ANOTHER MILE!
HEY THERE.
SHS

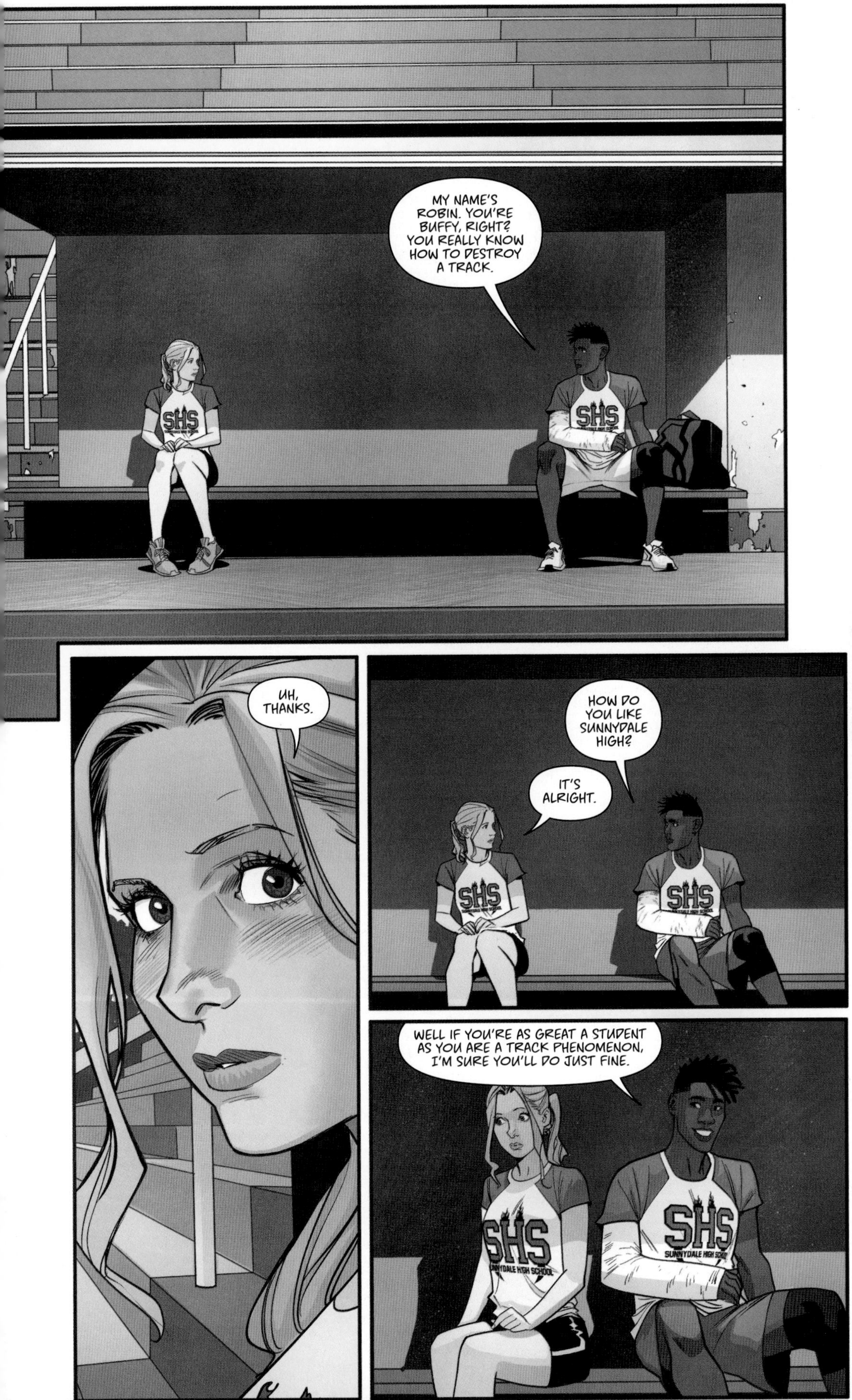
MY NAME'S ROBIN. YOU'RE BUFFY, RIGHT? YOU REALLY KNOW HOW TO DESTROY A TRACK.
UH, THANKS.
HOW DO YOU LIKE SUNNYDALE HIGH?
IT'S ALRIGHT.
WELL IF YOU'RE AS GREAT A STUDENT AS YOU ARE A TRACK PHENOMENON, I'M SURE YOU'LL DO JUST FINE.

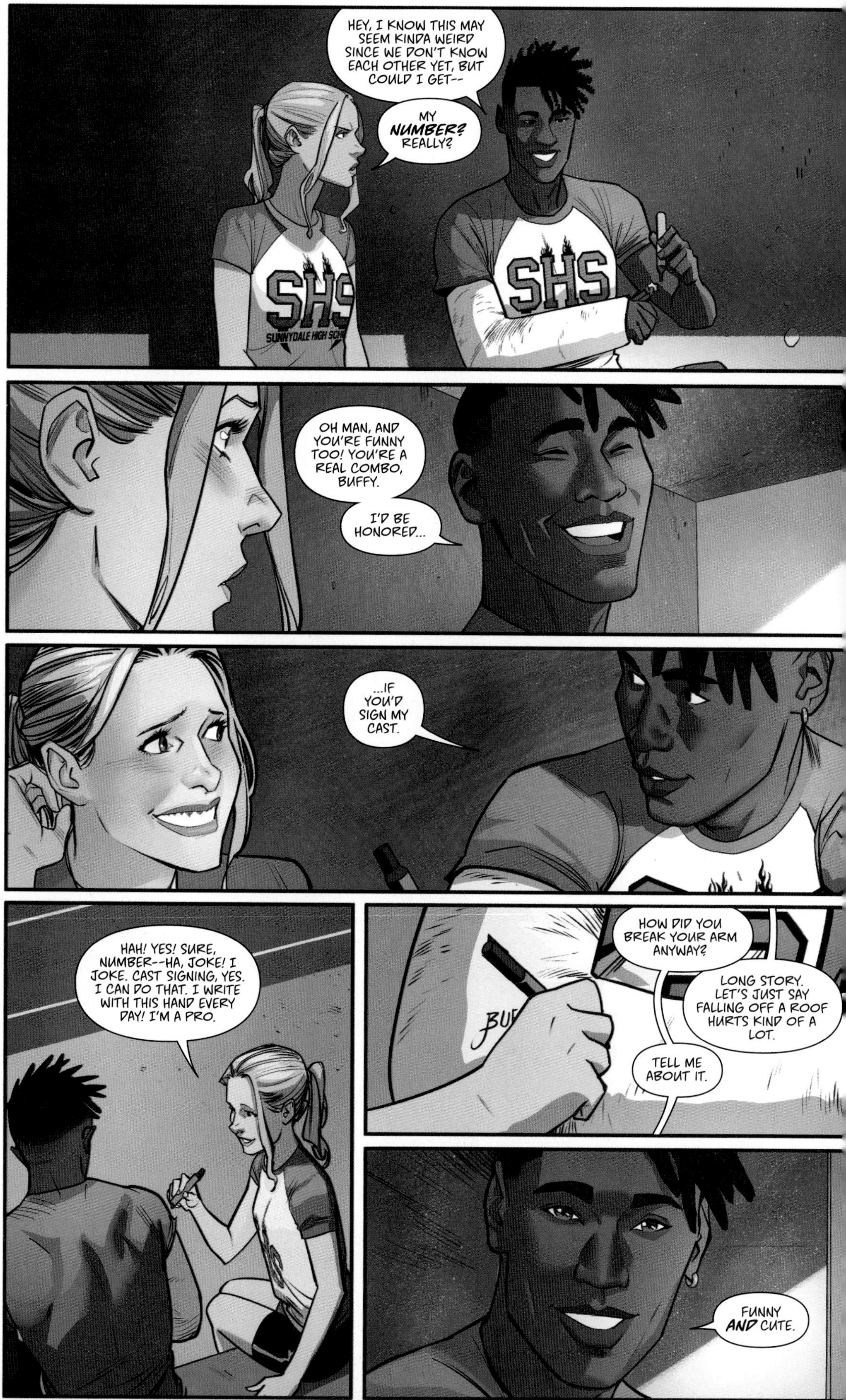
HEY, I KNOW THIS MAY SEEM KINDA WEIRD SINCE WE DON'T KNOW EACH OTHER YET, BUT COULD I GET--
MY NUMBER? REALLY?
SHS
SHS
SUNNYDALE HIGH SCH
OH MAN, AND YOU'RE FUNNY TOO! YOU'RE A REAL COMBO, BUFFY.
I'D BE HONORED...
...IF YOU'D SIGN MY CAST.
HAH! YES! SURE, NUMBER--HA, JOKE! I JOKE. CAST SIGNING, YES. I CAN DO THAT. I WRITE WITH THIS HAND EVERY DAY! I'M A PRO.
HOW DID YOU BREAK YOUR ARM ANYWAY?
LONG STORY. LET'S JUST SAY FALLING OFF A ROOF HURTS KIND OF A LOT.
TELL ME ABOUT IT.
FUNNY AND CUTE.

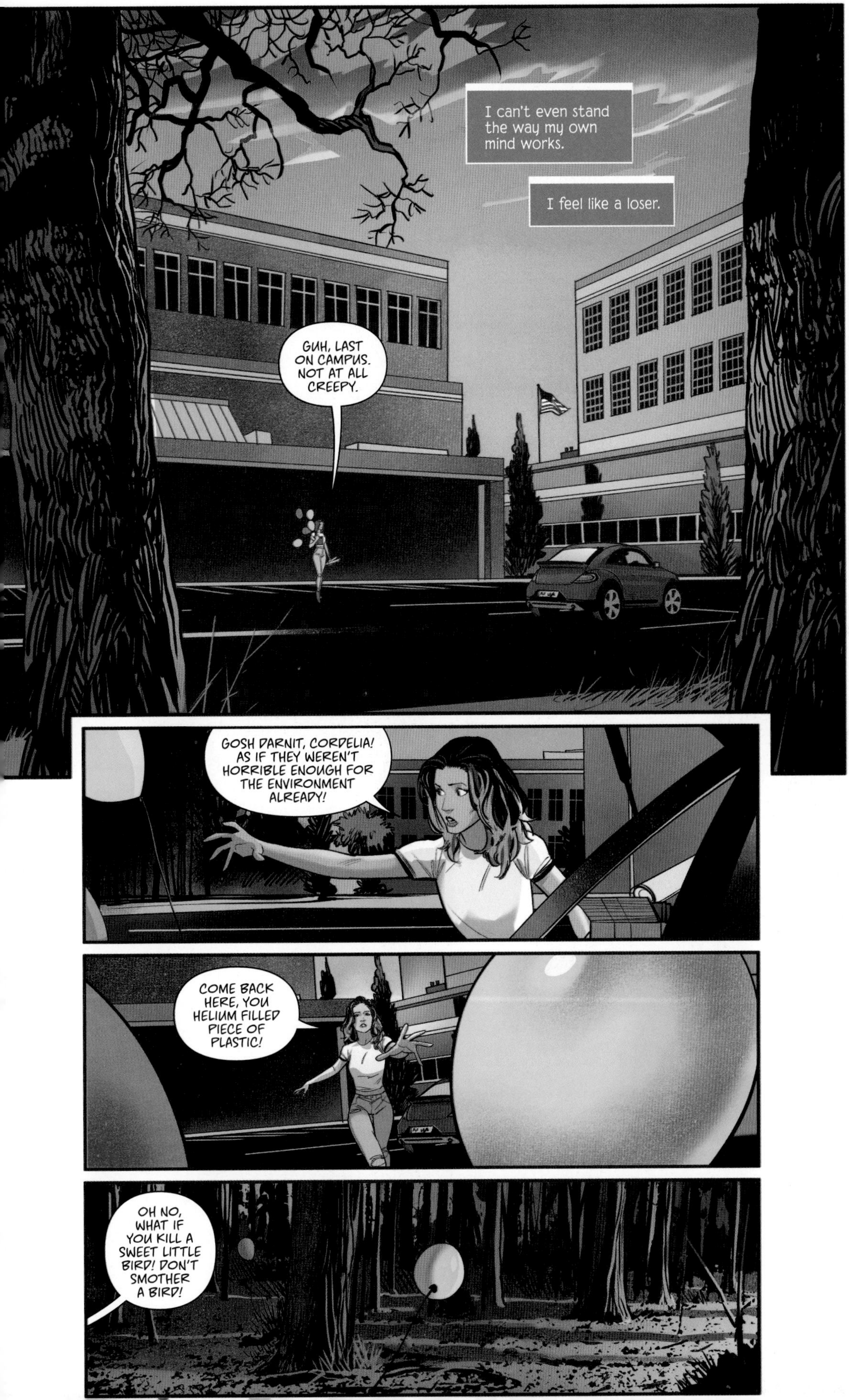
I can't even stand the way my own mind works.
I feel like a loser.
GUH, LAST ON CAMPUS. NOT AT ALL CREEPY.
GOSH DARNIT, CORDELIA! AS IF THEY WEREN'T HORRIBLE ENOUGH FOR THE ENVIRONMENT ALREADY!
COME BACK HERE, YOU HELIUM FILLED PIECE OF PLASTIC!
OH NO, WHAT IF YOU KILL A SWEET LITTLE BIRD! DON'T SMOTHER A BIRD!

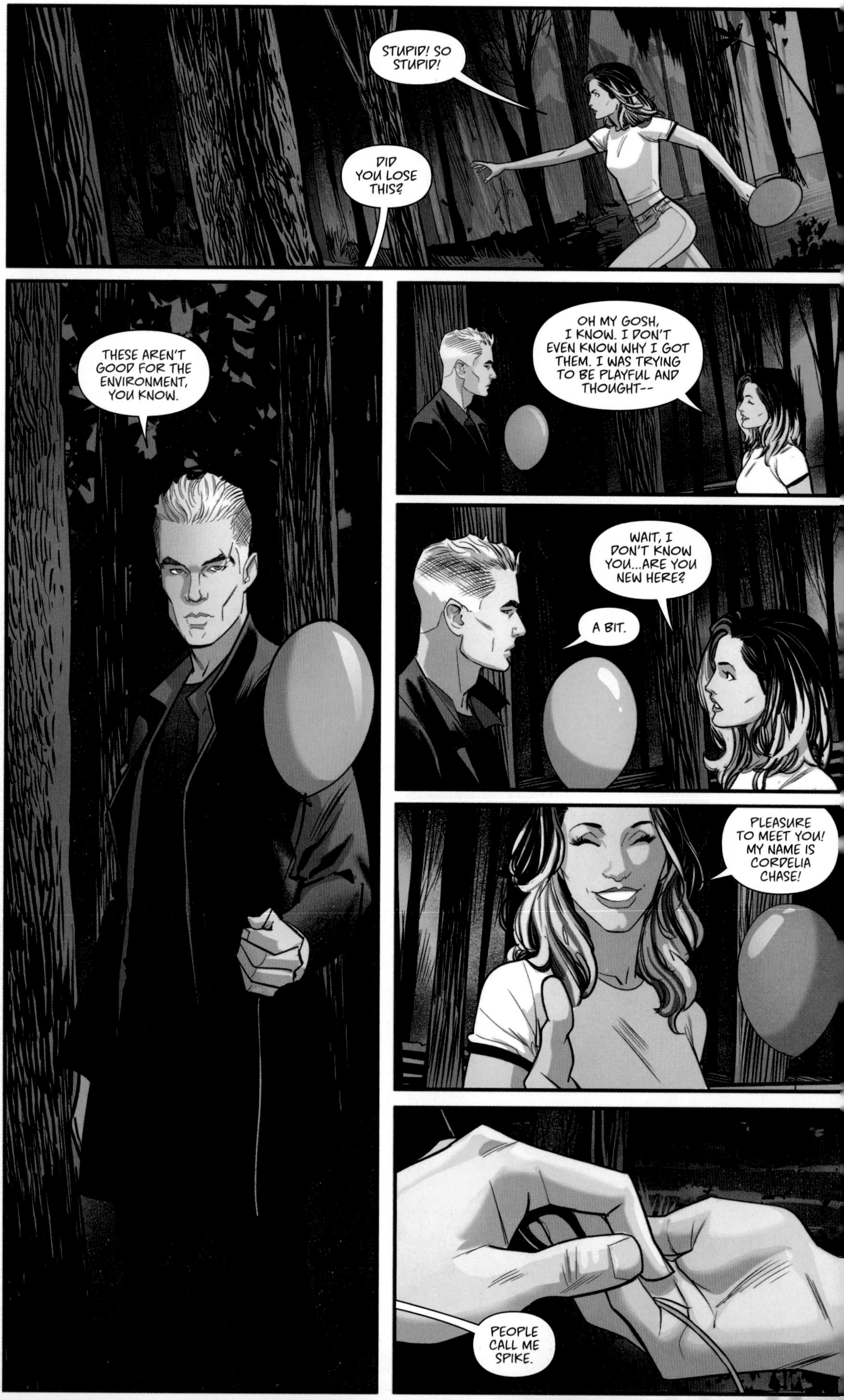
STUPID! SO STUPID!
DID YOU LOSE THIS?
THESE AREN'T GOOD FOR THE ENVIRONMENT, YOU KNOW.
OH MY GOSH, I KNOW. I DON'T EVEN KNOW WHY I GOT THEM. I WAS TRYING TO BE PLAYFUL AND THOUGHT--
WAIT, I DON'T KNOW YOU...ARE YOU NEW HERE?
A BIT.
PLEASURE TO MEET YOU! MY NAME IS CORDELIA CHASE!
PEOPLE CALL ME SPIKE.

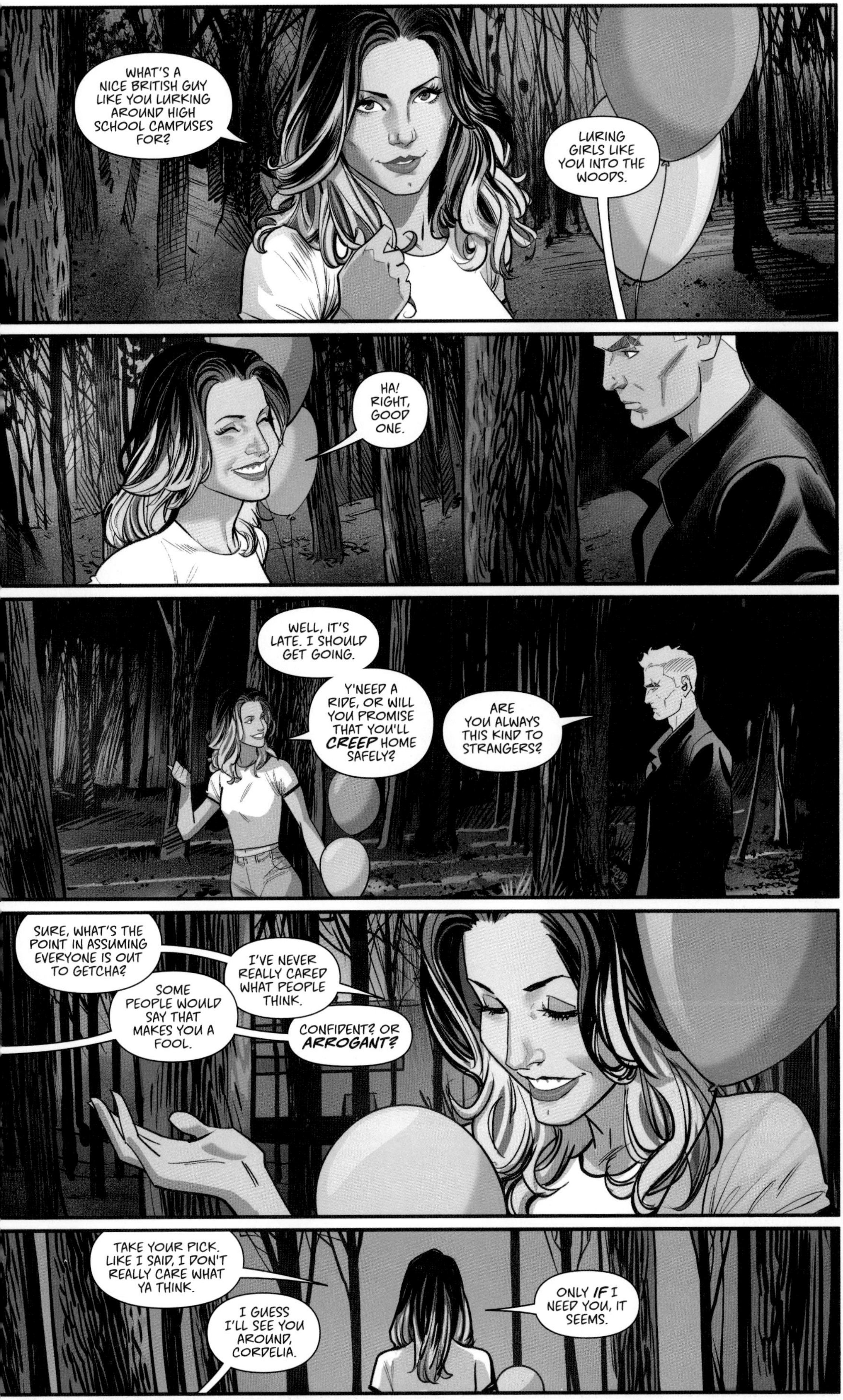
WHAT'S A NICE BRITISH GUY LIKE YOU LURKING AROUND HIGH SCHOOL CAMPUSES FOR?
LURING GIRLS LIKE YOU INTO THE WOODS.
HA! RIGHT, GOOD ONE.
WELL, IT'S LATE. I SHOULD GET GOING.
Y'NEED A RIDE, OR WILL YOU PROMISE THAT YOU'LL CREEP HOME SAFELY?
ARE YOU ALWAYS THIS KIND TO STRANGERS?
SURE, WHAT'S THE POINT IN ASSUMING EVERYONE IS OUT TO GETCHA?
I'VE NEVER REALLY CARED WHAT PEOPLE THINK.
SOME PEOPLE WOULD SAY THAT MAKES YOU A FOOL.
CONFIDENT? OR ARROGANT?
TAKE YOUR PICK. LIKE I SAID, I DON'T REALLY CARE WHAT YA THINK.
I GUESS I'LL SEE YOU AROUND, CORDELIA.
ONLY IF I NEED YOU, IT SEEMS.

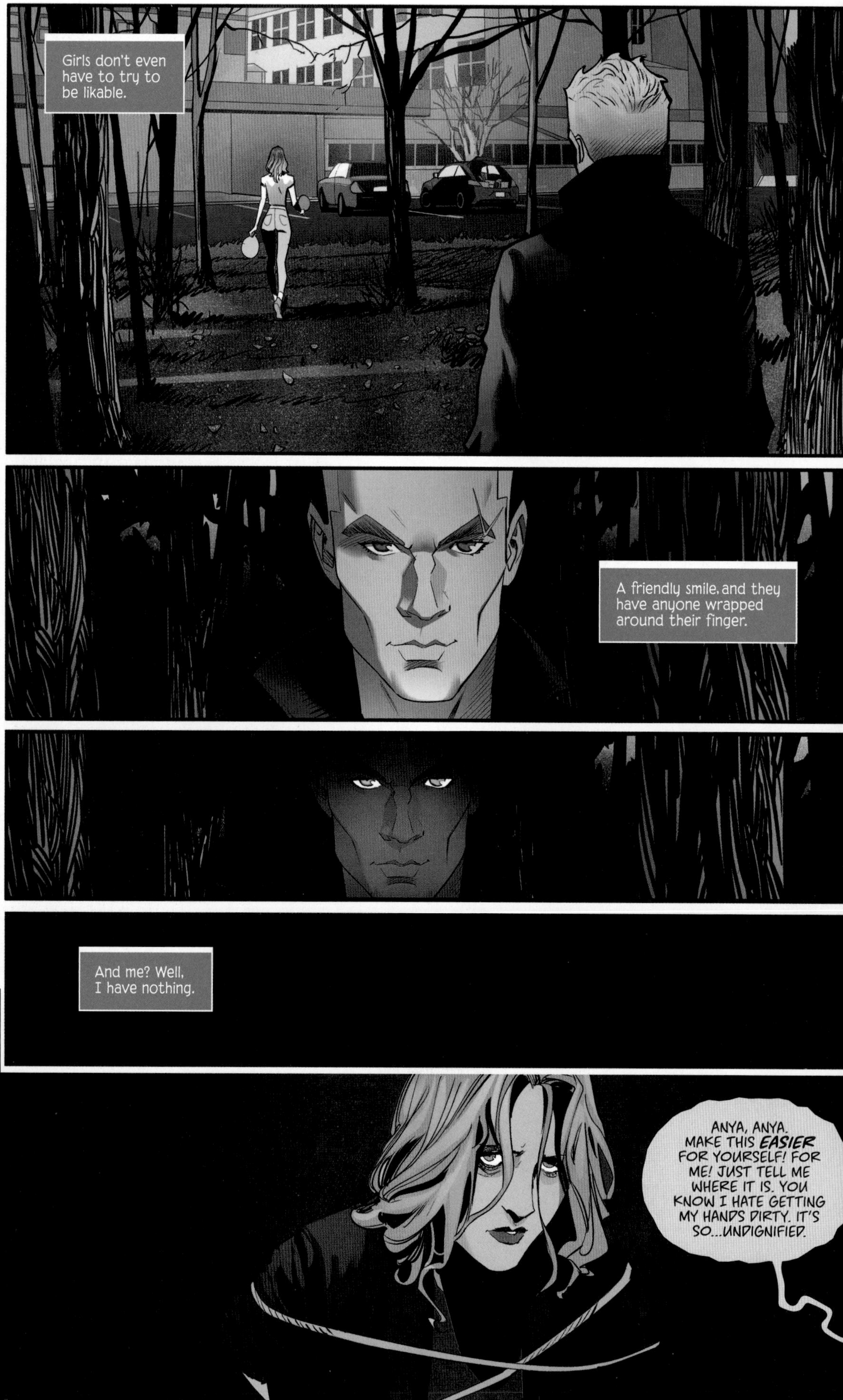
Girls don't even have to try to be likable.
A friendly smile, and they have anyone wrapped around their finger.
And me? Well, I have nothing.
ANYA, ANYA. MAKE THIS EASIER FOR YOURSELF! FOR ME! JUST TELL ME WHERE IT IS. YOU KNOW I HATE GETTING MY HANDS DIRTY. IT'S SO...UNDIGNIFIED.

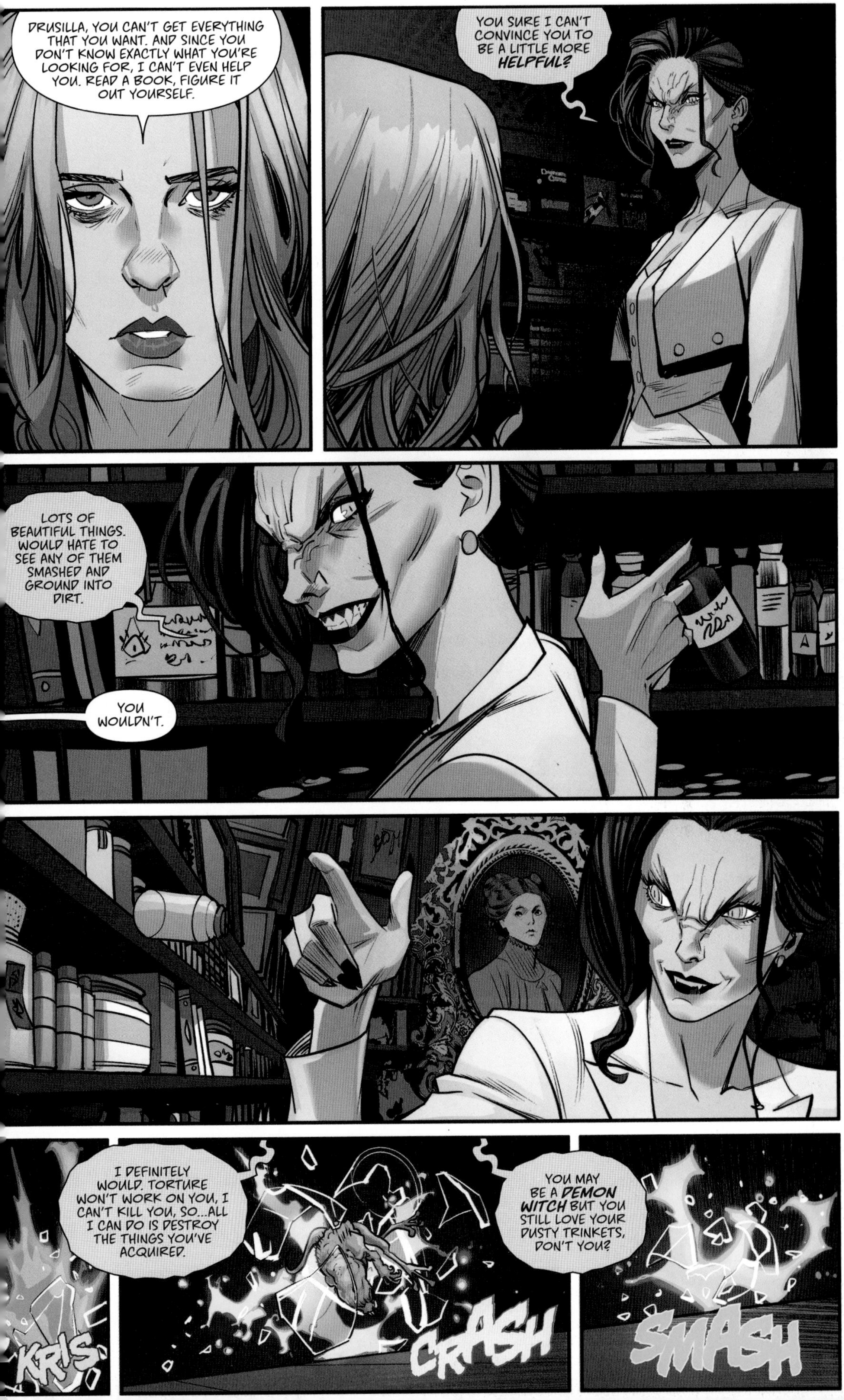
DRUSILLA, YOU CAN'T GET EVERYTHING THAT YOU WANT. AND SINCE YOU DON'T KNOW EXACTLY WHAT YOU'RE LOOKING FOR, I CAN'T EVEN HELP YOU. READ A BOOK, FIGURE IT OUT YOURSELF.
YOU SURE I CAN'T CONVINCE YOU TO BE A LITTLE MORE **HELPFUL?**
LOTS OF BEAUTIFUL THINGS. WOULD HATE TO SEE ANY OF THEM SMASHED AND GROUND INTO DIRT.
YOU WOULDN'T.
I DEFINITELY WOULD. TORTURE WON'T WORK ON YOU, I CAN'T KILL YOU, SO...ALL I CAN DO IS DESTROY THE THINGS YOU'VE ACQUIRED.
YOU MAY BE A **DEMON WITCH** BUT YOU STILL LOVE YOUR DUSTY TRINKETS, DON'T YOU?
KRIS
CRASH
SMASH

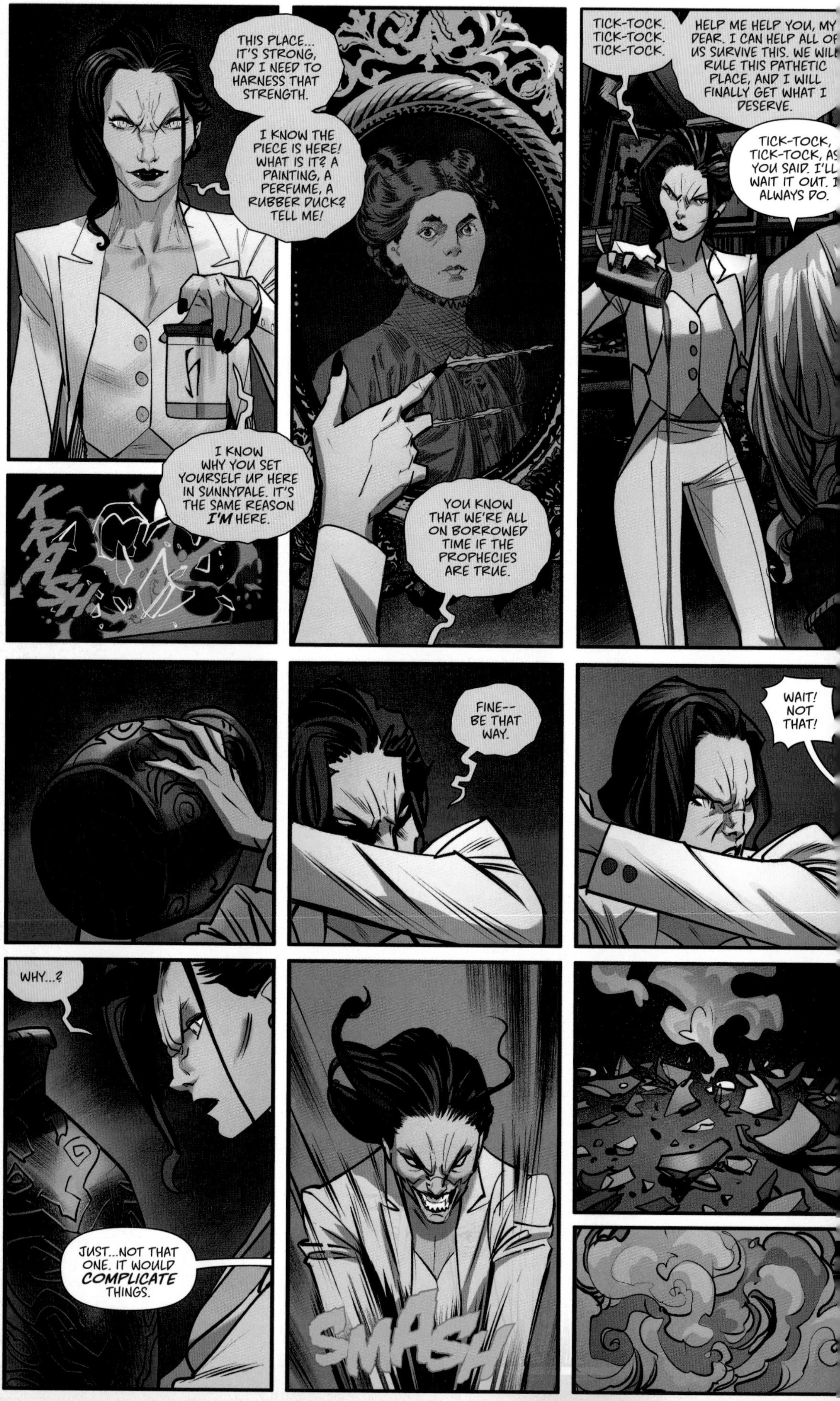
THIS PLACE... IT'S STRONG, AND I NEED TO HARNESS THAT STRENGTH.
I KNOW THE PIECE IS HERE! WHAT IS IT? A PAINTING, A PERFUME, A RUBBER DUCK? TELL ME!
KRASH
I KNOW WHY YOU SET YOURSELF UP HERE IN SUNNYDALE. IT'S THE SAME REASON I'M HERE.
YOU KNOW THAT WE'RE ALL ON BORROWED TIME IF THE PROPHECIES ARE TRUE.
TICK-TOCK. TICK-TOCK. TICK-TOCK.
HELP ME HELP YOU, MY DEAR. I CAN HELP ALL OF US SURVIVE THIS. WE WILL RULE THIS PATHETIC PLACE, AND I WILL FINALLY GET WHAT I DESERVE.
TICK-TOCK, TICK-TOCK, AS YOU SAID. I'LL WAIT IT OUT. I ALWAYS DO.
FINE-- BE THAT WAY.
WAIT! NOT THAT!
WHY...?
JUST...NOT THAT ONE. IT WOULD COMPLICATE THINGS.
SMASH

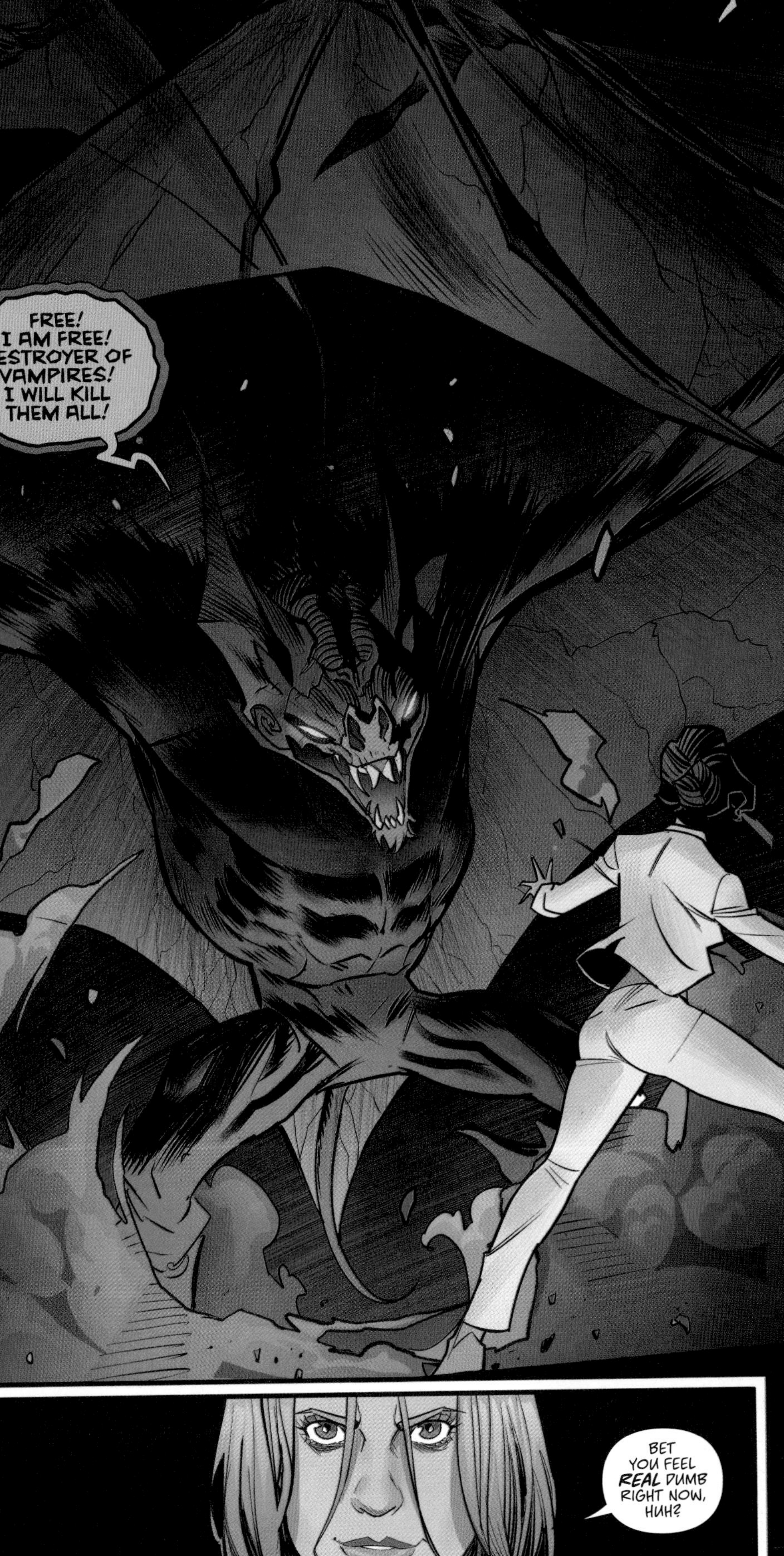
FREE! I AM FREE! ESTROYER OF VAMPIRES! I WILL KILL THEM ALL!
BET YOU FEEL **REAL** DUMB RIGHT NOW, HUH?

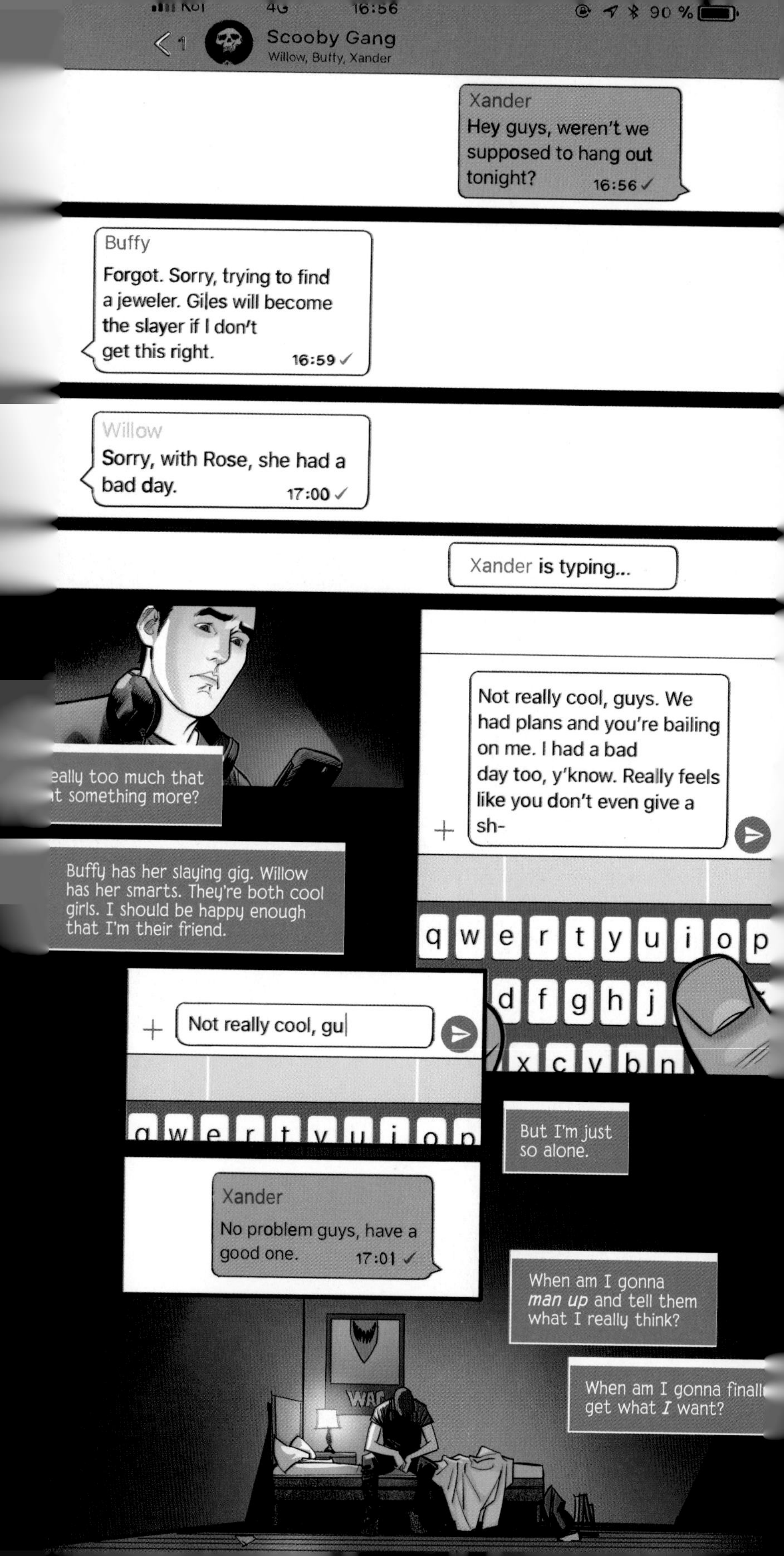
Kol 4G 16:56 90 %
Scooby Gang
Willow, Buffy, Xander
Xander
Hey guys, weren't we supposed to hang out tonight? 16:56
Buffy
Forgot. Sorry, trying to find a jeweler. Giles will become the slayer if I don't get this right. 16:59
Willow
Sorry, with Rose, she had a bad day. 17:00
Xander is typing...
Not really cool, guys. We had plans and you're bailing on me. I had a bad day too, y'know. Really feels like you don't even give a sh-
eally too much that
t something more?
Buffy has her slaying gig. Willow has her smarts. They're both cool girls. I should be happy enough that I'm their friend.
Not really cool, gu
But I'm just so alone.
Xander
No problem guys, have a good one. 17:01
When am I gonna *man up* and tell them what I really think?
When am I gonna finall get what *I* want?

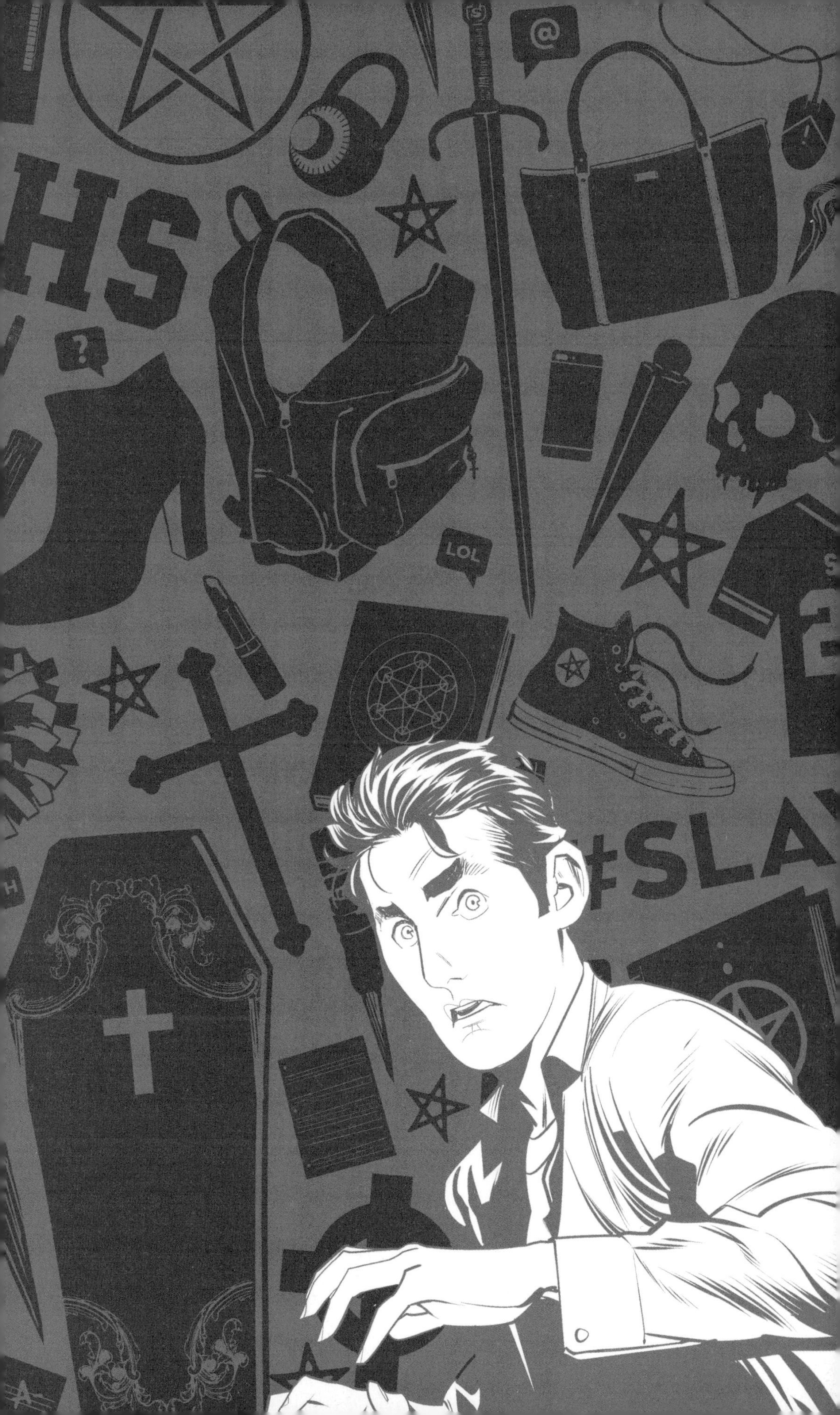
HS
?
LOL
#SLA

THREE

Issue Three Cover by **Matthew Taylor**

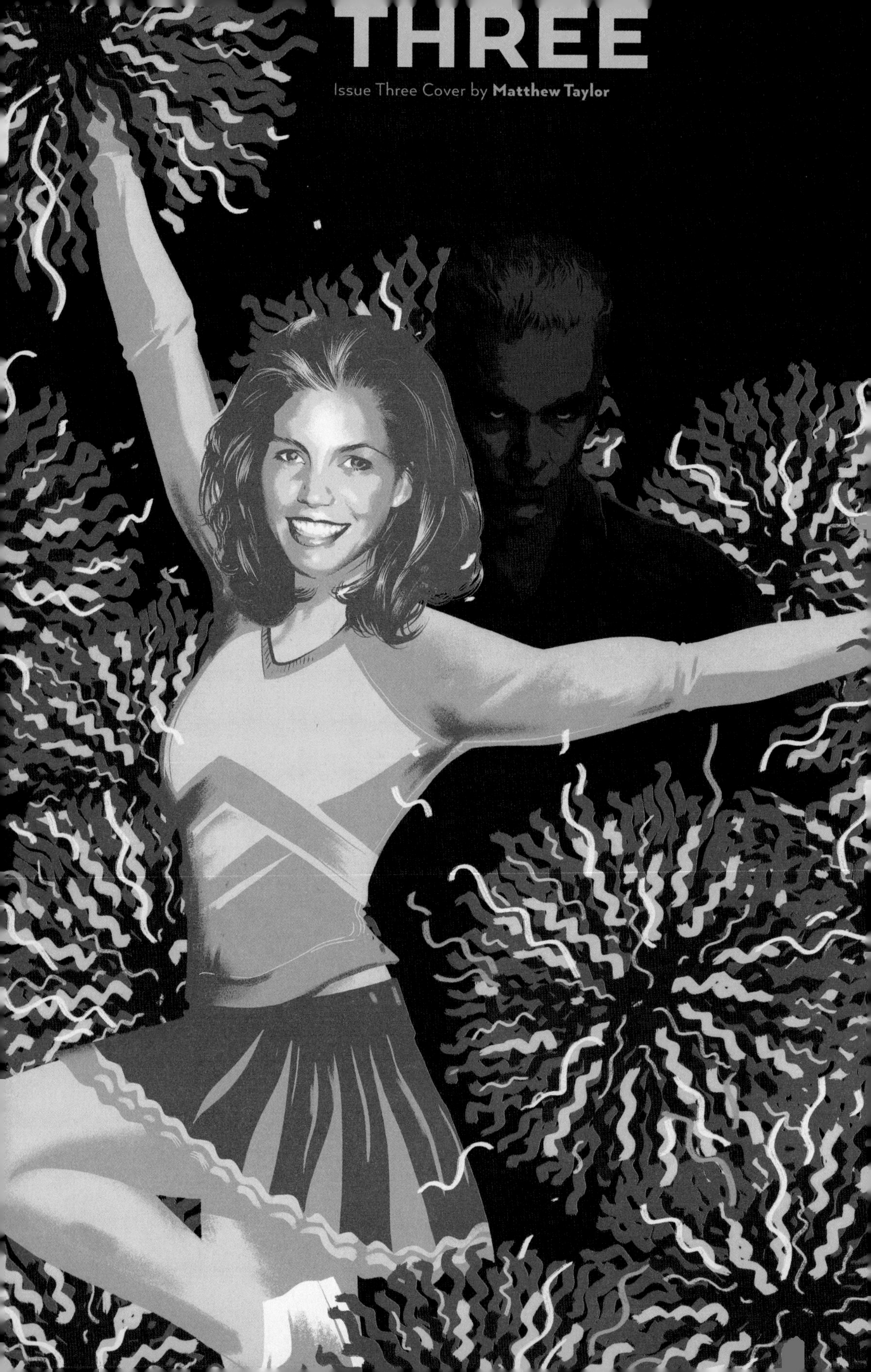

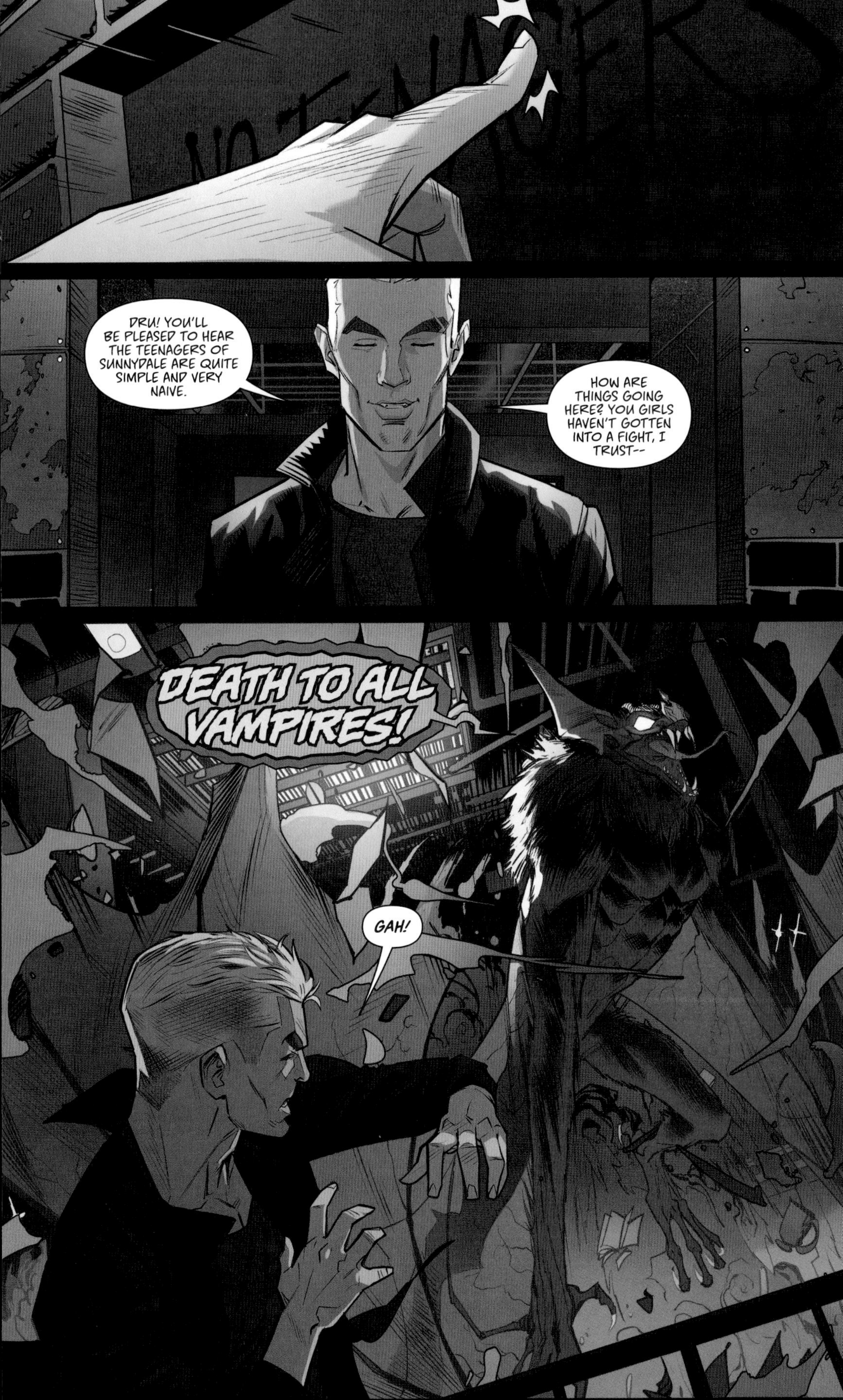
DRU! YOU'LL BE PLEASED TO HEAR THE TEENAGERS OF SUNNYDALE ARE QUITE SIMPLE AND VERY NAIVE.
HOW ARE THINGS GOING HERE? YOU GIRLS HAVEN'T GOTTEN INTO A FIGHT, I TRUST--
DEATH TO ALL VAMPIRES!
GAH!

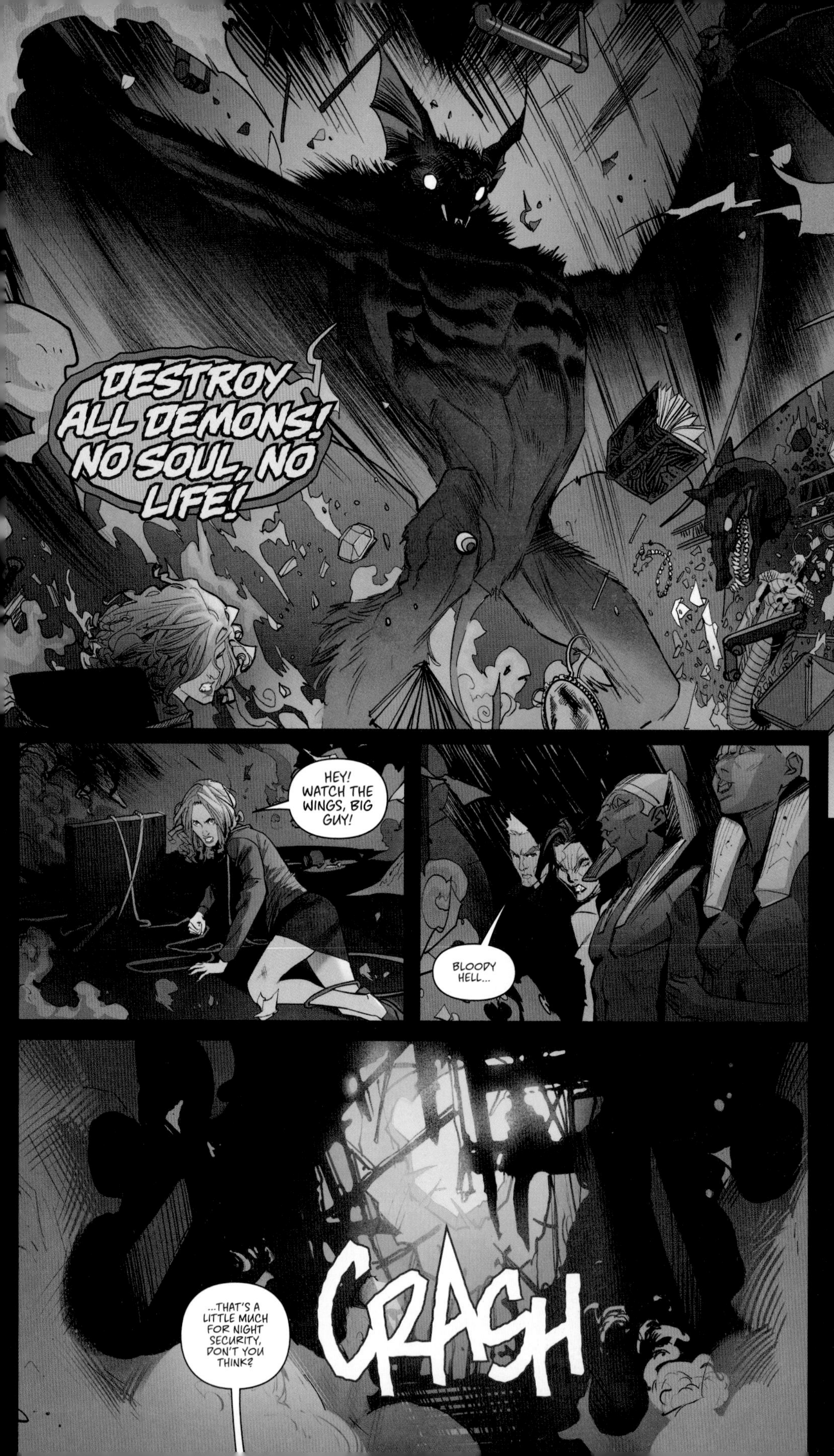
DESTROY ALL DEMONS! NO SOUL, NO LIFE!
HEY! WATCH THE WINGS, BIG GUY!
BLOODY HELL...
CRASH
...THAT'S A LITTLE MUCH FOR NIGHT SECURITY, DON'T YOU THINK?

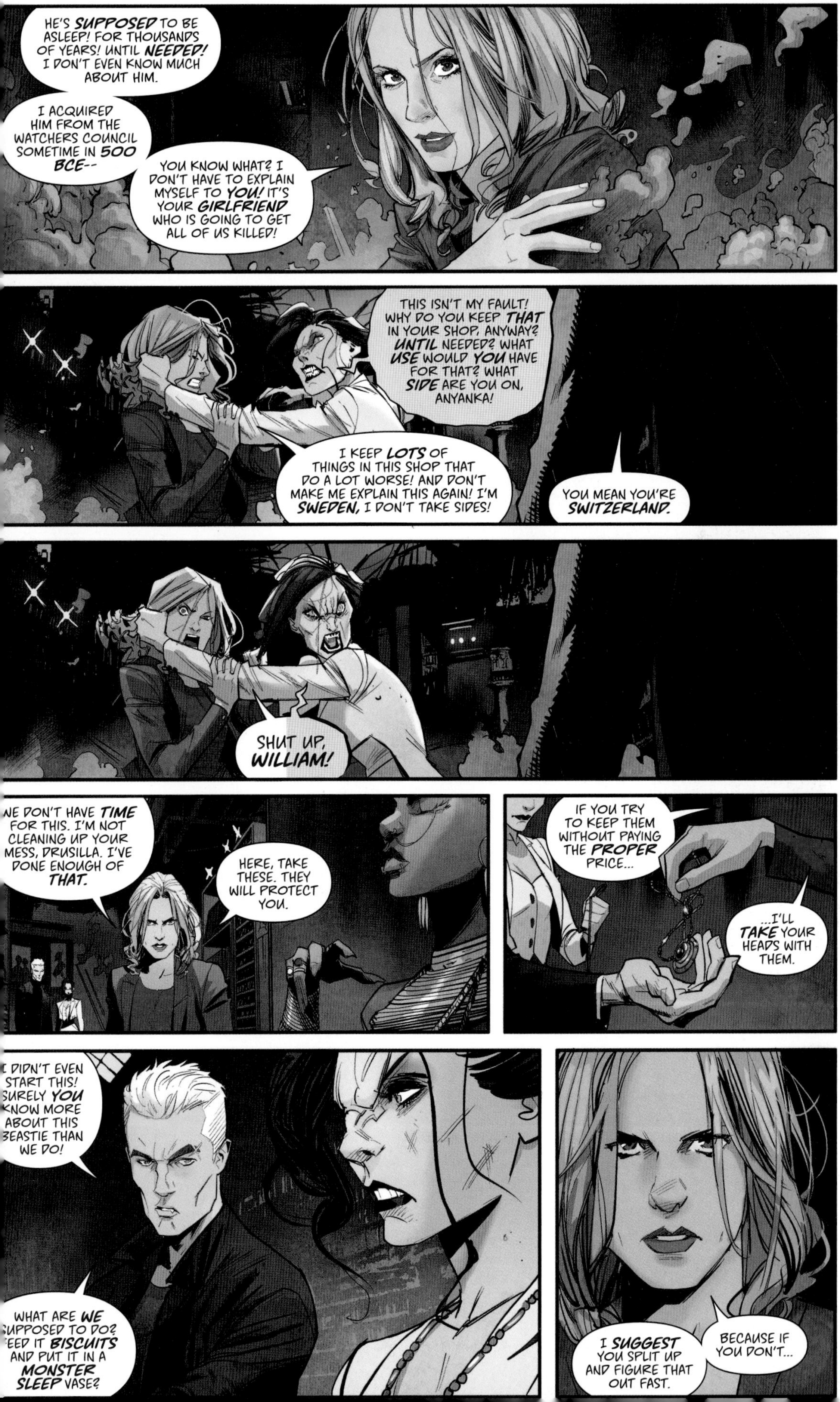

HE'S SUPPOSED TO BE ASLEEP! FOR THOUSANDS OF YEARS! UNTIL NEEDED! I DON'T EVEN KNOW MUCH ABOUT HIM.
I ACQUIRED HIM FROM THE WATCHERS COUNCIL SOMETIME IN 500 BCE--
YOU KNOW WHAT? I DON'T HAVE TO EXPLAIN MYSELF TO YOU! IT'S YOUR GIRLFRIEND WHO IS GOING TO GET ALL OF US KILLED!
THIS ISN'T MY FAULT! WHY DO YOU KEEP THAT IN YOUR SHOP, ANYWAY? UNTIL NEEDED? WHAT USE WOULD YOU HAVE FOR THAT? WHAT SIDE ARE YOU ON, ANYANKA!
I KEEP LOTS OF THINGS IN THIS SHOP THAT DO A LOT WORSE! AND DON'T MAKE ME EXPLAIN THIS AGAIN! I'M SWEDEN, I DON'T TAKE SIDES!
YOU MEAN YOU'RE SWITZERLAND.
SHUT UP, WILLIAM!
WE DON'T HAVE TIME FOR THIS. I'M NOT CLEANING UP YOUR MESS, DRUSILLA. I'VE DONE ENOUGH OF THAT.
HERE, TAKE THESE. THEY WILL PROTECT YOU.
IF YOU TRY TO KEEP THEM WITHOUT PAYING THE PROPER PRICE...
...I'LL TAKE YOUR HEADS WITH THEM.
I DIDN'T EVEN START THIS! SURELY YOU KNOW MORE ABOUT THIS BEASTIE THAN WE DO!
WHAT ARE WE SUPPOSED TO DO? FEED IT BISCUITS AND PUT IT IN A MONSTER SLEEP VASE?
I SUGGEST YOU SPLIT UP AND FIGURE THAT OUT FAST.
BECAUSE IF YOU DON'T...

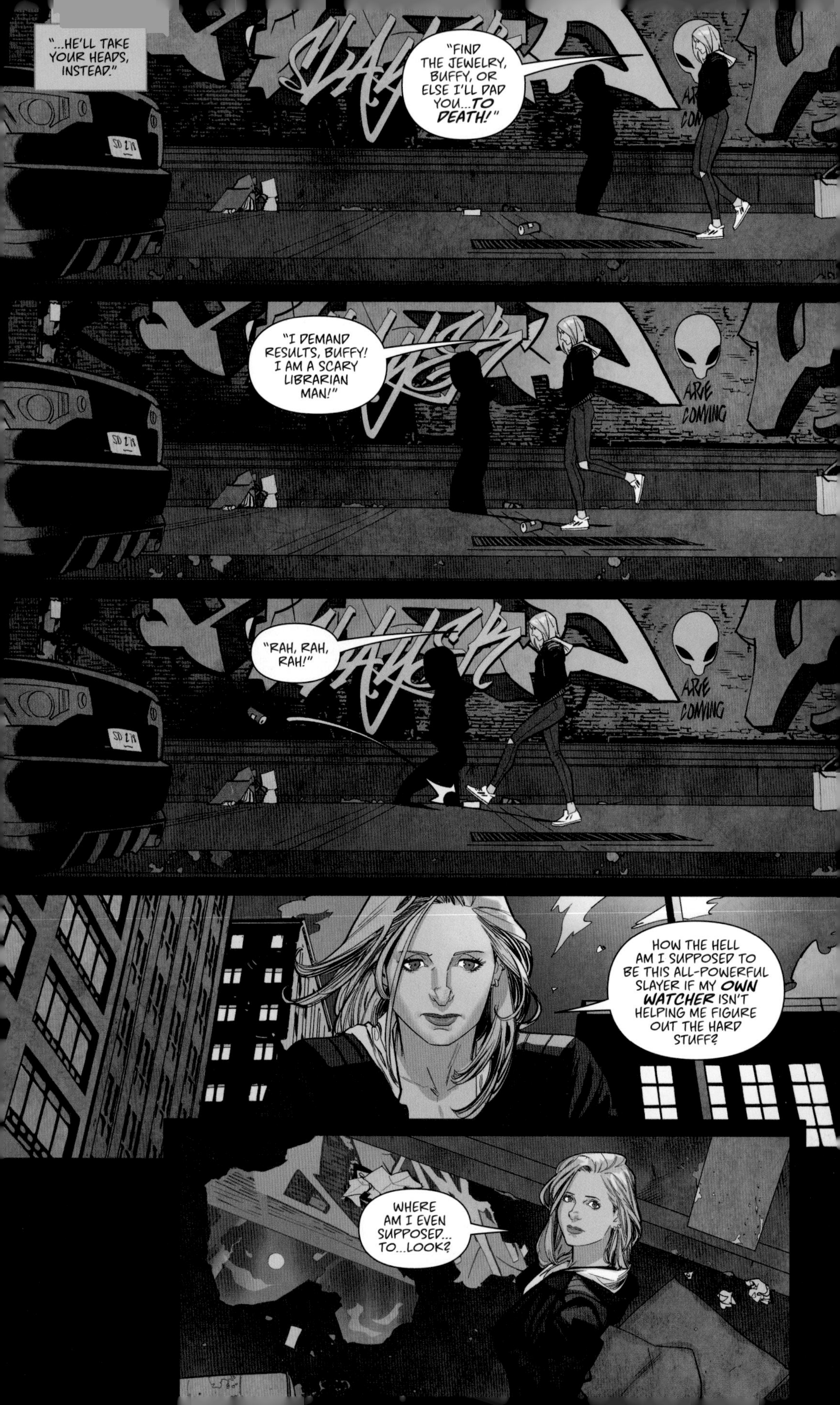
"...HE'LL TAKE YOUR HEADS, INSTEAD."
SLAYER
"FIND THE JEWELRY, BUFFY, OR ELSE I'LL DAD YOU...TO DEATH!"
"I DEMAND RESULTS, BUFFY! I AM A SCARY LIBRARIAN MAN!"
ARE COMING
"RAH, RAH, RAH!"
ARE COMING
HOW THE HELL AM I SUPPOSED TO BE THIS ALL-POWERFUL SLAYER IF MY OWN WATCHER ISN'T HELPING ME FIGURE OUT THE HARD STUFF?
WHERE AM I EVEN SUPPOSED... TO...LOOK?

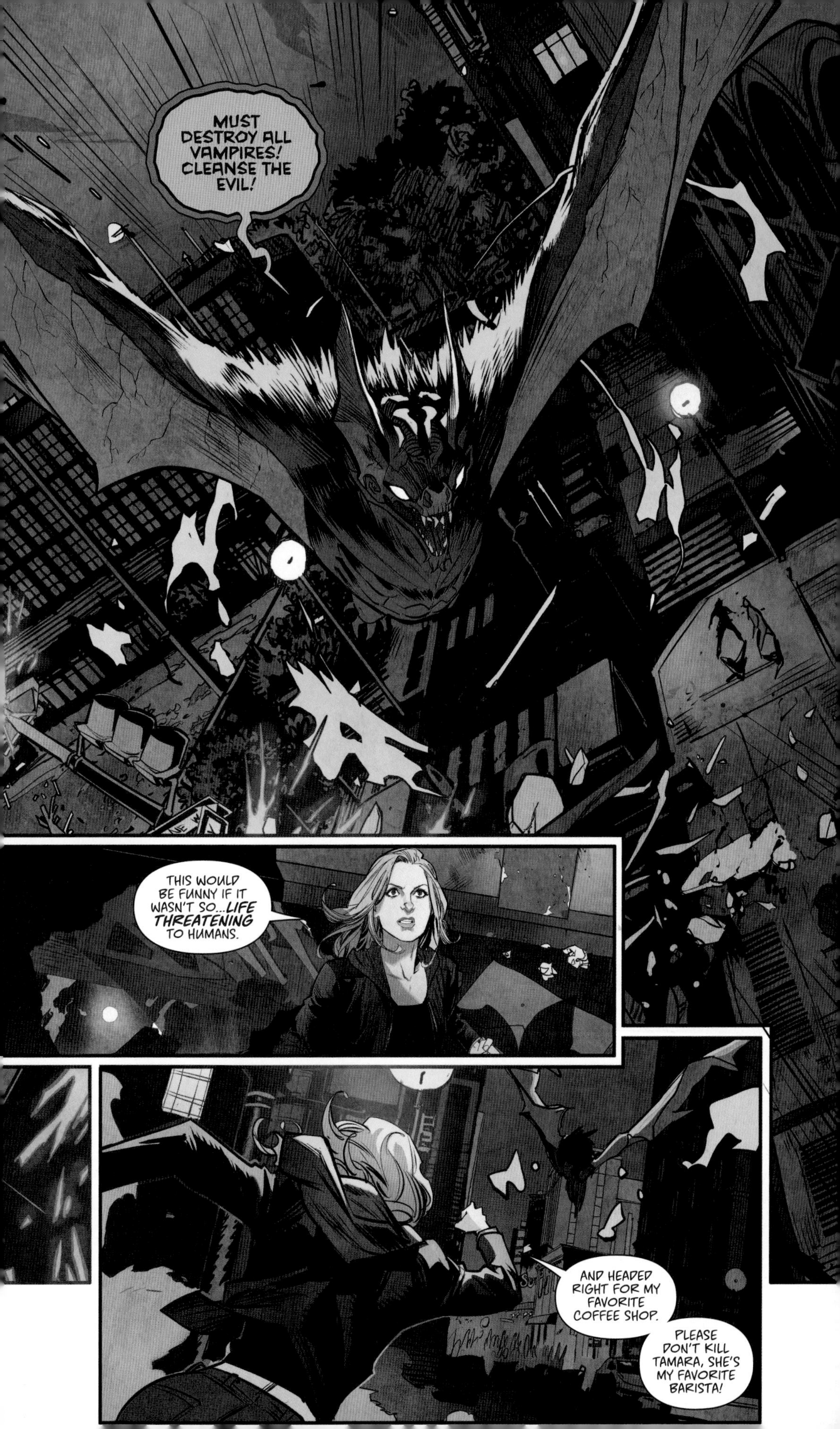
MUST DESTROY ALL VAMPIRES! CLEANSE THE EVIL!
THIS WOULD BE FUNNY IF IT WASN'T SO...*LIFE THREATENING* TO HUMANS.
AND HEADED RIGHT FOR MY FAVORITE COFFEE SHOP.
PLEASE DON'T KILL TAMARA, SHE'S MY FAVORITE BARISTA!

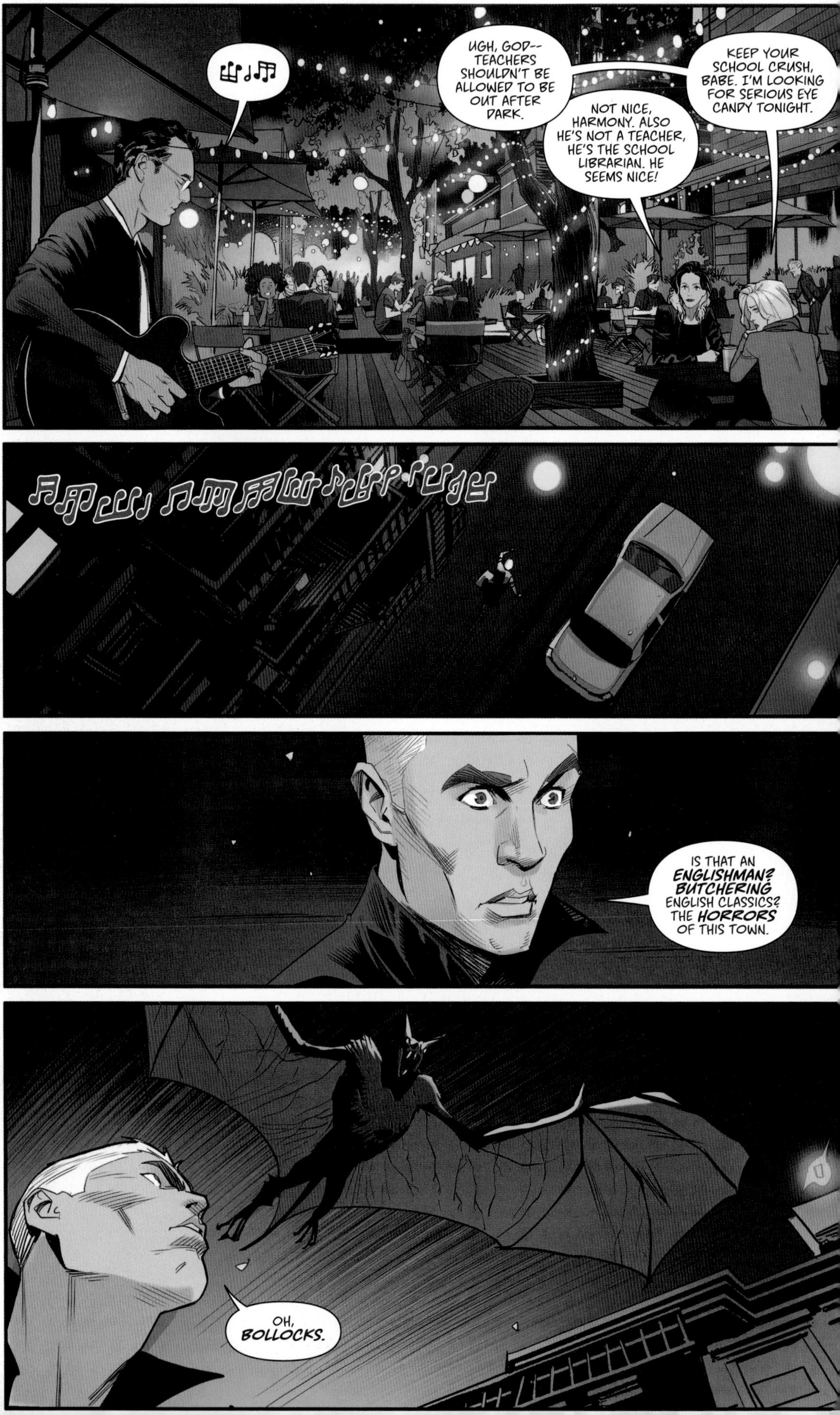
UGH, GOD-- TEACHERS SHOULDN'T BE ALLOWED TO BE OUT AFTER DARK.
KEEP YOUR SCHOOL CRUSH, BABE. I'M LOOKING FOR SERIOUS EYE CANDY TONIGHT.
NOT NICE, HARMONY. ALSO HE'S NOT A TEACHER, HE'S THE SCHOOL LIBRARIAN. HE SEEMS NICE!
IS THAT AN ENGLISHMAN? BUTCHERING ENGLISH CLASSICS? THE HORRORS OF THIS TOWN.
OH, BOLLOCKS.

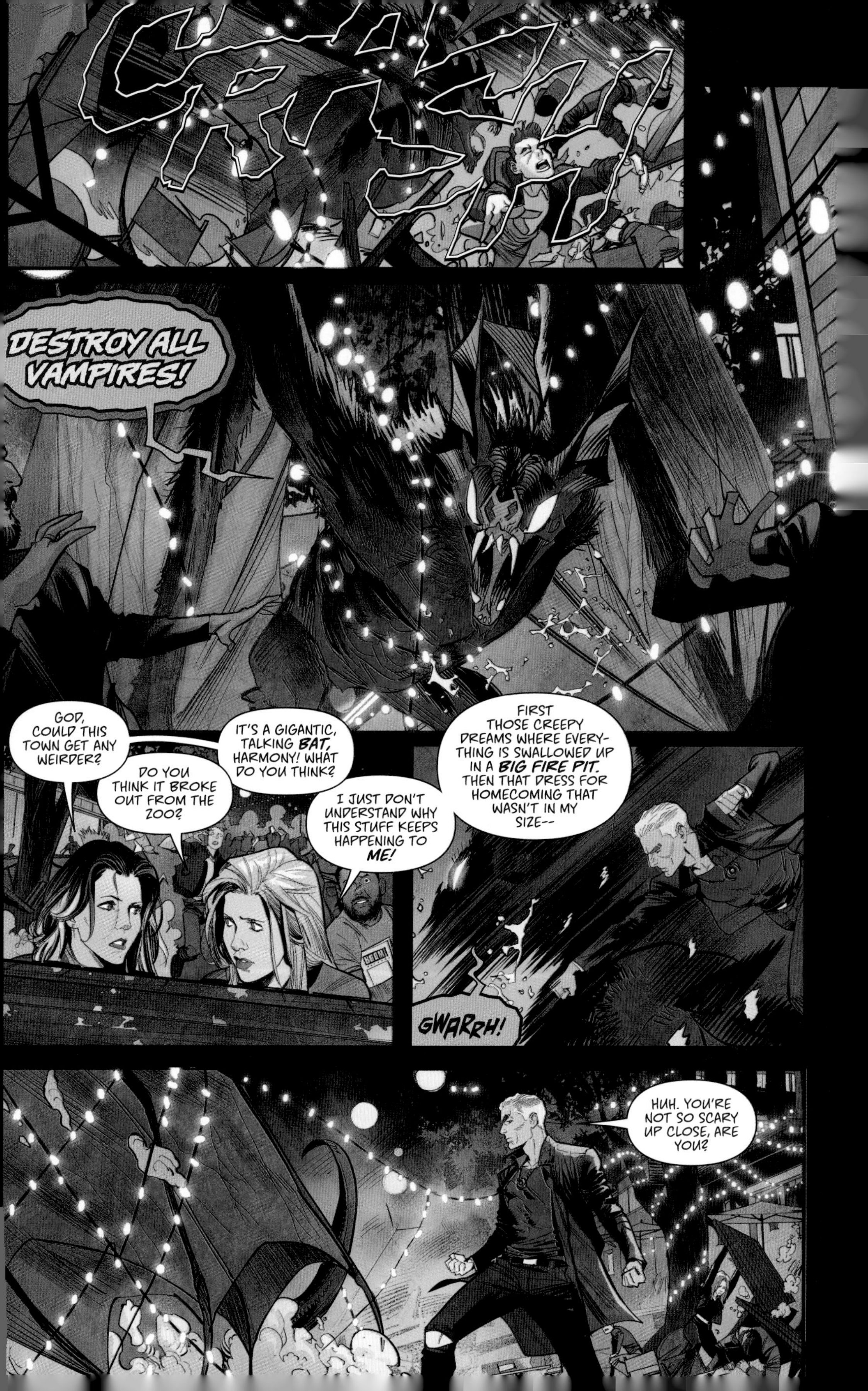
CRASH
DESTROY ALL VAMPIRES!
GOD, COULD THIS TOWN GET ANY WEIRDER?
IT'S A GIGANTIC, TALKING BAT, HARMONY! WHAT DO YOU THINK?
DO YOU THINK IT BROKE OUT FROM THE ZOO?
I JUST DON'T UNDERSTAND WHY THIS STUFF KEEPS HAPPENING TO ME!
FIRST THOSE CREEPY DREAMS WHERE EVERY-THING IS SWALLOWED UP IN A BIG FIRE PIT. THEN THAT DRESS FOR HOMECOMING THAT WASN'T IN MY SIZE--
GWARRH!
HUH. YOU'RE NOT SO SCARY UP CLOSE, ARE YOU?

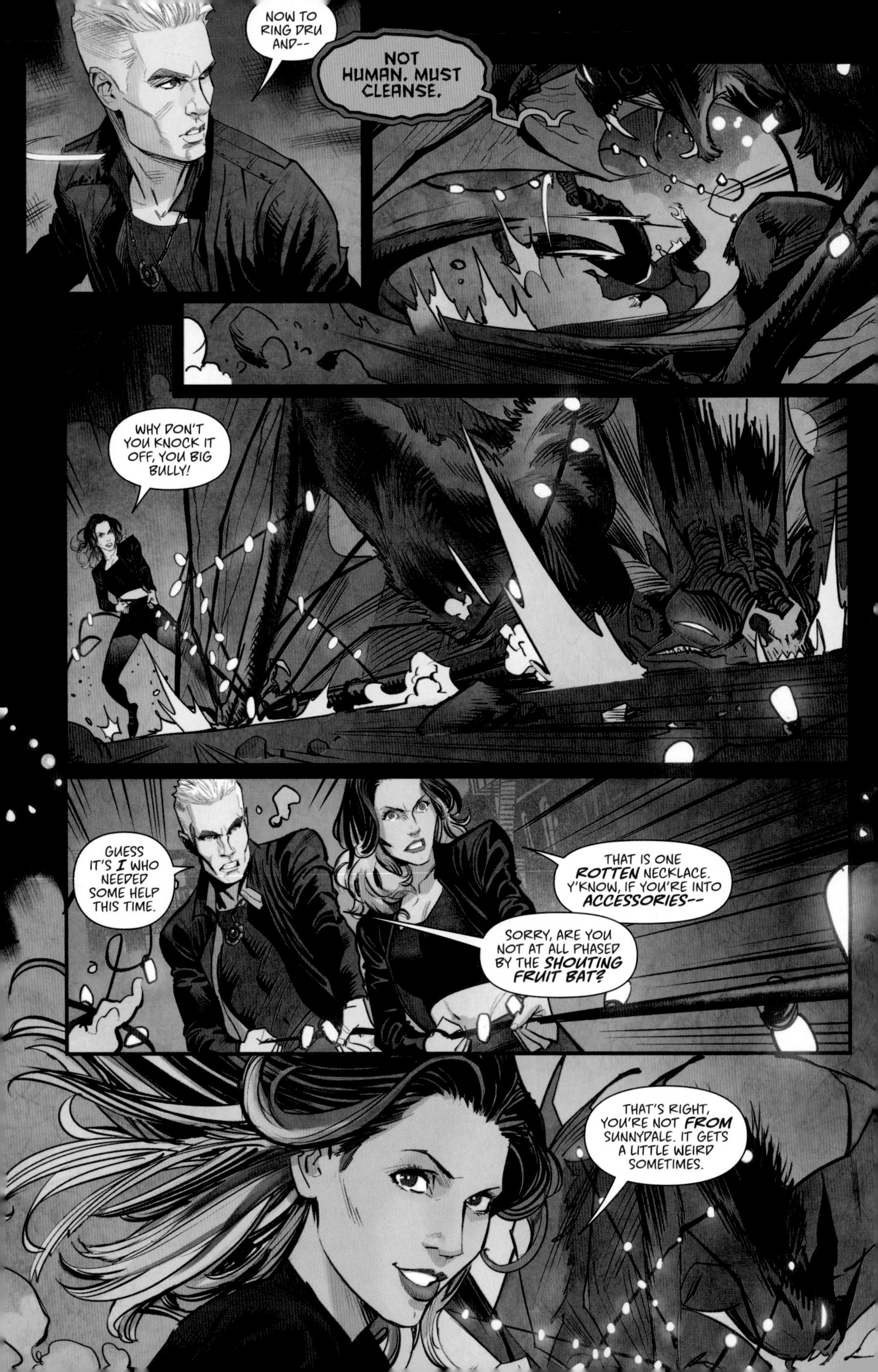
NOW TO RING DRU AND--
NOT HUMAN. MUST CLEANSE.
WHY DON'T YOU KNOCK IT OFF, YOU BIG BULLY!
GUESS IT'S *I* WHO NEEDED SOME HELP THIS TIME.
THAT IS ONE ***ROTTEN*** NECKLACE. Y'KNOW, IF YOU'RE INTO ***ACCESSORIES--***
SORRY, ARE YOU NOT AT ALL PHASED BY THE ***SHOUTING FRUIT BAT?***
THAT'S RIGHT, YOU'RE NOT ***FROM*** SUNNYDALE. IT GETS A LITTLE WEIRD SOMETIMES.

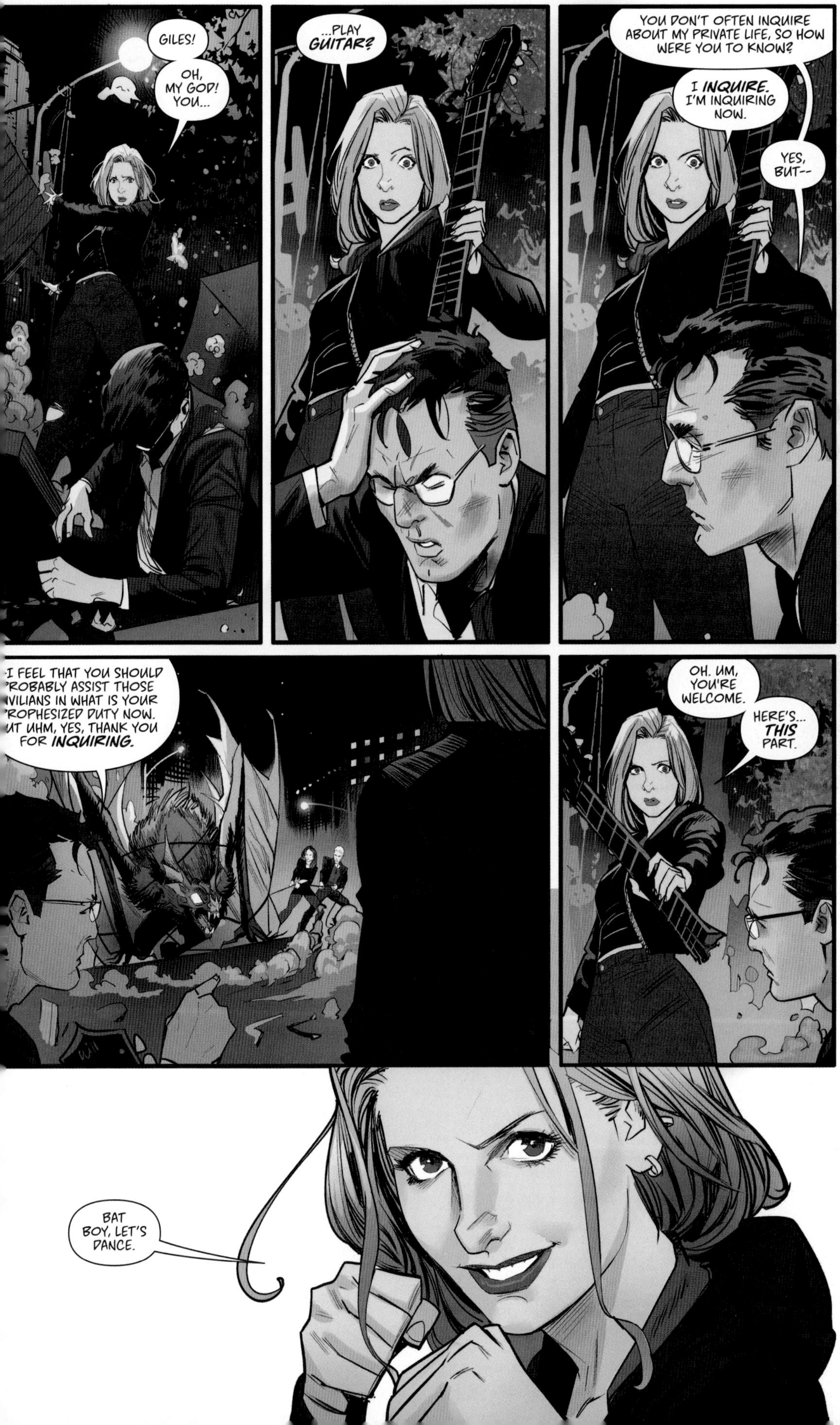

GILES!
OH, MY GOD! YOU...
...PLAY GUITAR?
YOU DON'T OFTEN INQUIRE ABOUT MY PRIVATE LIFE, SO HOW WERE YOU TO KNOW?
I INQUIRE. I'M INQUIRING NOW.
YES, BUT--
I FEEL THAT YOU SHOULD PROBABLY ASSIST THOSE VILIANS IN WHAT IS YOUR PROPHESIZED DUTY NOW. UT UHM, YES, THANK YOU FOR INQUIRING.
OH. UM, YOU'RE WELCOME.
HERE'S... THIS PART.
BAT BOY, LET'S DANCE.

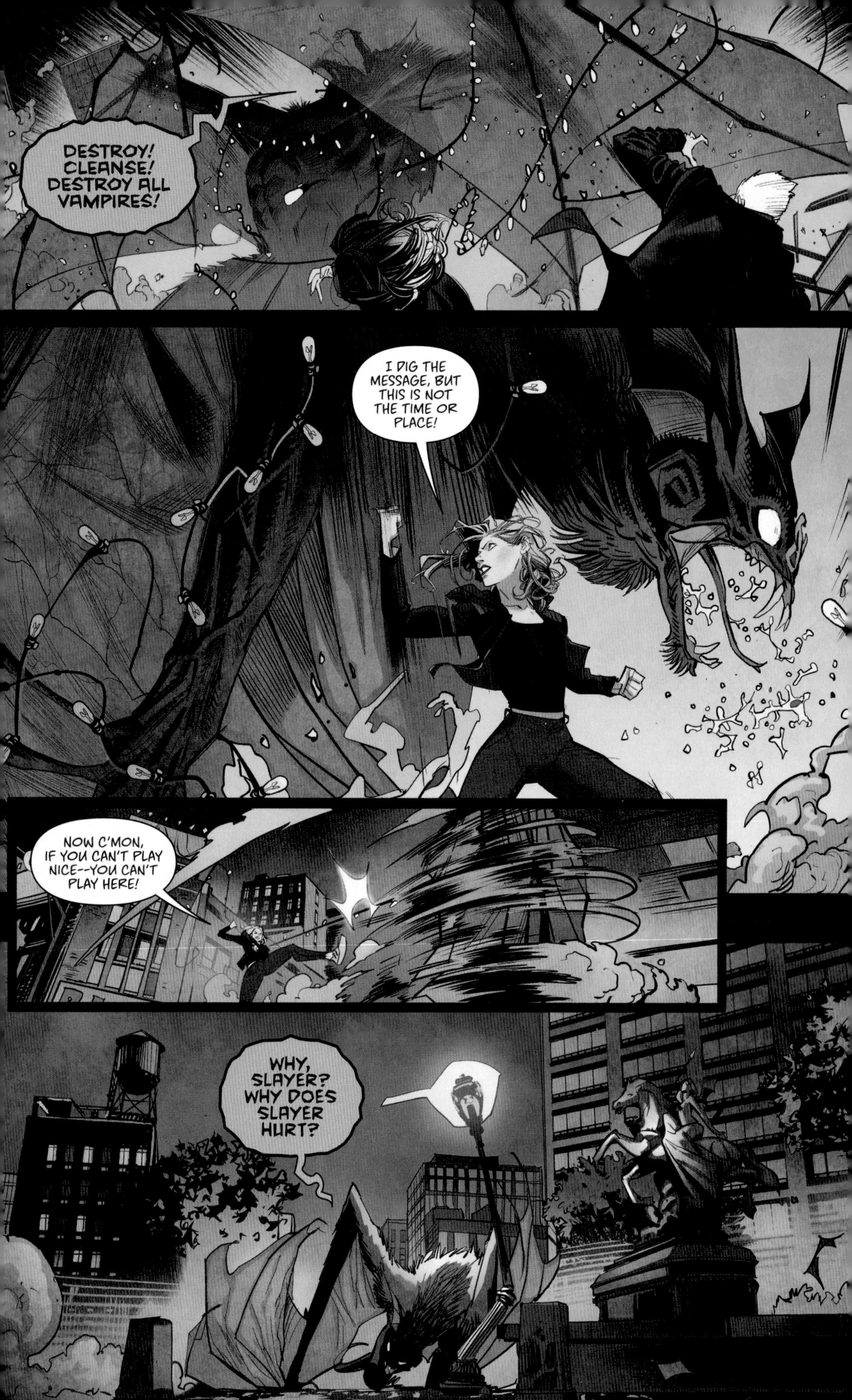
DESTROY! CLEANSE! DESTROY ALL VAMPIRES!
I DIG THE MESSAGE, BUT THIS IS NOT THE TIME OR PLACE!
NOW C'MON, IF YOU CAN'T PLAY NICE--YOU CAN'T PLAY HERE!
WHY, SLAYER? WHY DOES SLAYER HURT?

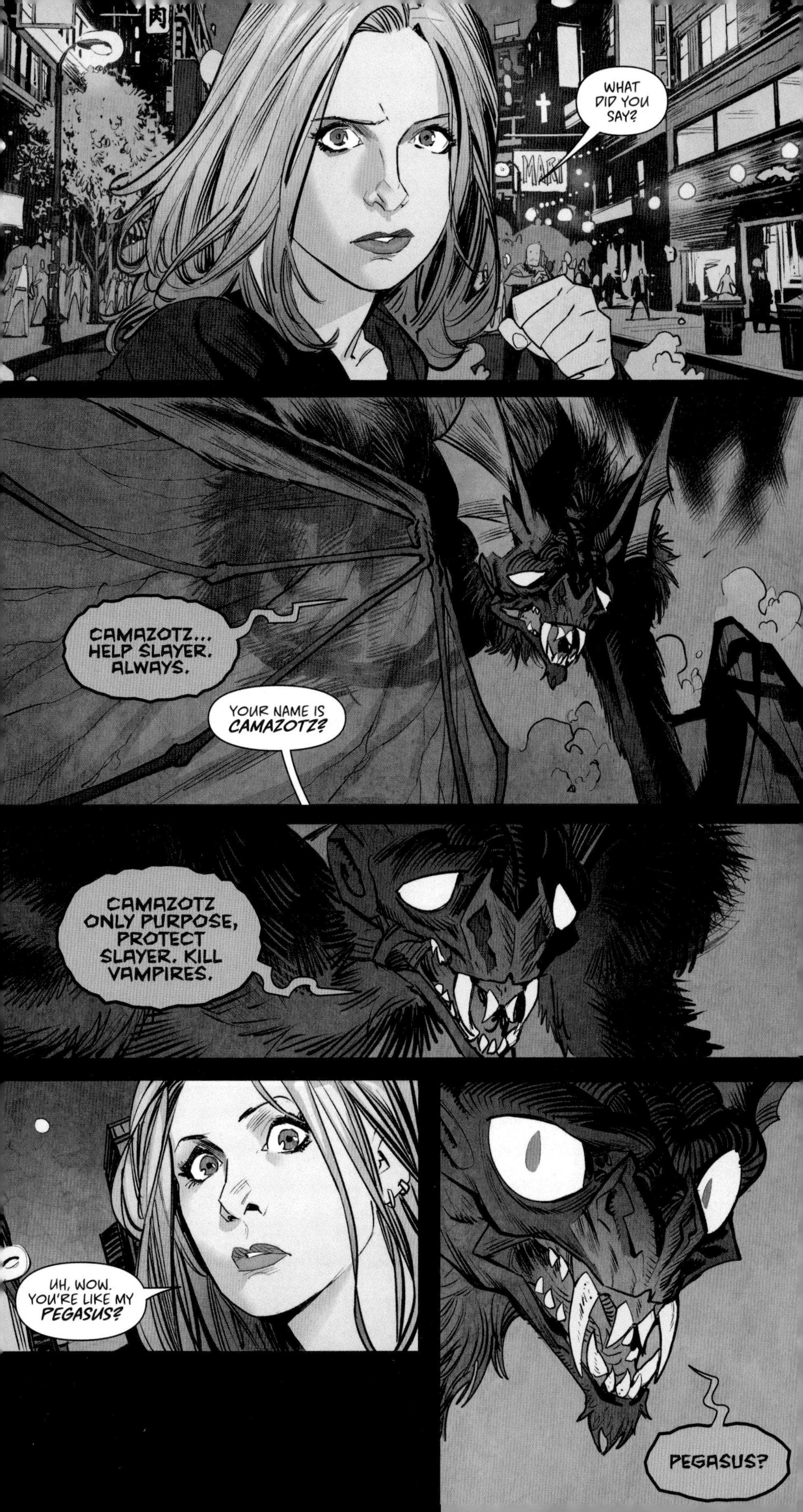
WHAT DID YOU SAY?
CAMAZOTZ... HELP SLAYER. ALWAYS.
YOUR NAME IS CAMAZOTZ?
CAMAZOTZ ONLY PURPOSE, PROTECT SLAYER. KILL VAMPIRES.
UH, WOW. YOU'RE LIKE MY PEGASUS?
PEGASUS?

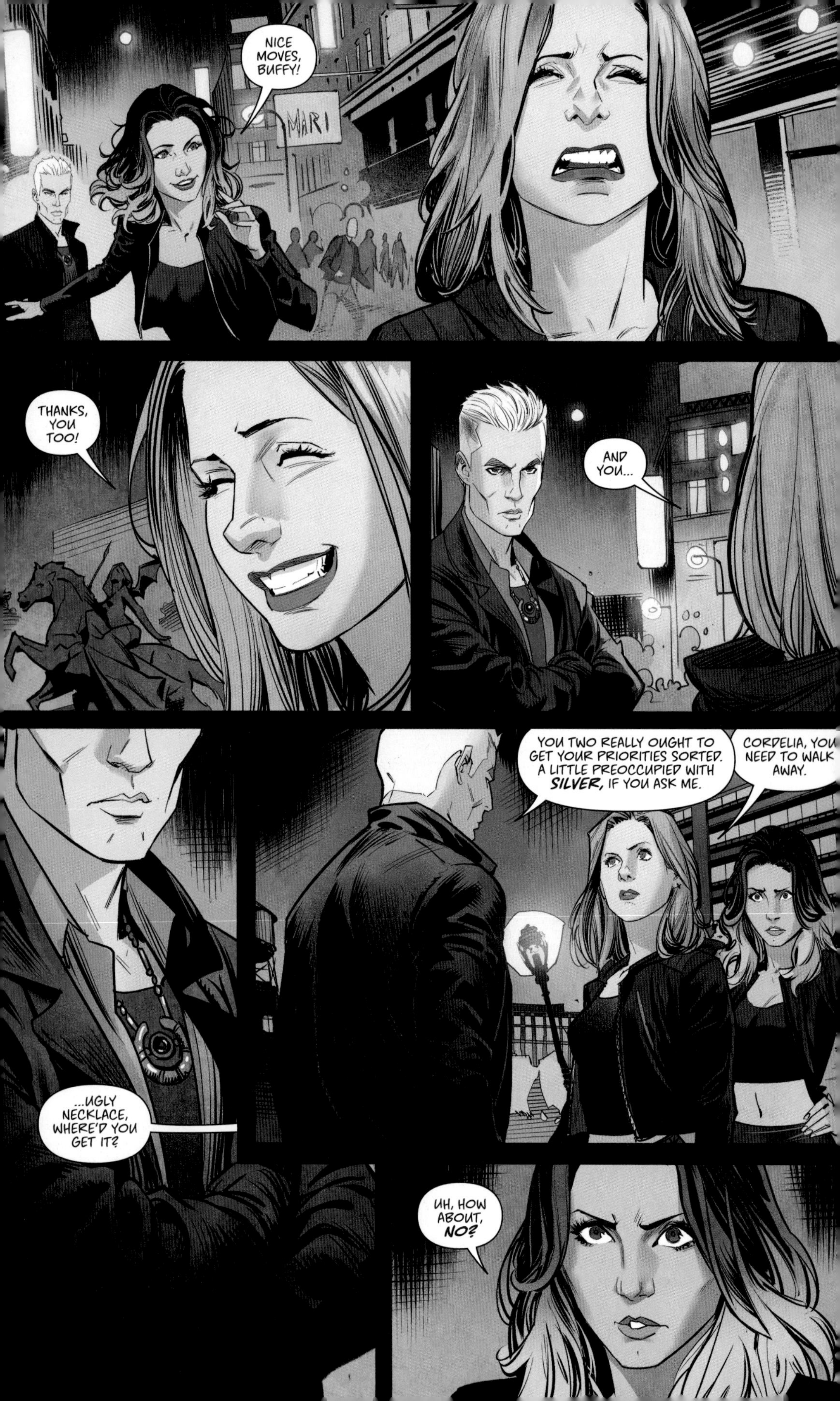
NICE MOVES, BUFFY!
THANKS, YOU TOO!
AND YOU...
...UGLY NECKLACE, WHERE'D YOU GET IT?
YOU TWO REALLY OUGHT TO GET YOUR PRIORITIES SORTED. A LITTLE PREOCCUPIED WITH SILVER, IF YOU ASK ME.
CORDELIA, YOU NEED TO WALK AWAY.
UH, HOW ABOUT, NO?

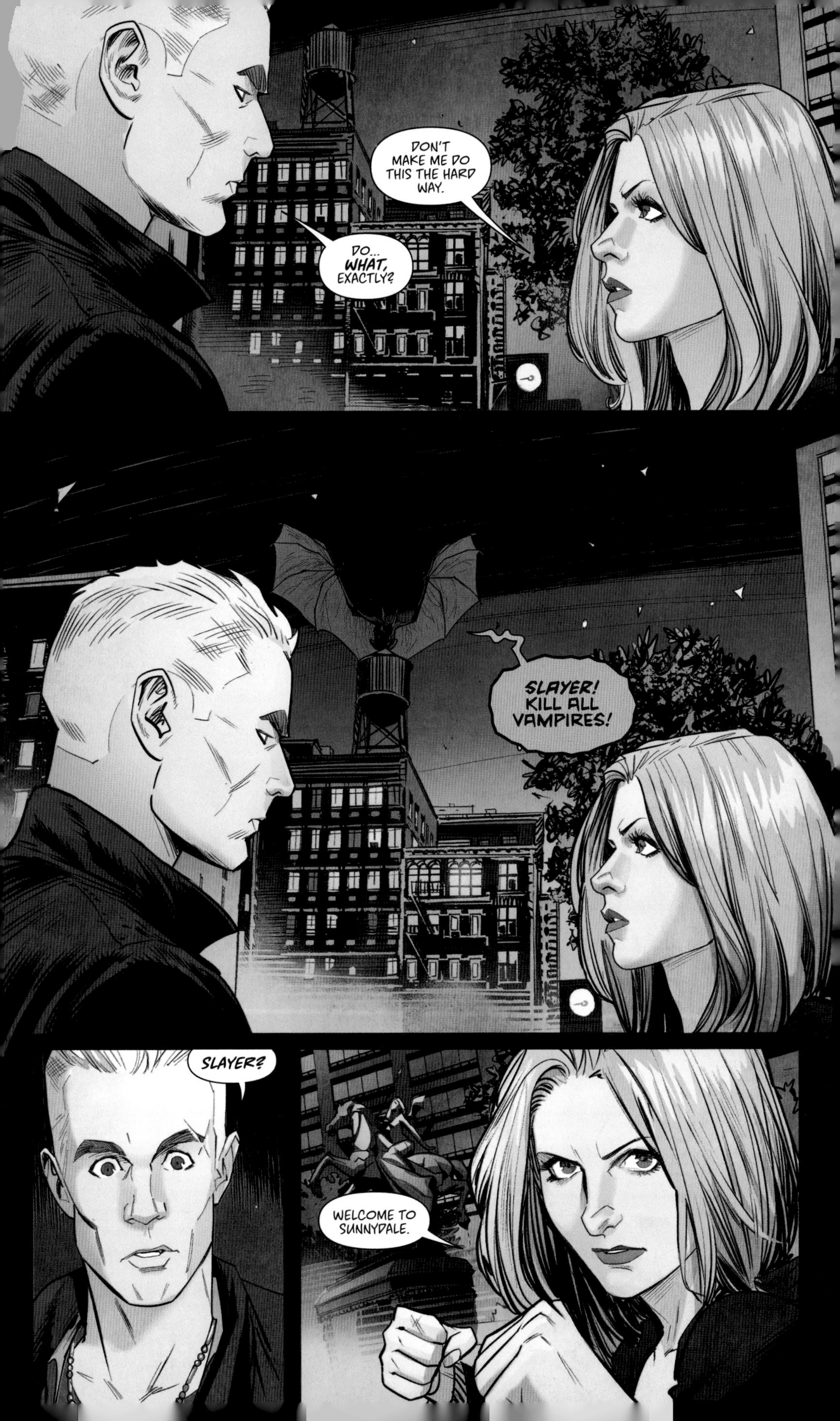
DON'T MAKE ME DO THIS THE HARD WAY.
DO... WHAT, EXACTLY?
SLAYER! KILL ALL VAMPIRES!
SLAYER?
WELCOME TO SUNNYDALE.

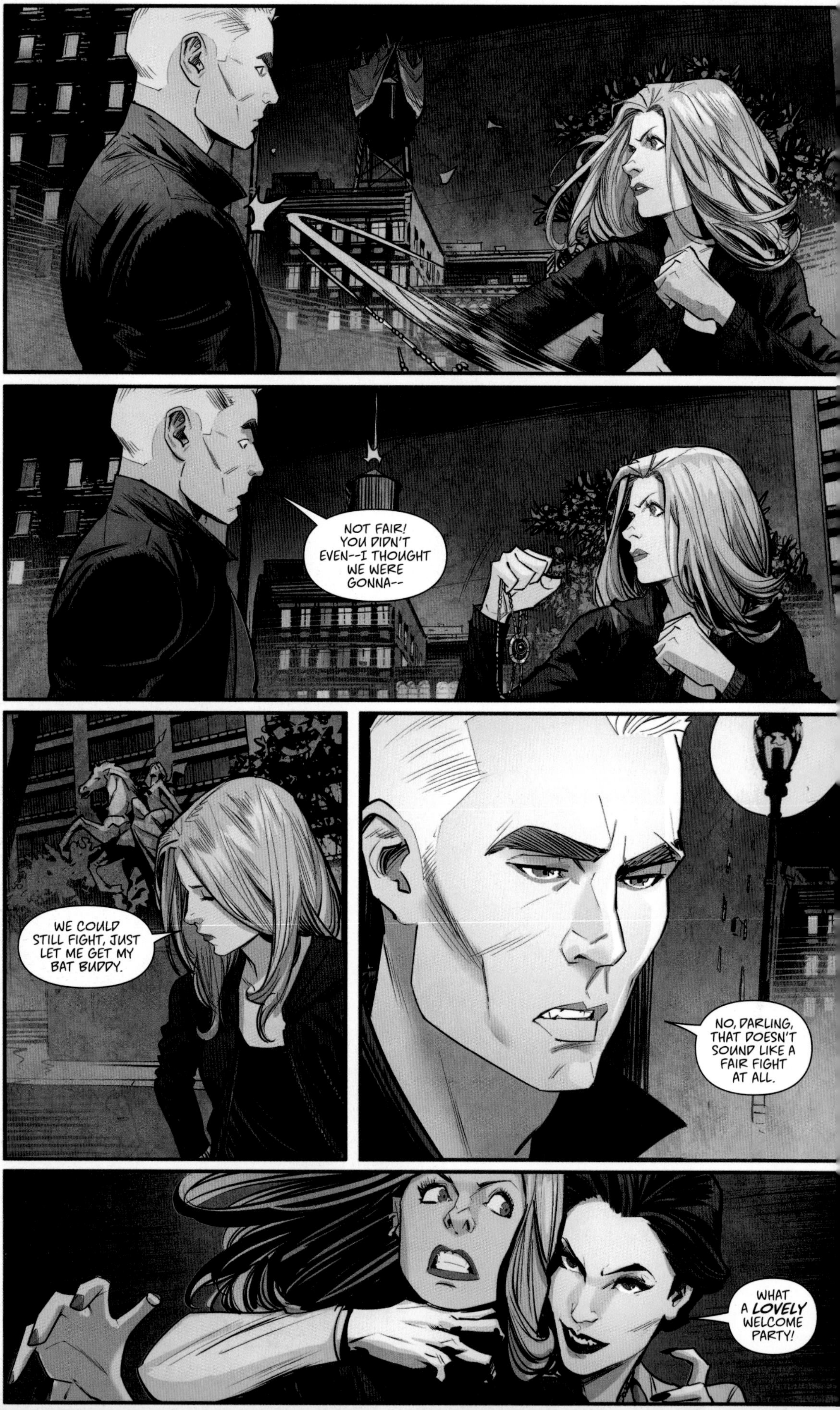
NOT FAIR! YOU DIDN'T EVEN--I THOUGHT WE WERE GONNA--
WE COULD STILL FIGHT, JUST LET ME GET MY BAT BUDDY.
NO, DARLING, THAT DOESN'T SOUND LIKE A FAIR FIGHT AT ALL.
WHAT A **LOVELY** WELCOME PARTY!

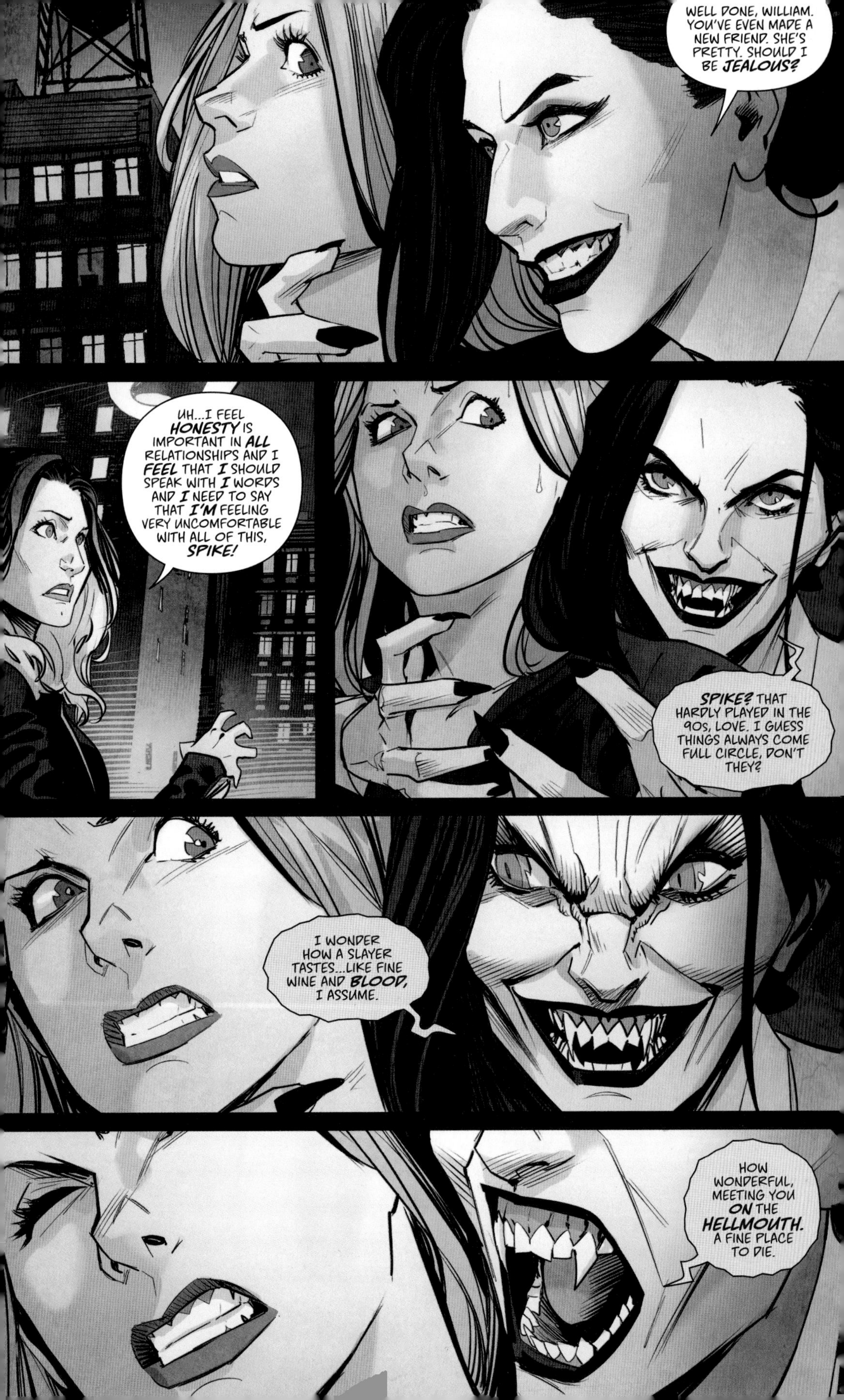
WELL DONE, WILLIAM. YOU'VE EVEN MADE A NEW FRIEND. SHE'S PRETTY. SHOULD I BE JEALOUS?
UH...I FEEL HONESTY IS IMPORTANT IN ALL RELATIONSHIPS AND I FEEL THAT I SHOULD SPEAK WITH I WORDS AND I NEED TO SAY THAT I'M FEELING VERY UNCOMFORTABLE WITH ALL OF THIS, SPIKE!
SPIKE? THAT HARDLY PLAYED IN THE 90s, LOVE. I GUESS THINGS ALWAYS COME FULL CIRCLE, DON'T THEY?
I WONDER HOW A SLAYER TASTES...LIKE FINE WINE AND BLOOD, I ASSUME.
HOW WONDERFUL, MEETING YOU ON THE HELLMOUTH. A FINE PLACE TO DIE.

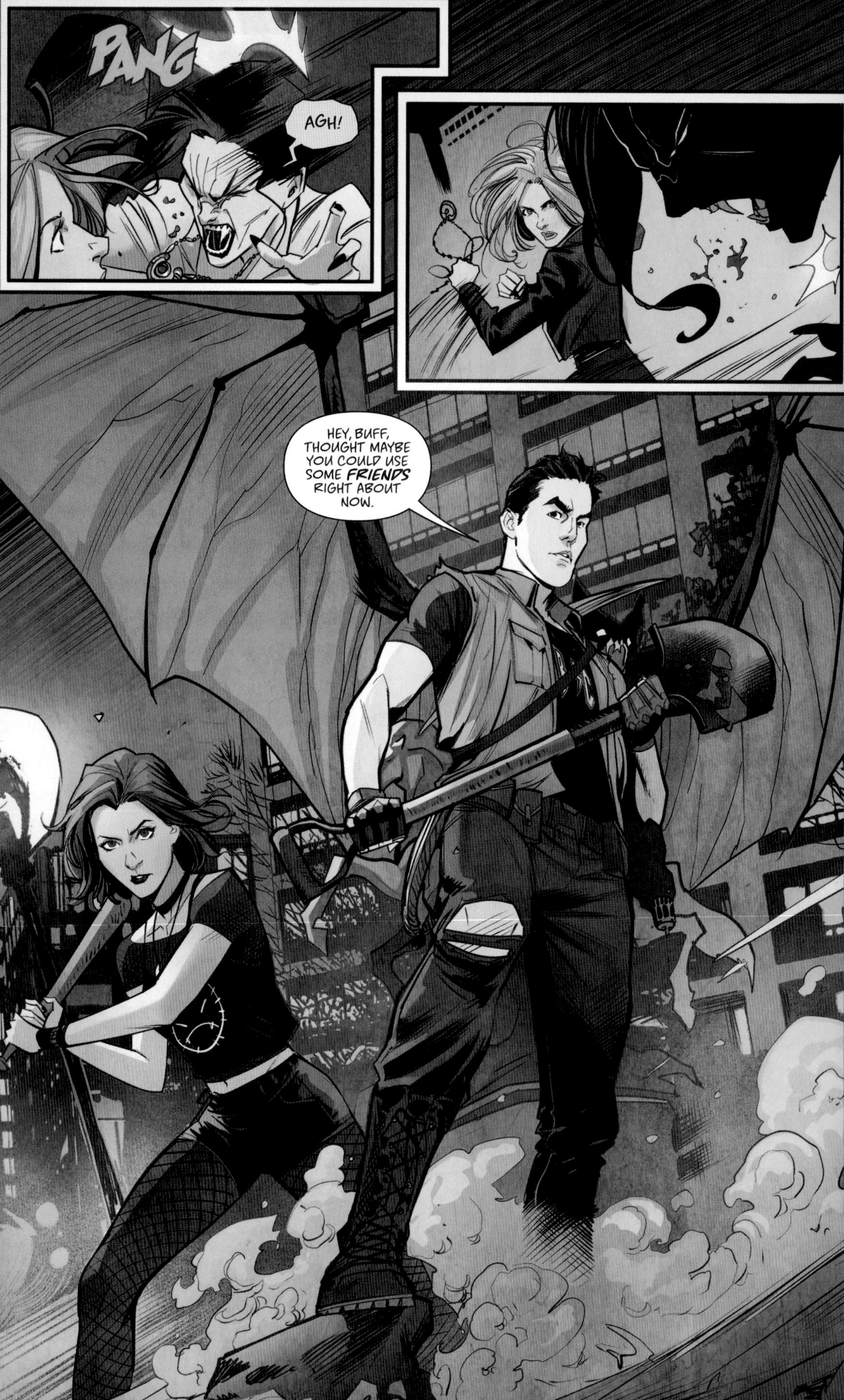
PANG
AGH!
HEY, BUFF, THOUGHT MAYBE YOU COULD USE SOME FRIENDS RIGHT ABOUT NOW.

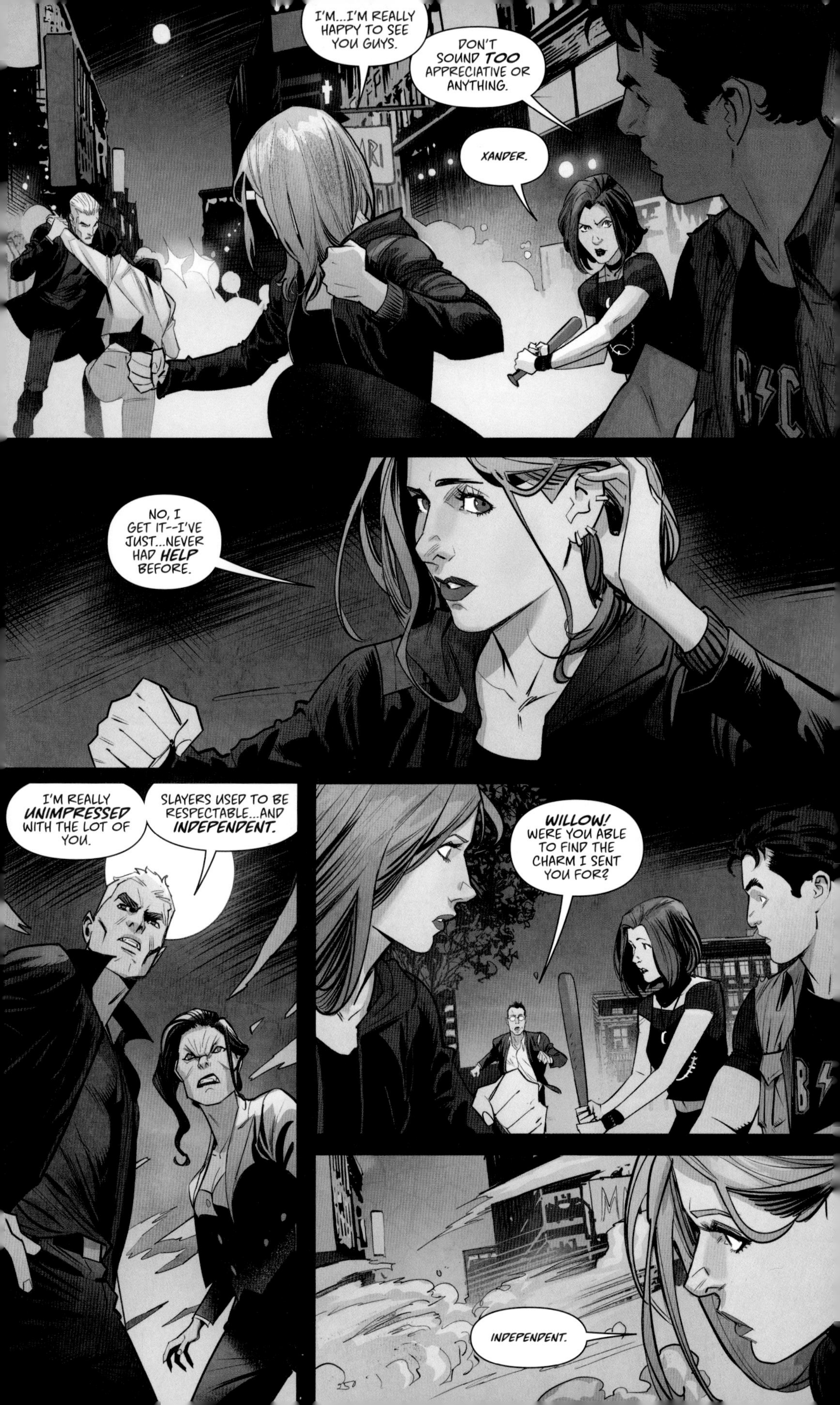
I'M...I'M REALLY HAPPY TO SEE YOU GUYS.
DON'T SOUND TOO APPRECIATIVE OR ANYTHING.
XANDER.
NO, I GET IT--I'VE JUST...NEVER HAD HELP BEFORE.
I'M REALLY UNIMPRESSED WITH THE LOT OF YOU.
SLAYERS USED TO BE RESPECTABLE...AND INDEPENDENT.
WILLOW! WERE YOU ABLE TO FIND THE CHARM I SENT YOU FOR?
INDEPENDENT.

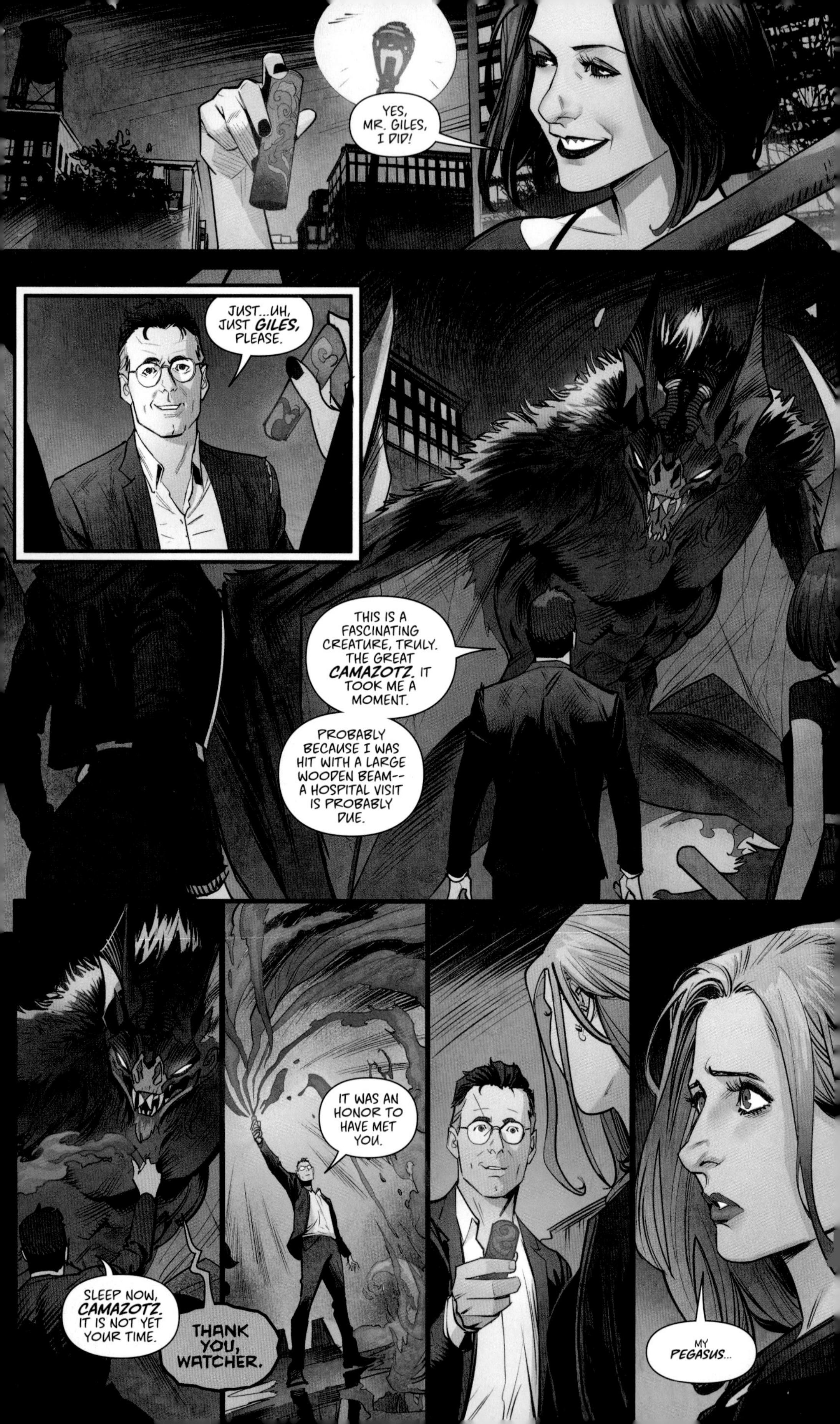
YES, MR. GILES, I DID!
JUST...UH, JUST *GILES,* PLEASE.
THIS IS A FASCINATING CREATURE, TRULY. THE GREAT *CAMAZOTZ.* IT TOOK ME A MOMENT.
PROBABLY BECAUSE I WAS HIT WITH A LARGE WOODEN BEAM-- A HOSPITAL VISIT IS PROBABLY DUE.
SLEEP NOW, *CAMAZOTZ.* IT IS NOT YET YOUR TIME.
THANK YOU, WATCHER.
IT WAS AN HONOR TO HAVE MET YOU.
MY *PEGASUS*...

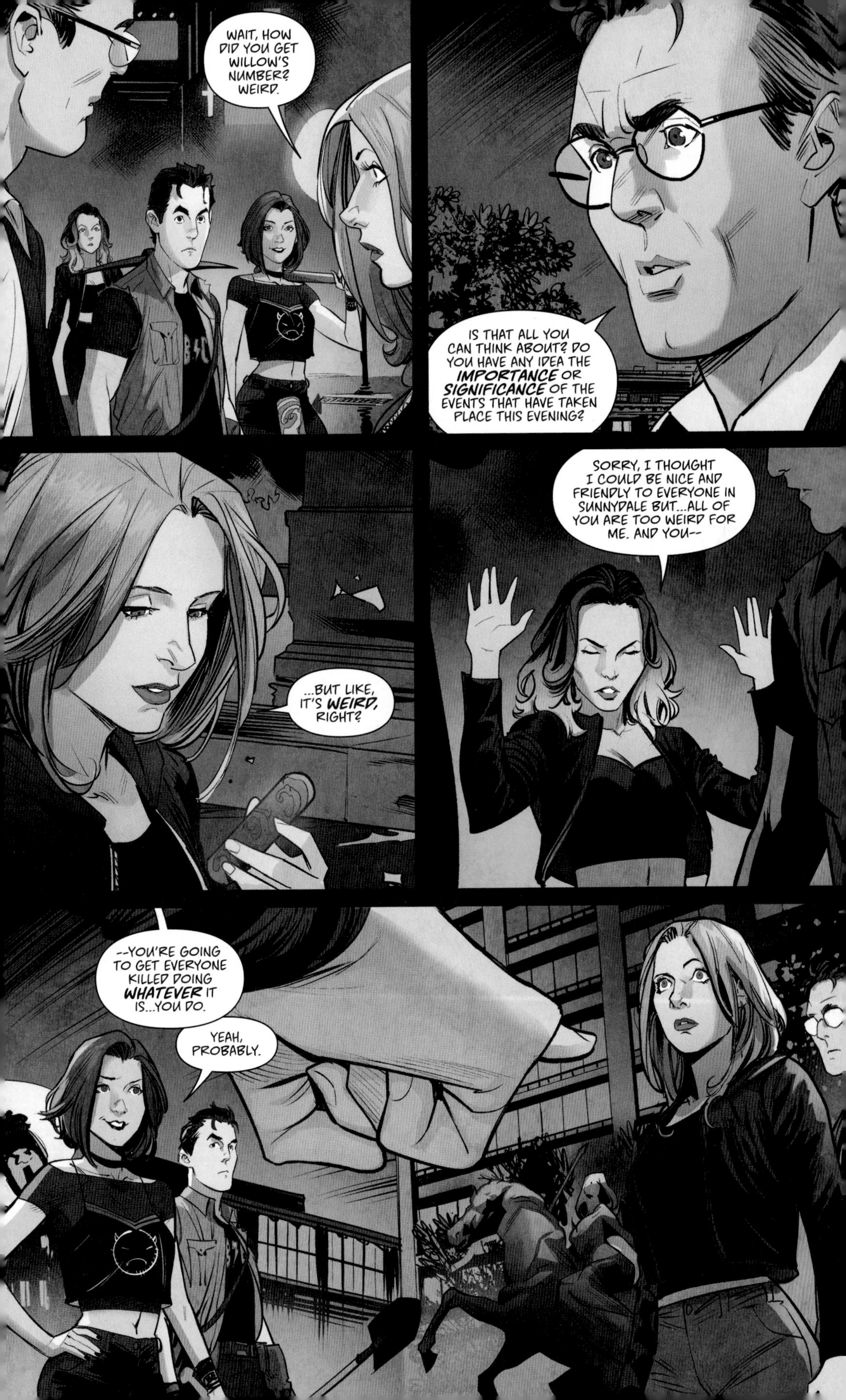
WAIT, HOW DID YOU GET WILLOW'S NUMBER? WEIRD.
IS THAT ALL YOU CAN THINK ABOUT? DO YOU HAVE ANY IDEA THE IMPORTANCE OR SIGNIFICANCE OF THE EVENTS THAT HAVE TAKEN PLACE THIS EVENING?
...BUT LIKE, IT'S WEIRD, RIGHT?
SORRY, I THOUGHT I COULD BE NICE AND FRIENDLY TO EVERYONE IN SUNNYDALE BUT...ALL OF YOU ARE TOO WEIRD FOR ME. AND YOU--
--YOU'RE GOING TO GET EVERYONE KILLED DOING WHATEVER IT IS...YOU DO.
YEAH, PROBABLY.

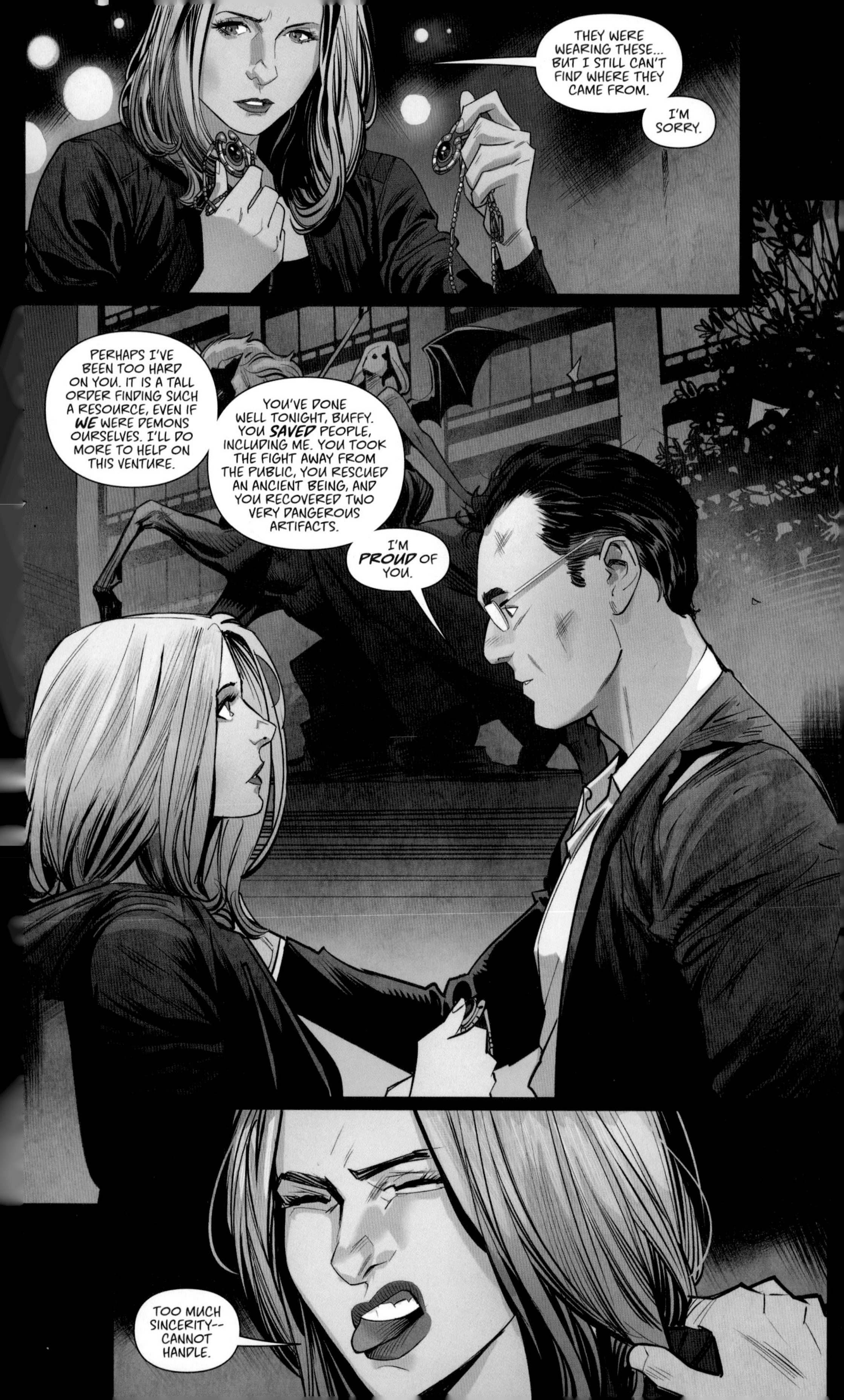
THEY WERE WEARING THESE... BUT I STILL CAN'T FIND WHERE THEY CAME FROM.
I'M SORRY.
PERHAPS I'VE BEEN TOO HARD ON YOU. IT IS A TALL ORDER FINDING SUCH A RESOURCE, EVEN IF WE WERE DEMONS OURSELVES. I'LL DO MORE TO HELP ON THIS VENTURE.
YOU'VE DONE WELL TONIGHT, BUFFY. YOU SAVED PEOPLE, INCLUDING ME. YOU TOOK THE FIGHT AWAY FROM THE PUBLIC, YOU RESCUED AN ANCIENT BEING, AND YOU RECOVERED TWO VERY DANGEROUS ARTIFACTS.
I'M PROUD OF YOU.
TOO MUCH SINCERITY-- CANNOT HANDLE.

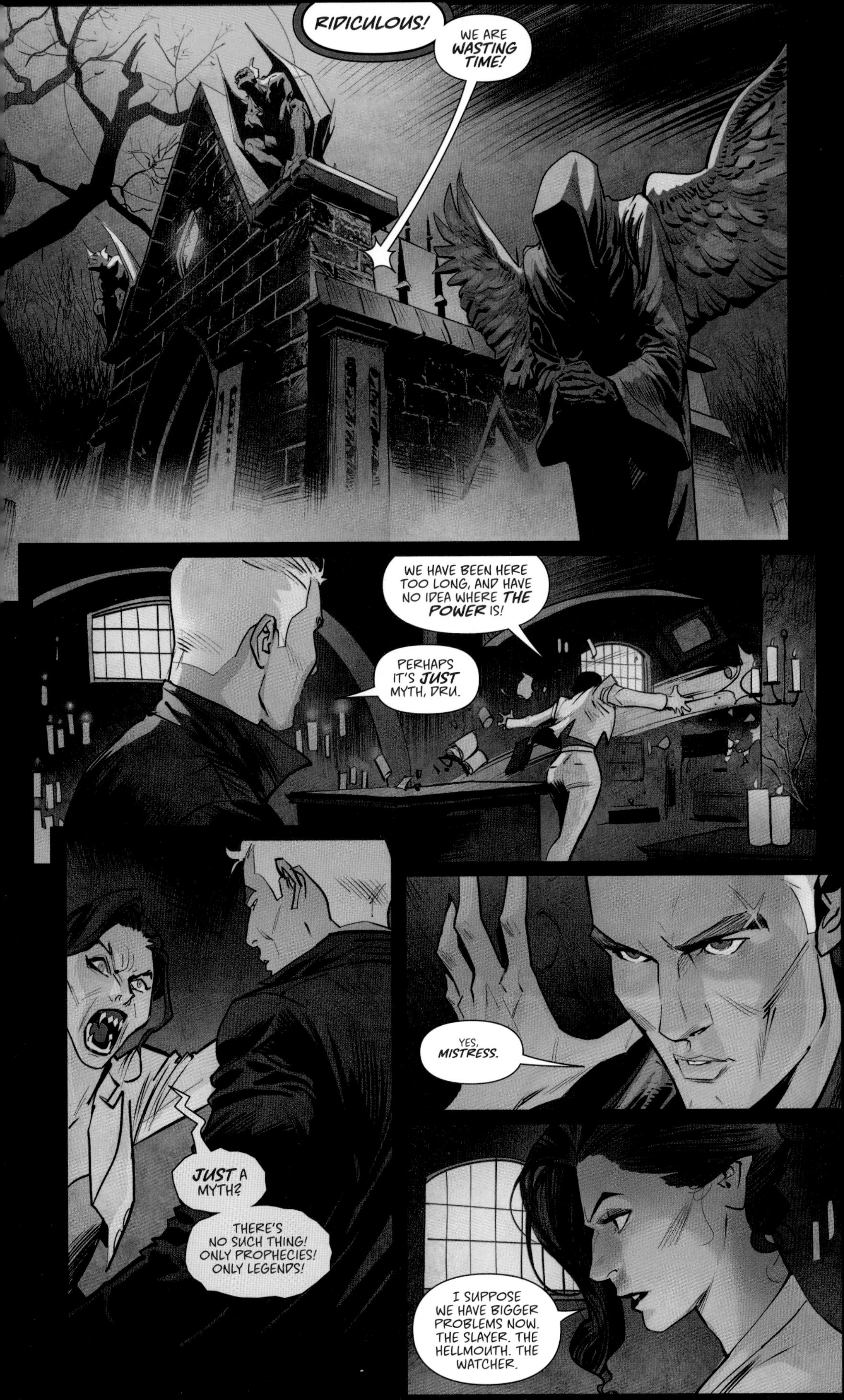
RIDICULOUS!
WE ARE WASTING TIME!
WE HAVE BEEN HERE TOO LONG, AND HAVE NO IDEA WHERE THE POWER IS!
PERHAPS IT'S JUST MYTH, DRU.
JUST A MYTH?
THERE'S NO SUCH THING! ONLY PROPHECIES! ONLY LEGENDS!
YES, MISTRESS.
I SUPPOSE WE HAVE BIGGER PROBLEMS NOW. THE SLAYER. THE HELLMOUTH. THE WATCHER.

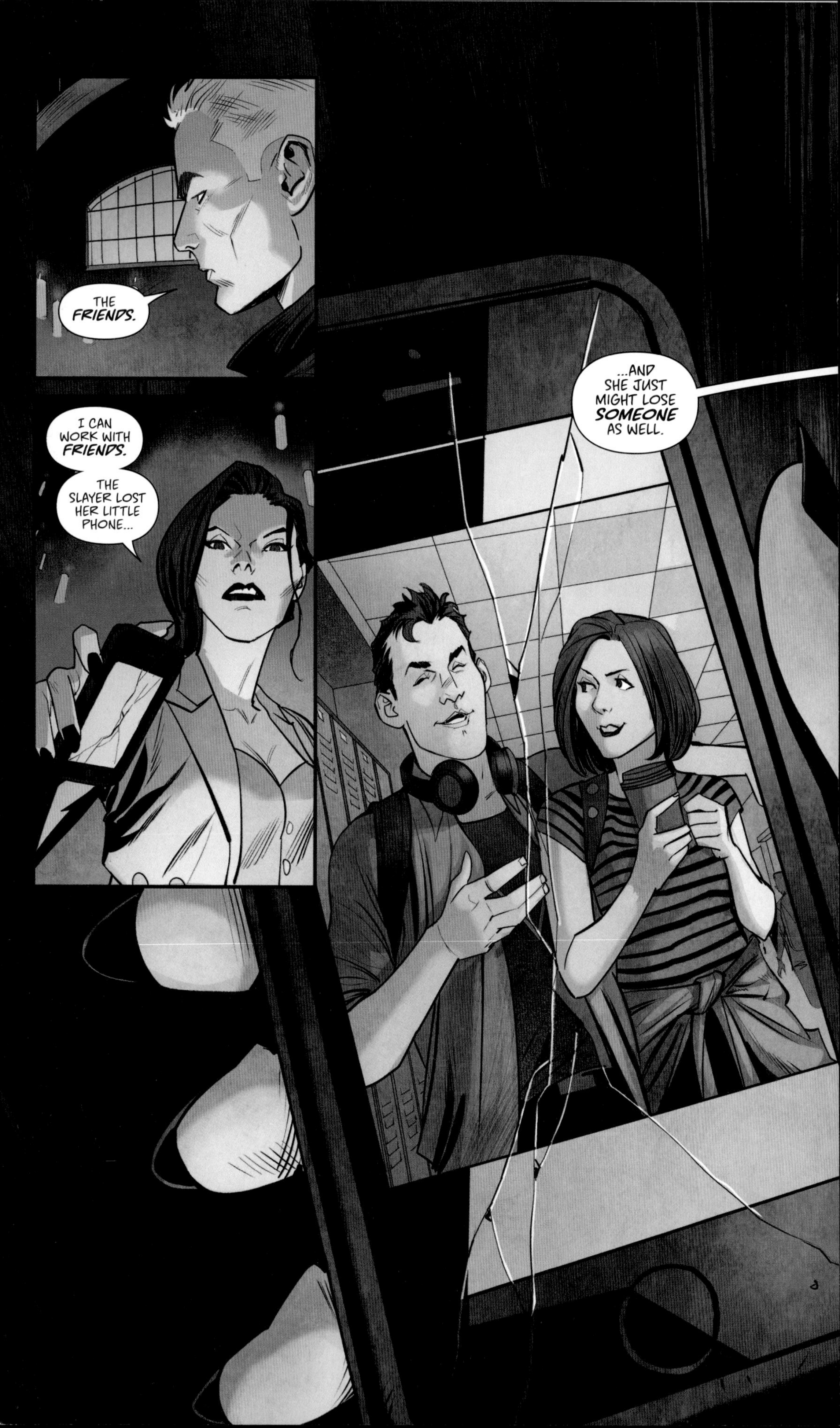
THE FRIENDS.
I CAN WORK WITH FRIENDS.
THE SLAYER LOST HER LITTLE PHONE...
...AND SHE JUST MIGHT LOSE SOMEONE AS WELL.

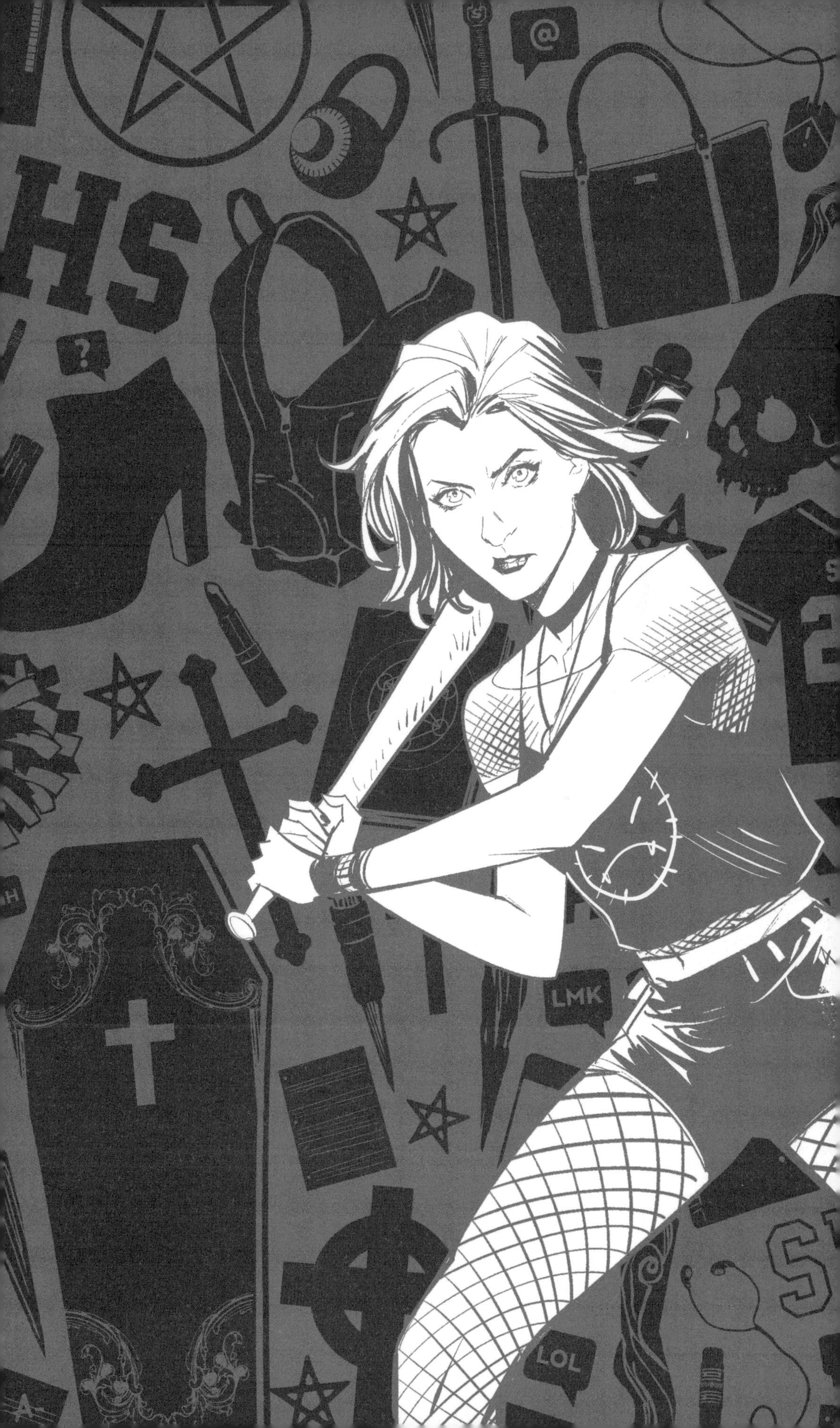
HS
@
?
LMK
LOL

CHAPTER
FOUR

Issue Four Cover by **Matthew Taylor**

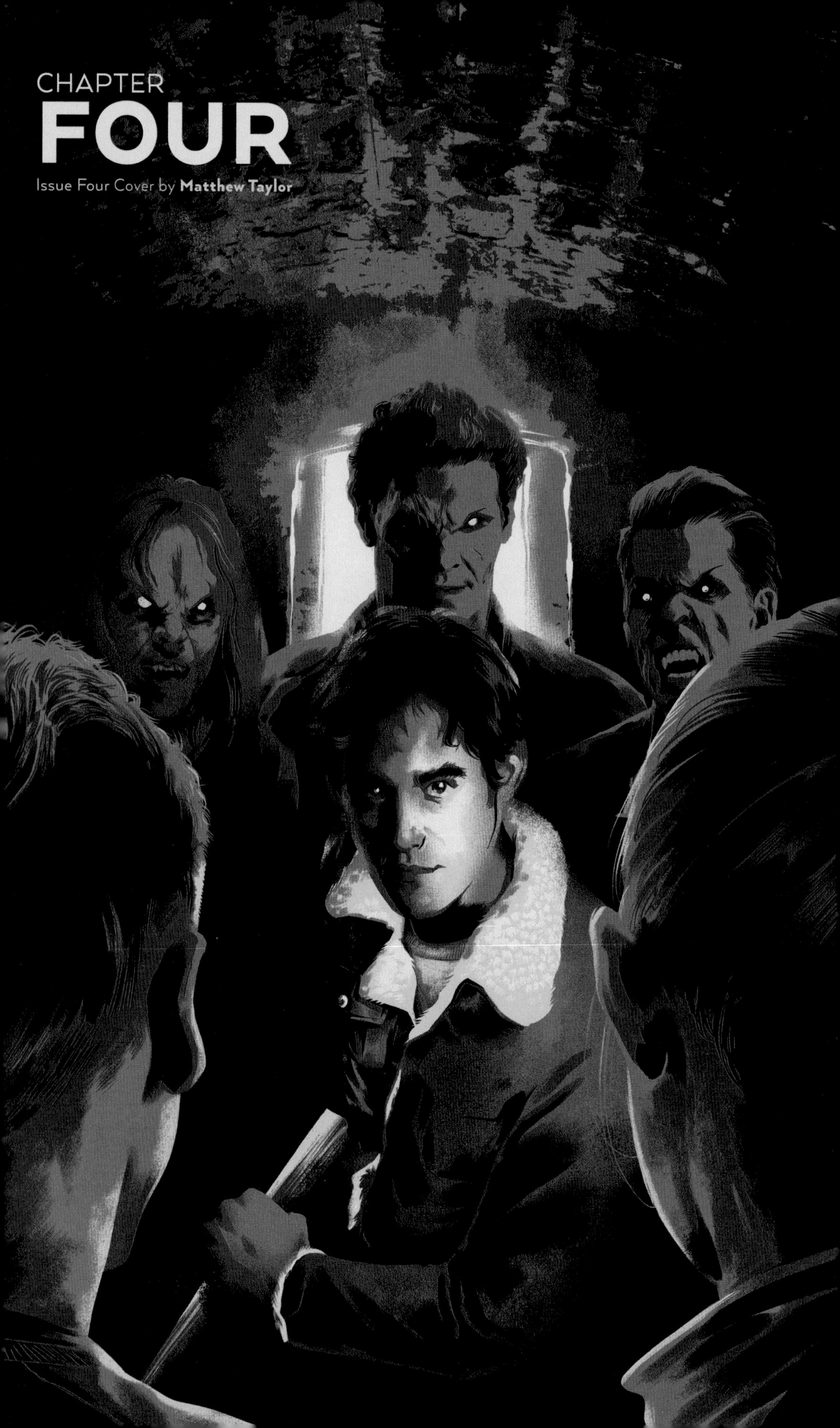

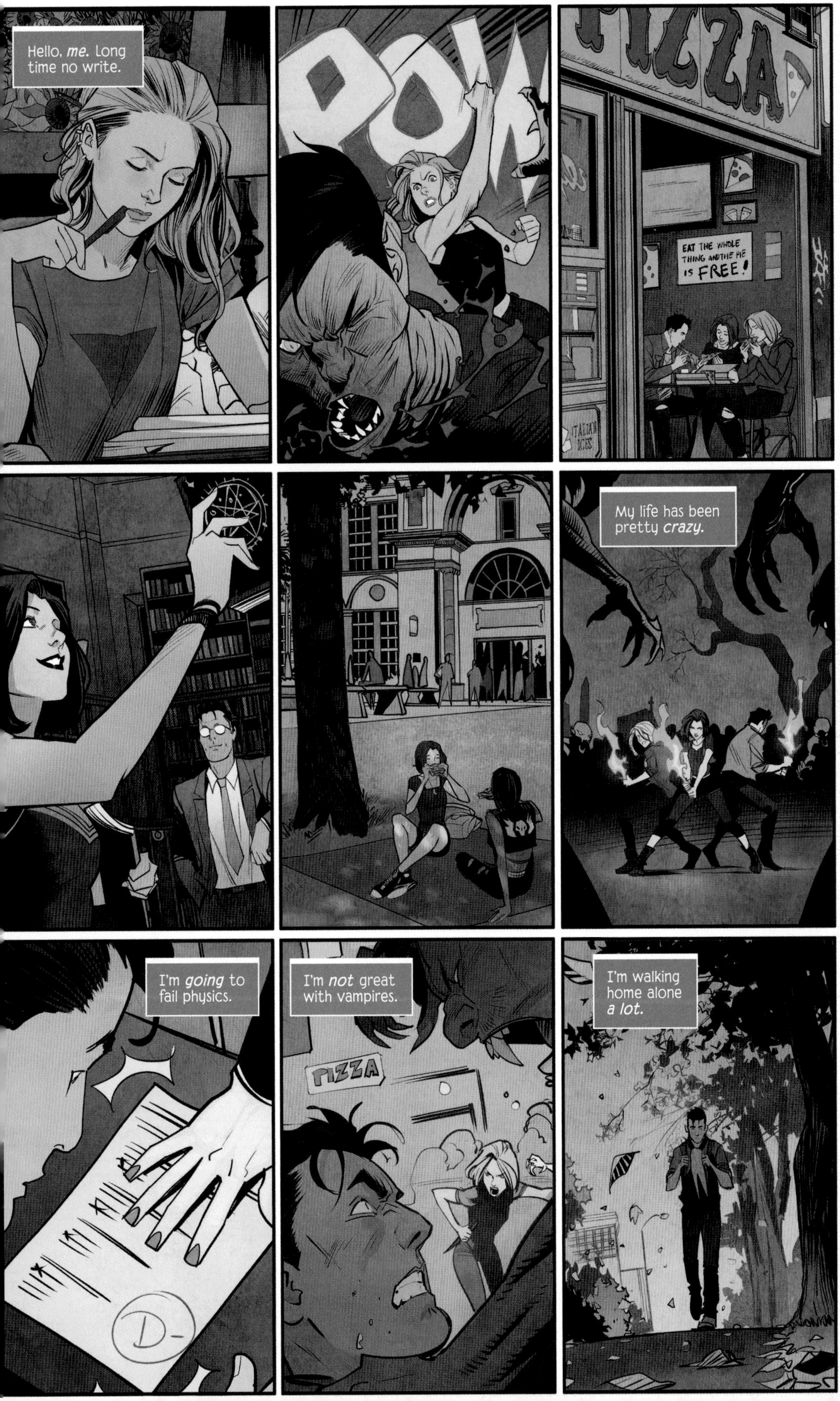
Hello, *me.* Long time no write.
POW
PIZZA
EAT THE WHOLE THING AND THE PIE IS FREE!
ITALIAN ICES
My life has been pretty *crazy.*
I'm *going* to fail physics.
D-
I'm *not* great with vampires.
PIZZA
I'm walking home alone *a lot.*

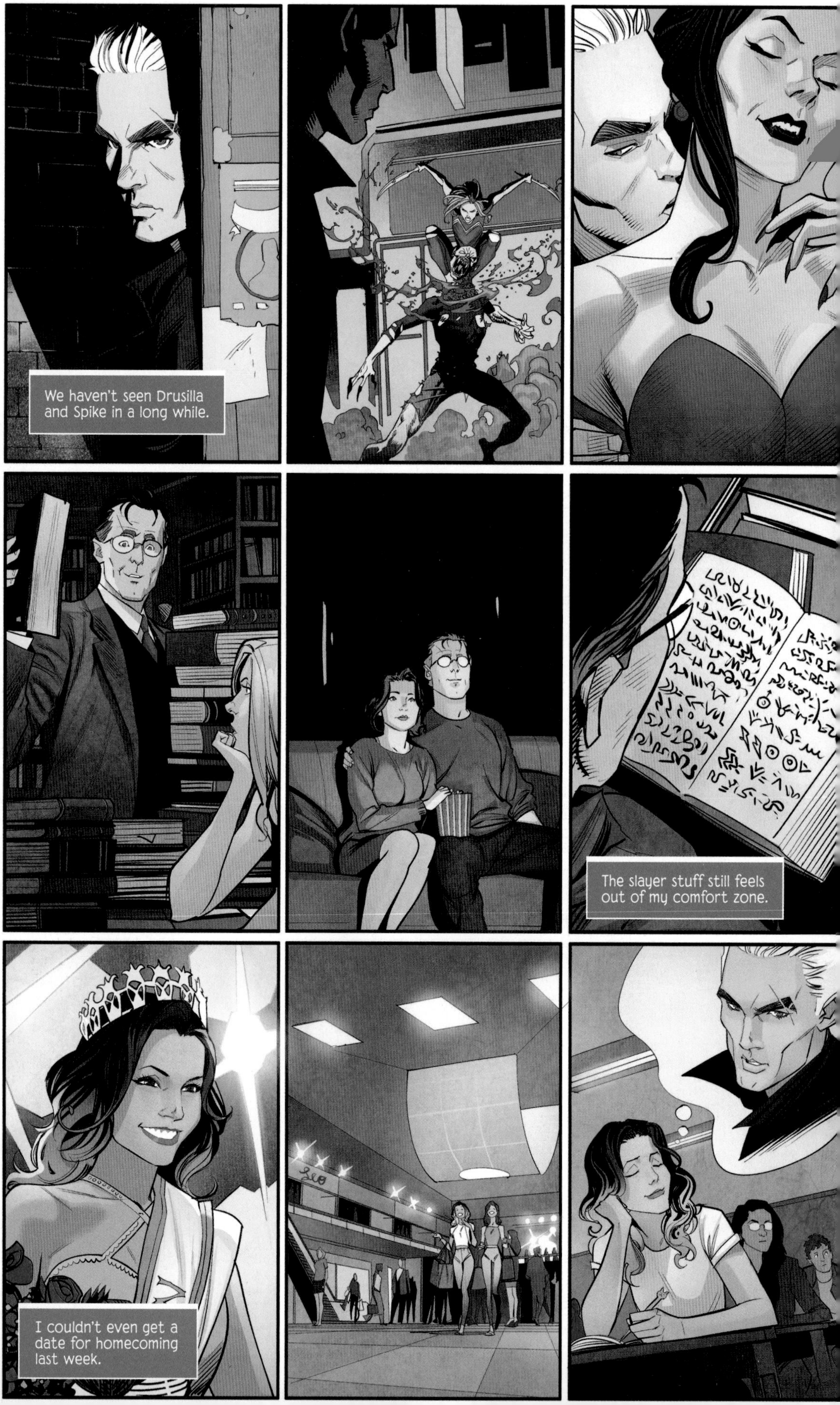
We haven't seen Drusilla and Spike in a long while.
The slayer stuff still feels out of my comfort zone.
I couldn't even get a date for homecoming last week.

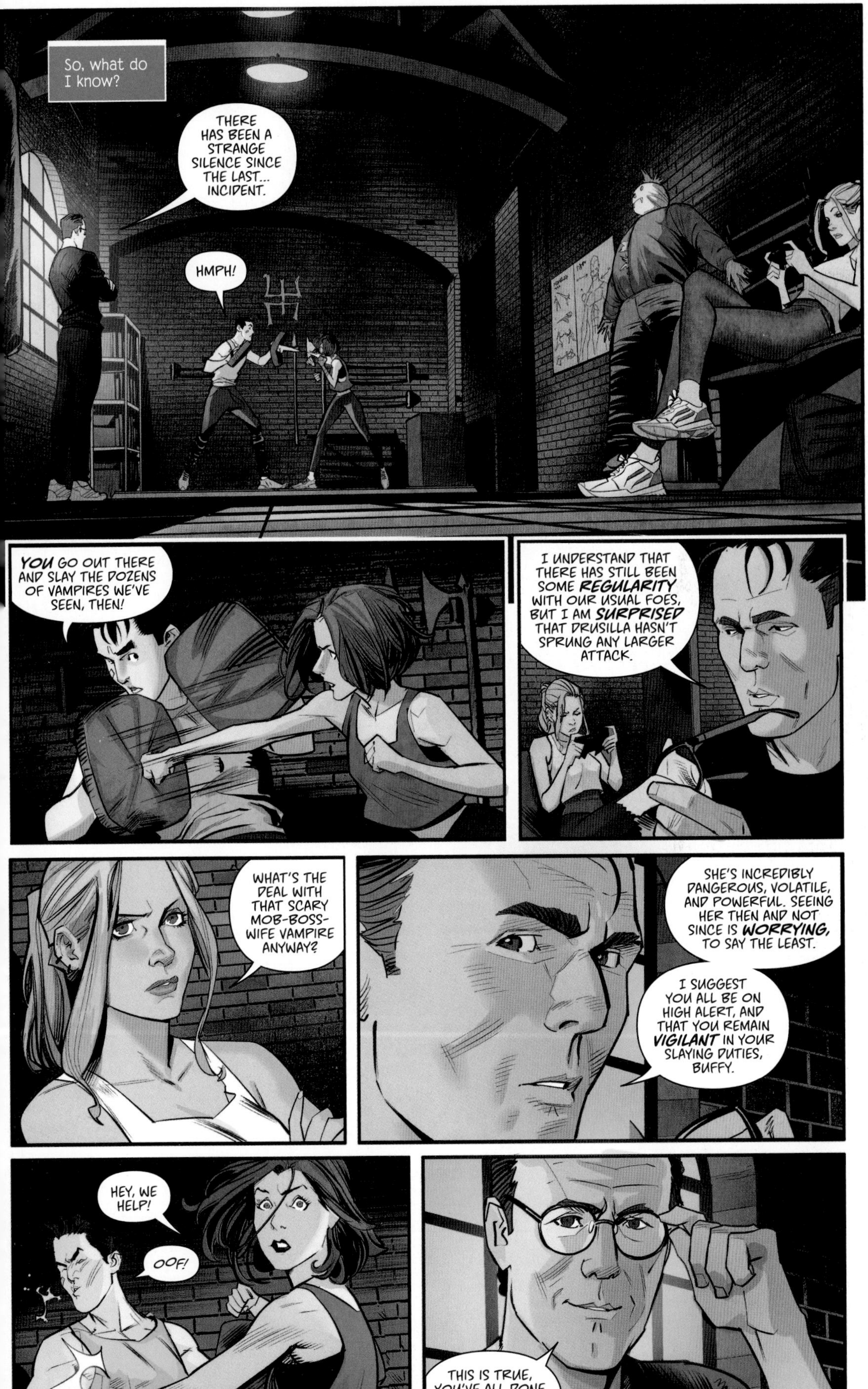
So, what do I know?
THERE HAS BEEN A STRANGE SILENCE SINCE THE LAST... INCIDENT.
HMPH!
YOU GO OUT THERE AND SLAY THE DOZENS OF VAMPIRES WE'VE SEEN, THEN!
I UNDERSTAND THAT THERE HAS STILL BEEN SOME REGULARITY WITH OUR USUAL FOES, BUT I AM SURPRISED THAT DRUSILLA HASN'T SPRUNG ANY LARGER ATTACK.
WHAT'S THE DEAL WITH THAT SCARY MOB-BOSS-WIFE VAMPIRE ANYWAY?
SHE'S INCREDIBLY DANGEROUS, VOLATILE, AND POWERFUL. SEEING HER THEN AND NOT SINCE IS WORRYING, TO SAY THE LEAST.
I SUGGEST YOU ALL BE ON HIGH ALERT, AND THAT YOU REMAIN VIGILANT IN YOUR SLAYING DUTIES, BUFFY.
HEY, WE HELP!
OOF!
THIS IS TRUE, YOU'VE ALL DONE GREAT WORK THESE PAST FEW WEEKS.

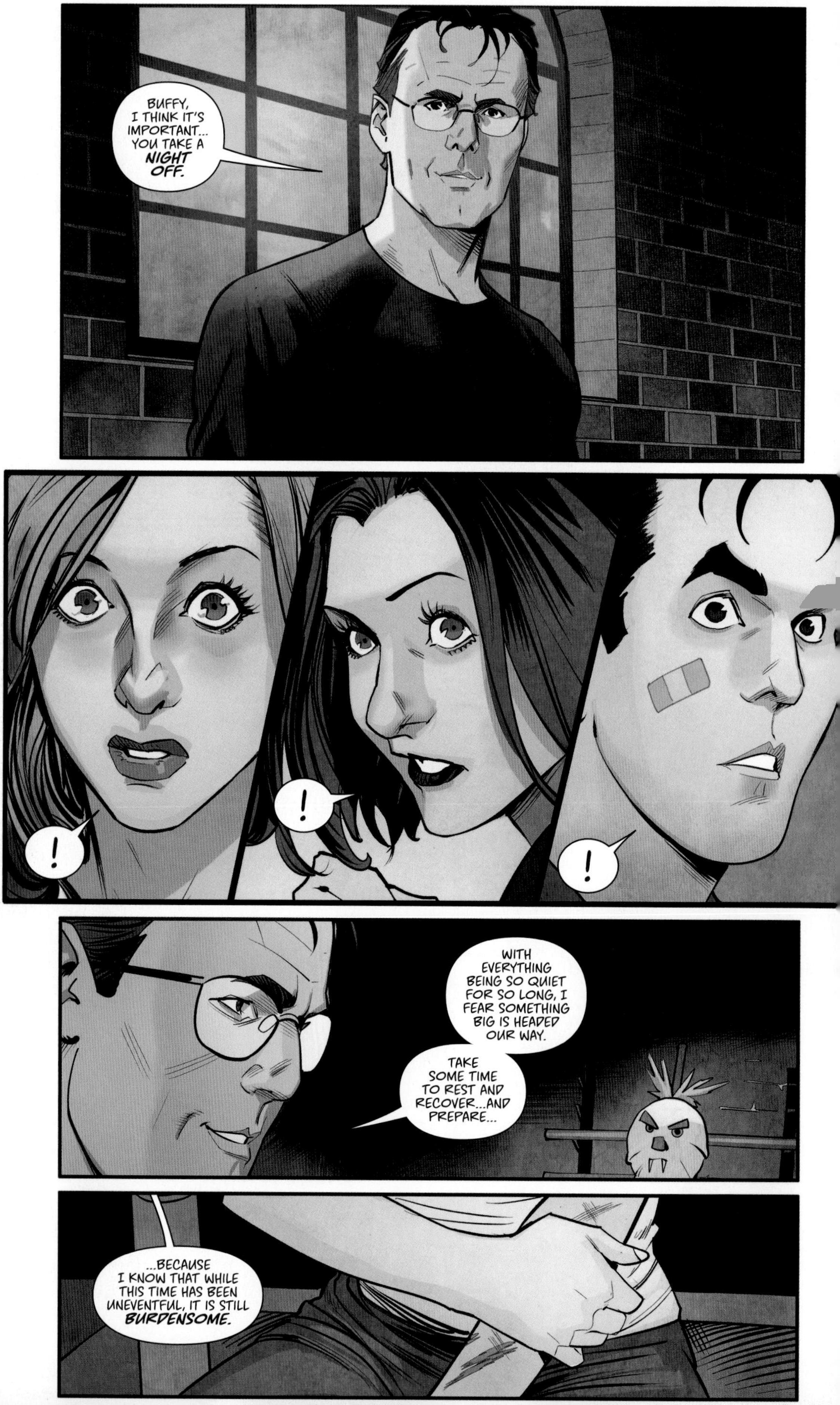
BUFFY, I THINK IT'S IMPORTANT... YOU TAKE A ***NIGHT OFF.***
!
!
!
WITH EVERYTHING BEING SO QUIET FOR SO LONG, I FEAR SOMETHING BIG IS HEADED OUR WAY.
TAKE SOME TIME TO REST AND RECOVER...AND PREPARE...
...BECAUSE I KNOW THAT WHILE THIS TIME HAS BEEN UNEVENTFUL, IT IS STILL ***BURDENSOME.***

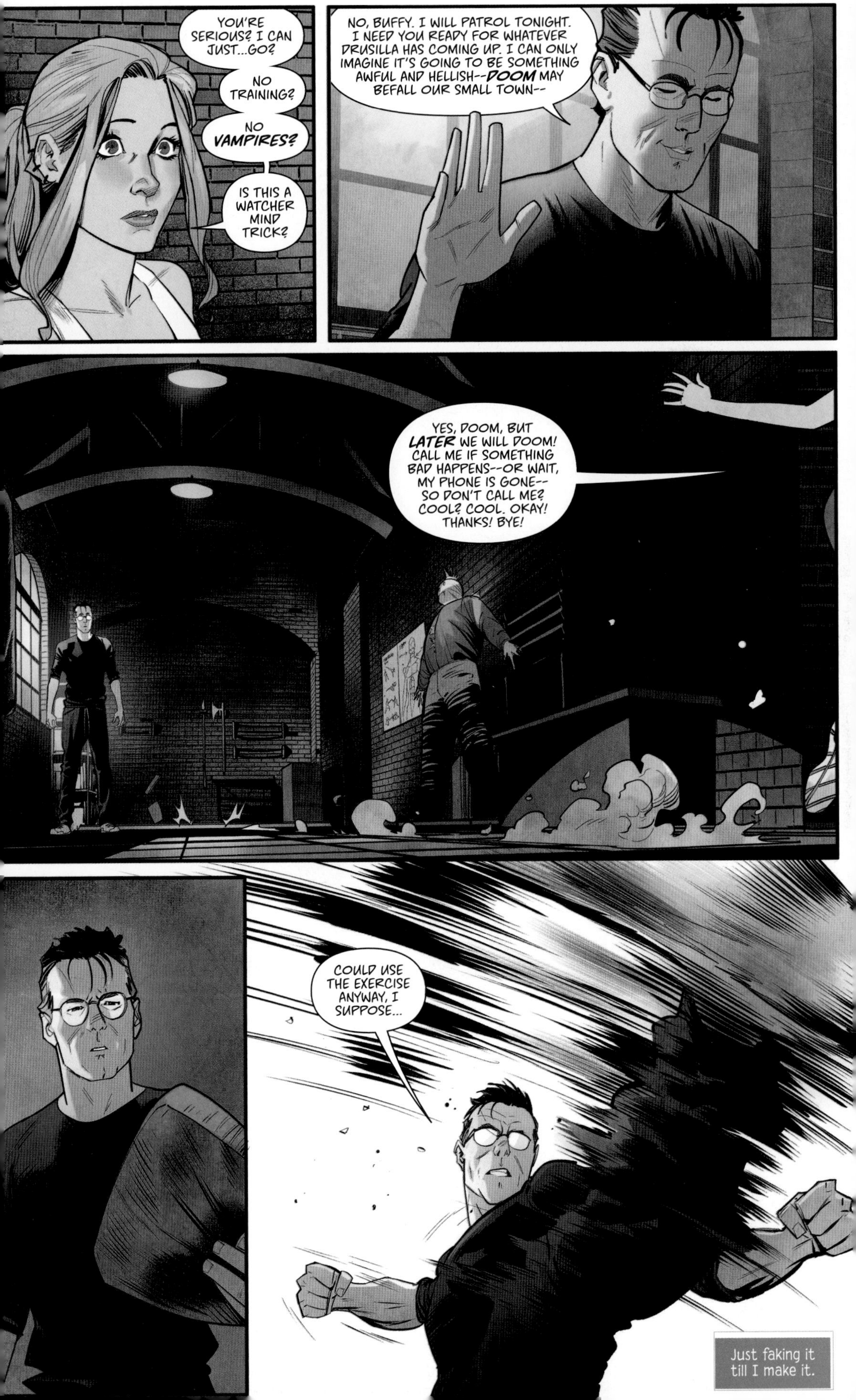
YOU'RE SERIOUS? I CAN JUST...GO?
NO TRAINING?
NO VAMPIRES?
IS THIS A WATCHER MIND TRICK?
NO, BUFFY. I WILL PATROL TONIGHT. I NEED YOU READY FOR WHATEVER DRUSILLA HAS COMING UP. I CAN ONLY IMAGINE IT'S GOING TO BE SOMETHING AWFUL AND HELLISH--DOOM MAY BEFALL OUR SMALL TOWN--
YES, DOOM, BUT LATER WE WILL DOOM! CALL ME IF SOMETHING BAD HAPPENS--OR WAIT, MY PHONE IS GONE--SO DON'T CALL ME? COOL? COOL. OKAY! THANKS! BYE!
COULD USE THE EXERCISE ANYWAY, I SUPPOSE...
Just faking it till I make it.

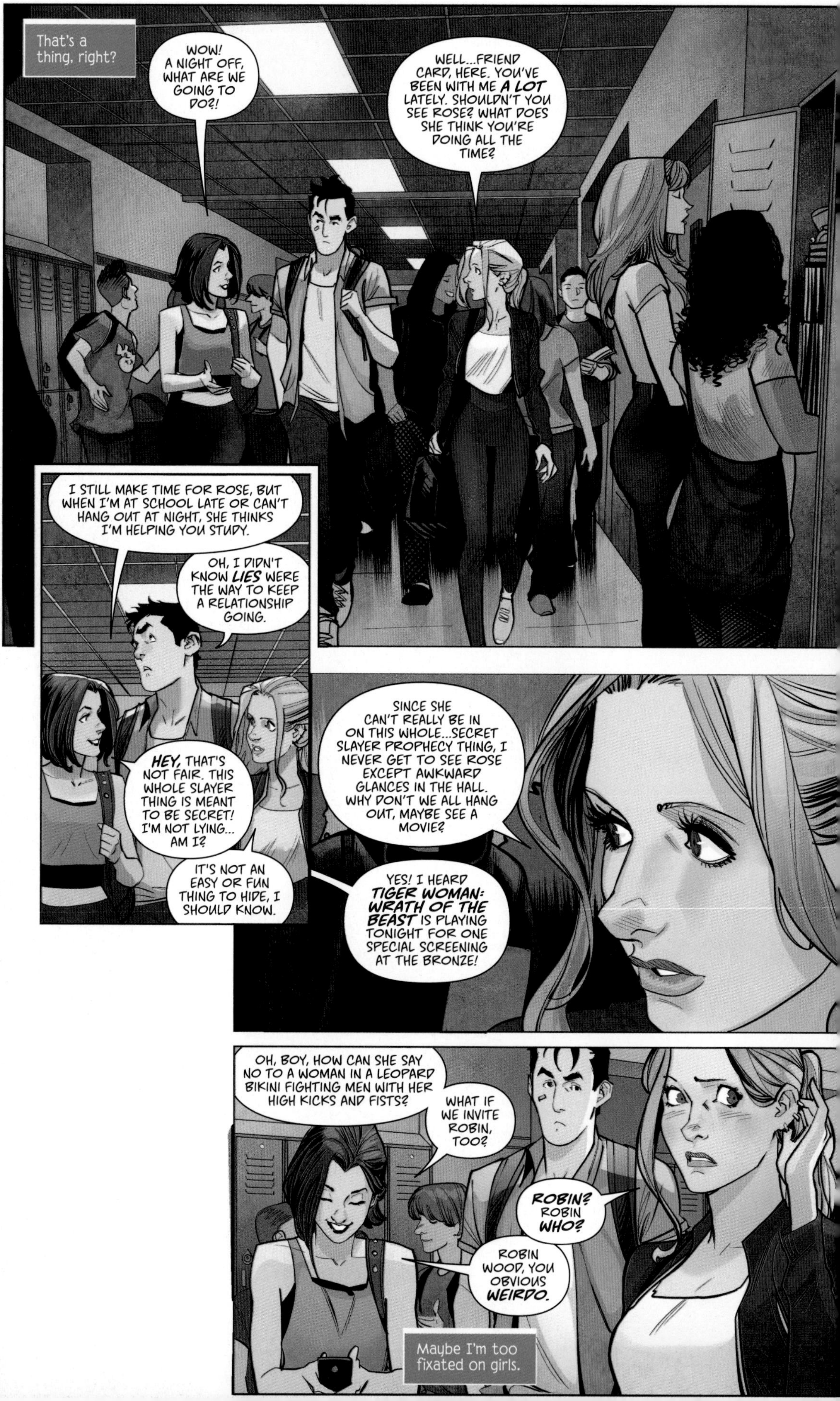
That's a thing, right?
WOW! A NIGHT OFF, WHAT ARE WE GOING TO DO?!
WELL...FRIEND CARD, HERE. YOU'VE BEEN WITH ME A LOT LATELY. SHOULDN'T YOU SEE ROSE? WHAT DOES SHE THINK YOU'RE DOING ALL THE TIME?
I STILL MAKE TIME FOR ROSE, BUT WHEN I'M AT SCHOOL LATE OR CAN'T HANG OUT AT NIGHT, SHE THINKS I'M HELPING YOU STUDY.
OH, I DIDN'T KNOW LIES WERE THE WAY TO KEEP A RELATIONSHIP GOING.
HEY, THAT'S NOT FAIR. THIS WHOLE SLAYER THING IS MEANT TO BE SECRET! I'M NOT LYING... AM I?
IT'S NOT AN EASY OR FUN THING TO HIDE, I SHOULD KNOW.
SINCE SHE CAN'T REALLY BE IN ON THIS WHOLE...SECRET SLAYER PROPHECY THING, I NEVER GET TO SEE ROSE EXCEPT AWKWARD GLANCES IN THE HALL. WHY DON'T WE ALL HANG OUT, MAYBE SEE A MOVIE?
YES! I HEARD TIGER WOMAN: WRATH OF THE BEAST IS PLAYING TONIGHT FOR ONE SPECIAL SCREENING AT THE BRONZE!
OH, BOY, HOW CAN SHE SAY NO TO A WOMAN IN A LEOPARD BIKINI FIGHTING MEN WITH HER HIGH KICKS AND FISTS?
WHAT IF WE INVITE ROBIN, TOO?
ROBIN? ROBIN WHO?
ROBIN WOOD, YOU OBVIOUS WEIRDO.
Maybe I'm too fixated on girls.

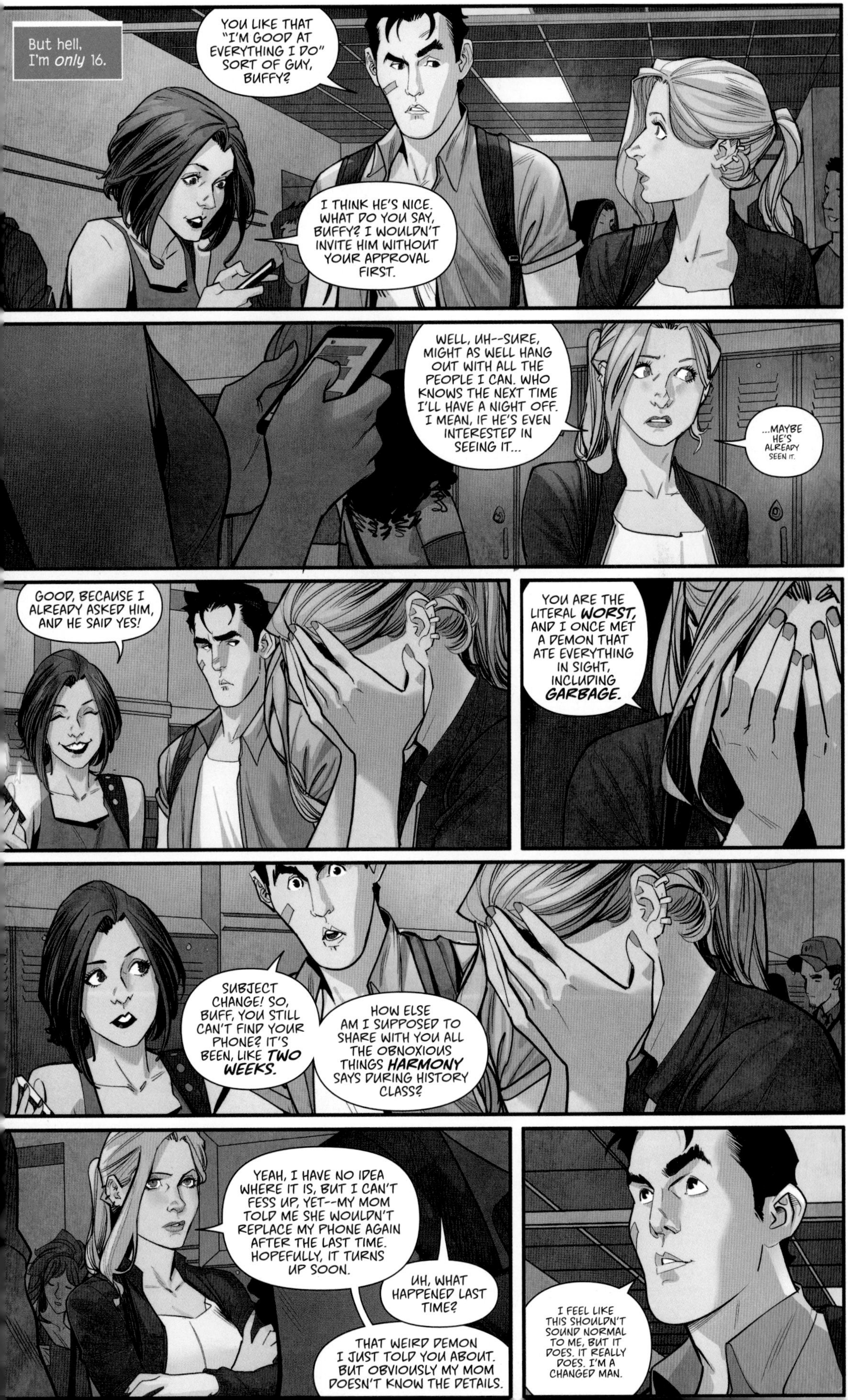

But hell, I'm *only* 16.
YOU LIKE THAT "I'M GOOD AT EVERYTHING I DO" SORT OF GUY, BUFFY?
I THINK HE'S NICE. WHAT DO YOU SAY, BUFFY? I WOULDN'T INVITE HIM WITHOUT YOUR APPROVAL FIRST.
WELL, UH--SURE, MIGHT AS WELL HANG OUT WITH ALL THE PEOPLE I CAN. WHO KNOWS THE NEXT TIME I'LL HAVE A NIGHT OFF. I MEAN, IF HE'S EVEN INTERESTED IN SEEING IT...
...MAYBE HE'S ALREADY SEEN IT.
GOOD, BECAUSE I ALREADY ASKED HIM, AND HE SAID YES!
YOU ARE THE LITERAL **WORST,** AND I ONCE MET A DEMON THAT ATE EVERYTHING IN SIGHT, INCLUDING **GARBAGE.**
SUBJECT CHANGE! SO, BUFF, YOU STILL CAN'T FIND YOUR PHONE? IT'S BEEN, LIKE **TWO WEEKS.**
HOW ELSE AM I SUPPOSED TO SHARE WITH YOU ALL THE OBNOXIOUS THINGS **HARMONY** SAYS DURING HISTORY CLASS?
YEAH, I HAVE NO IDEA WHERE IT IS, BUT I CAN'T FESS UP, YET--MY MOM TOLD ME SHE WOULDN'T REPLACE MY PHONE AGAIN AFTER THE LAST TIME. HOPEFULLY, IT TURNS UP SOON.
UH, WHAT HAPPENED LAST TIME?
THAT WEIRD DEMON I JUST TOLD YOU ABOUT. BUT OBVIOUSLY MY MOM DOESN'T KNOW THE DETAILS.
I FEEL LIKE THIS SHOULDN'T SOUND NORMAL TO ME, BUT IT DOES. IT REALLY DOES. I'M A CHANGED MAN.

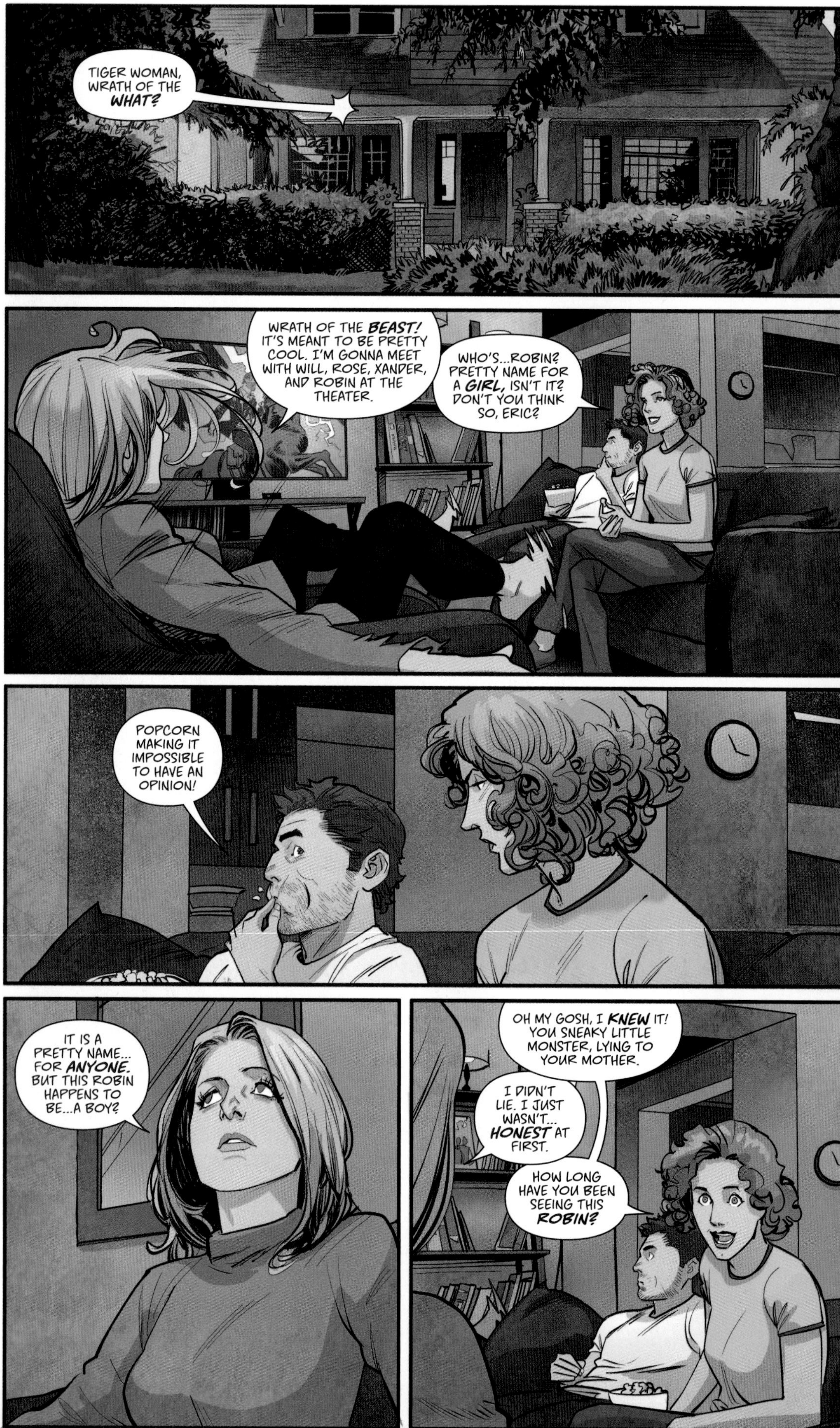
TIGER WOMAN, WRATH OF THE WHAT?
WRATH OF THE BEAST! IT'S MEANT TO BE PRETTY COOL. I'M GONNA MEET WITH WILL, ROSE, XANDER, AND ROBIN AT THE THEATER.
WHO'S...ROBIN? PRETTY NAME FOR A GIRL, ISN'T IT? DON'T YOU THINK SO, ERIC?
POPCORN MAKING IT IMPOSSIBLE TO HAVE AN OPINION!
IT IS A PRETTY NAME... FOR ANYONE. BUT THIS ROBIN HAPPENS TO BE...A BOY?
OH MY GOSH, I KNEW IT! YOU SNEAKY LITTLE MONSTER, LYING TO YOUR MOTHER.
I DIDN'T LIE. I JUST WASN'T... HONEST AT FIRST.
HOW LONG HAVE YOU BEEN SEEING THIS ROBIN?

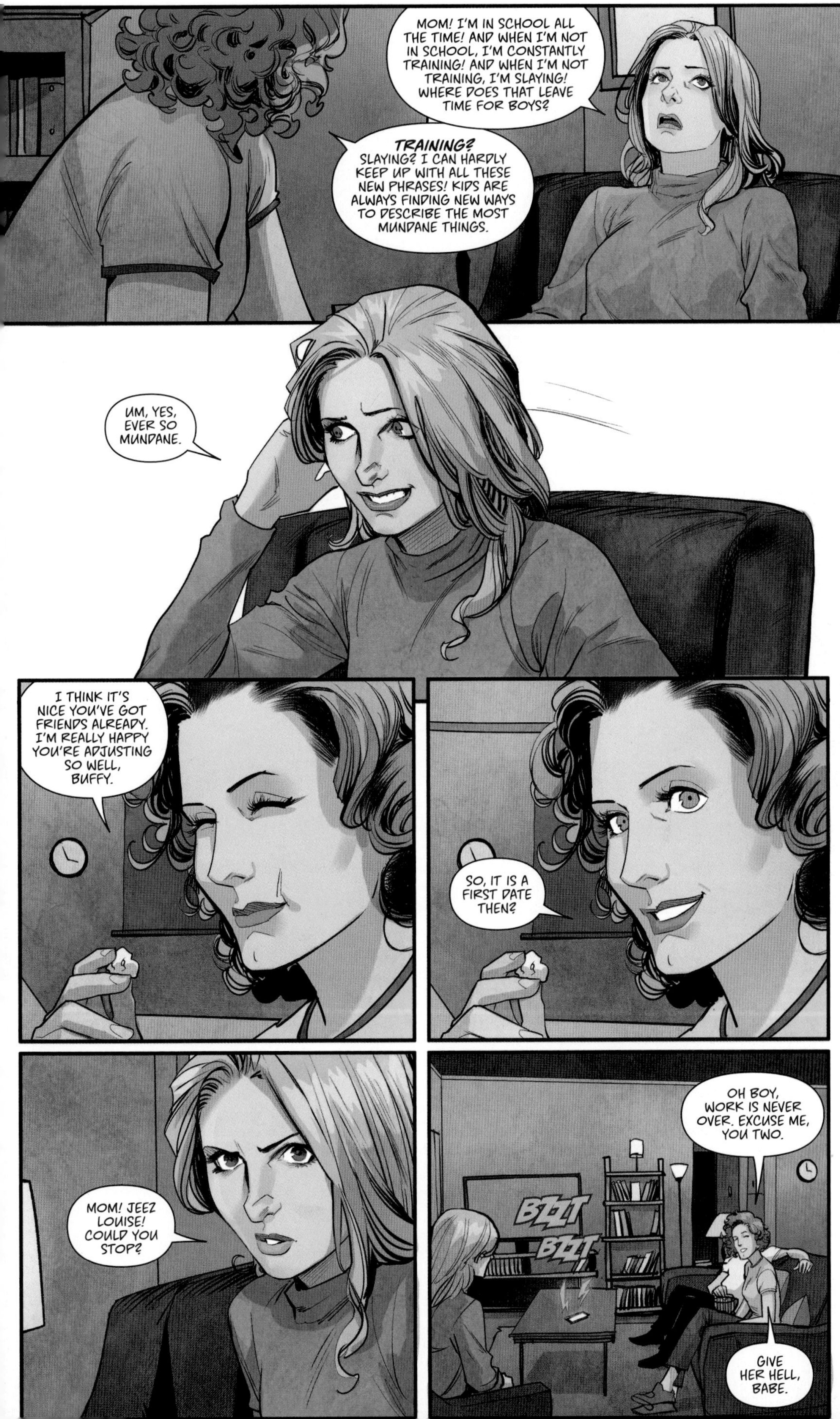
MOM! I'M IN SCHOOL ALL THE TIME! AND WHEN I'M NOT IN SCHOOL, I'M CONSTANTLY TRAINING! AND WHEN I'M NOT TRAINING, I'M SLAYING! WHERE DOES THAT LEAVE TIME FOR BOYS?
TRAINING? SLAYING? I CAN HARDLY KEEP UP WITH ALL THESE NEW PHRASES! KIDS ARE ALWAYS FINDING NEW WAYS TO DESCRIBE THE MOST MUNDANE THINGS.
UM, YES, EVER SO MUNDANE.
I THINK IT'S NICE YOU'VE GOT FRIENDS ALREADY. I'M REALLY HAPPY YOU'RE ADJUSTING SO WELL, BUFFY.
SO, IT IS A FIRST DATE THEN?
MOM! JEEZ LOUISE! COULD YOU STOP?
OH BOY, WORK IS NEVER OVER. EXCUSE ME, YOU TWO.
BZZT
BZZT
GIVE HER HELL, BABE.

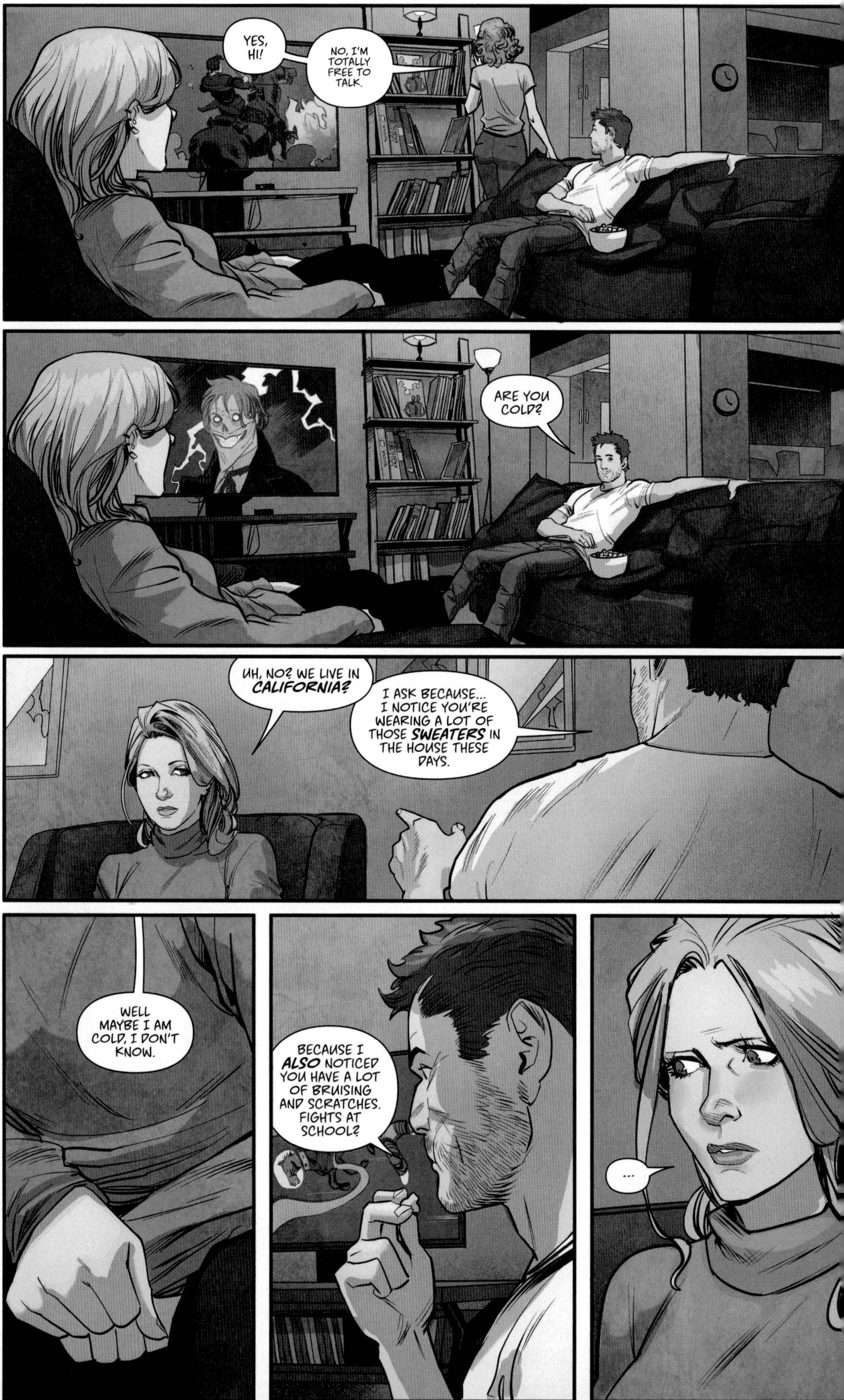
YES, HI!
NO, I'M TOTALLY FREE TO TALK.
ARE YOU COLD?
UH, NO? WE LIVE IN CALIFORNIA?
I ASK BECAUSE... I NOTICE YOU'RE WEARING A LOT OF THOSE SWEATERS IN THE HOUSE THESE DAYS.
WELL MAYBE I AM COLD, I DON'T KNOW.
BECAUSE I ALSO NOTICED YOU HAVE A LOT OF BRUISING AND SCRATCHES. FIGHTS AT SCHOOL?
...

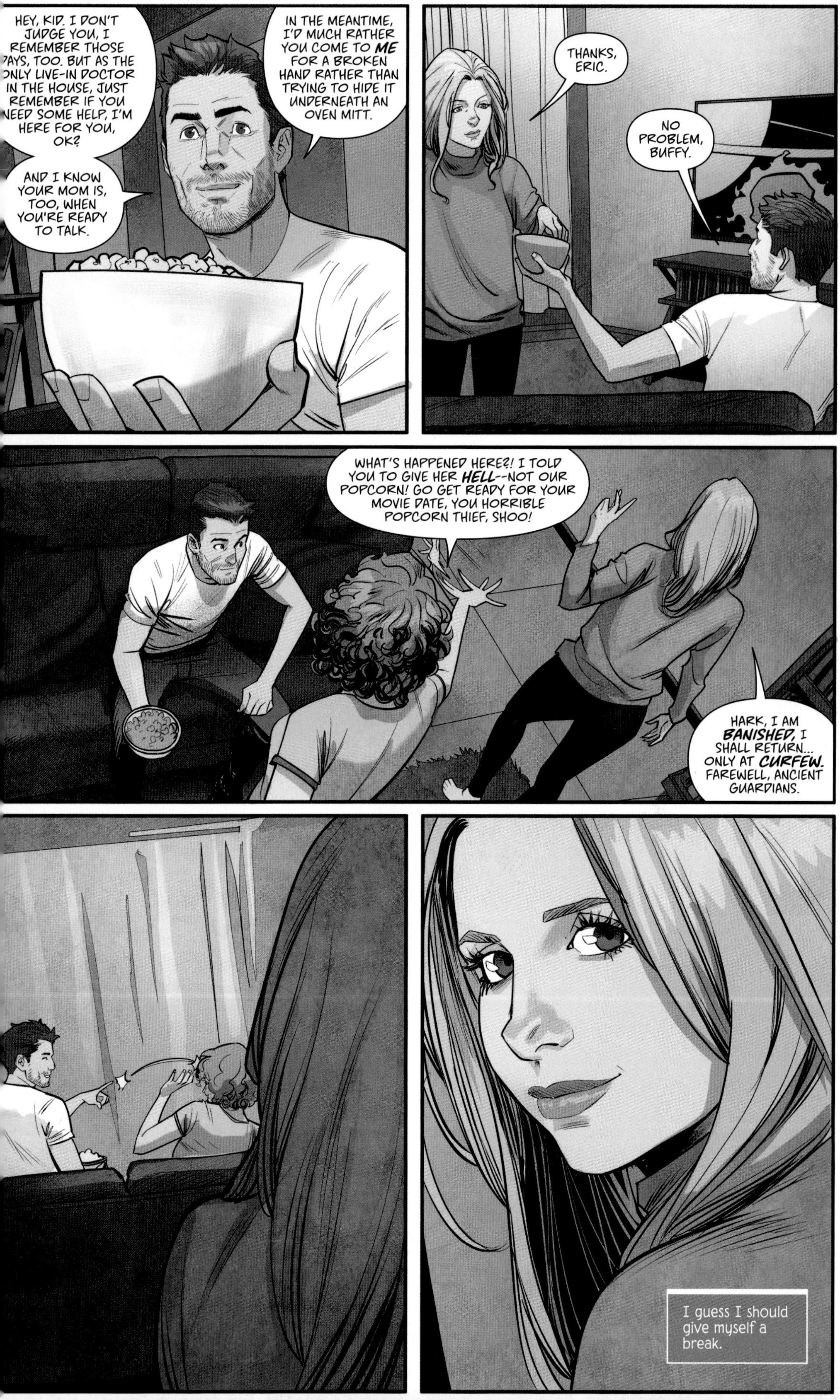

HEY, KID. I DON'T JUDGE YOU, I REMEMBER THOSE DAYS, TOO. BUT AS THE ONLY LIVE-IN DOCTOR IN THE HOUSE, JUST REMEMBER IF YOU NEED SOME HELP, I'M HERE FOR YOU, OK?
AND I KNOW YOUR MOM IS, TOO, WHEN YOU'RE READY TO TALK.
IN THE MEANTIME, I'D MUCH RATHER YOU COME TO ME FOR A BROKEN HAND RATHER THAN TRYING TO HIDE IT UNDERNEATH AN OVEN MITT.
THANKS, ERIC.
NO PROBLEM, BUFFY.
WHAT'S HAPPENED HERE?! I TOLD YOU TO GIVE HER HELL--NOT OUR POPCORN! GO GET READY FOR YOUR MOVIE DATE, YOU HORRIBLE POPCORN THIEF, SHOO!
HARK, I AM BANISHED, I SHALL RETURN... ONLY AT CURFEW. FAREWELL, ANCIENT GUARDIANS.
I guess I should give myself a break.

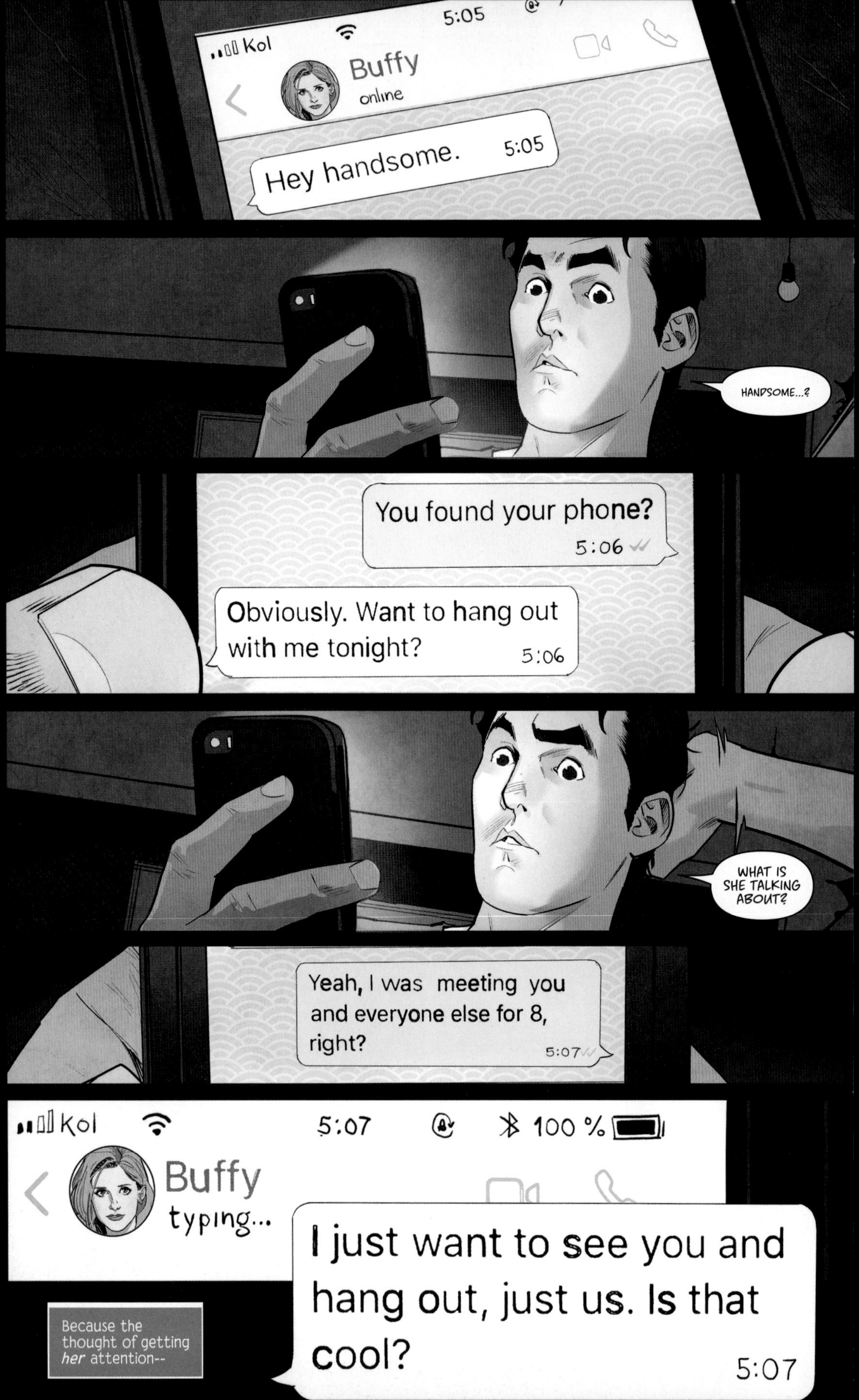

Kol
5:05
Buffy
online
Hey handsome. 5:05
HANDSOME...?
You found your phone? 5:06
Obviously. Want to hang out with me tonight? 5:06
WHAT IS SHE TALKING ABOUT?
Yeah, I was meeting you and everyone else for 8, right? 5:07
Kol
5:07
100 %
Buffy
typing...
I just want to see you and hang out, just us. Is that cool? 5:07
Because the thought of getting *her* attention--

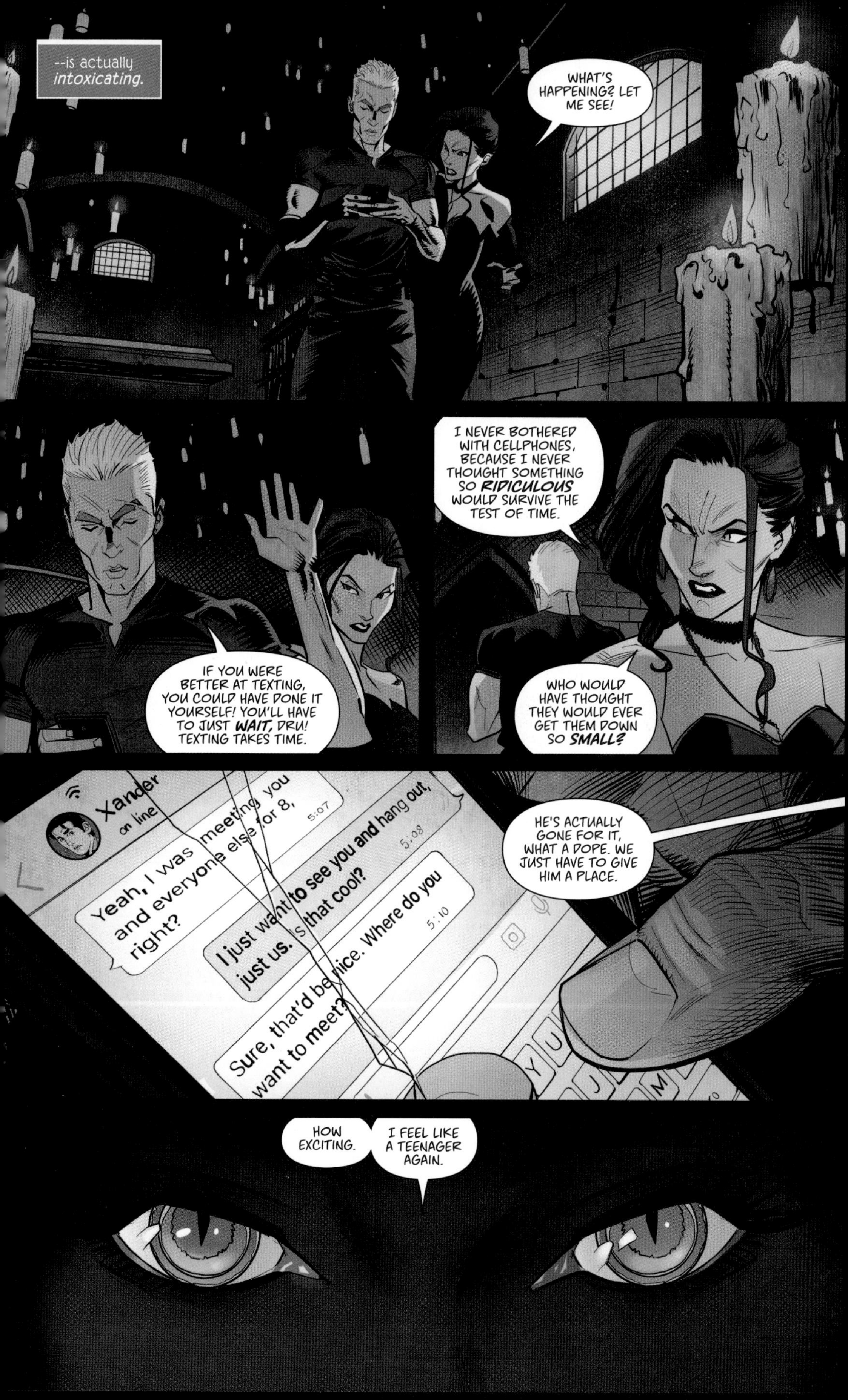
--is actually *intoxicating.*
WHAT'S HAPPENING? LET ME SEE!
IF YOU WERE BETTER AT TEXTING, YOU COULD HAVE DONE IT YOURSELF! YOU'LL HAVE TO JUST **WAIT,** DRU! TEXTING TAKES TIME.
I NEVER BOTHERED WITH CELLPHONES, BECAUSE I NEVER THOUGHT SOMETHING SO **RIDICULOUS** WOULD SURVIVE THE TEST OF TIME.
WHO WOULD HAVE THOUGHT THEY WOULD EVER GET THEM DOWN SO **SMALL?**
Xander
on line
Yeah, I was meeting you and everyone else for 8, right?
5:07
I just want to see you and hang out, just us. Is that cool?
5:08
Sure, that'd be nice. Where do you want to meet?
5:10
HE'S ACTUALLY GONE FOR IT, WHAT A DOPE. WE JUST HAVE TO GIVE HIM A PLACE.
HOW EXCITING.
I FEEL LIKE A TEENAGER AGAIN.

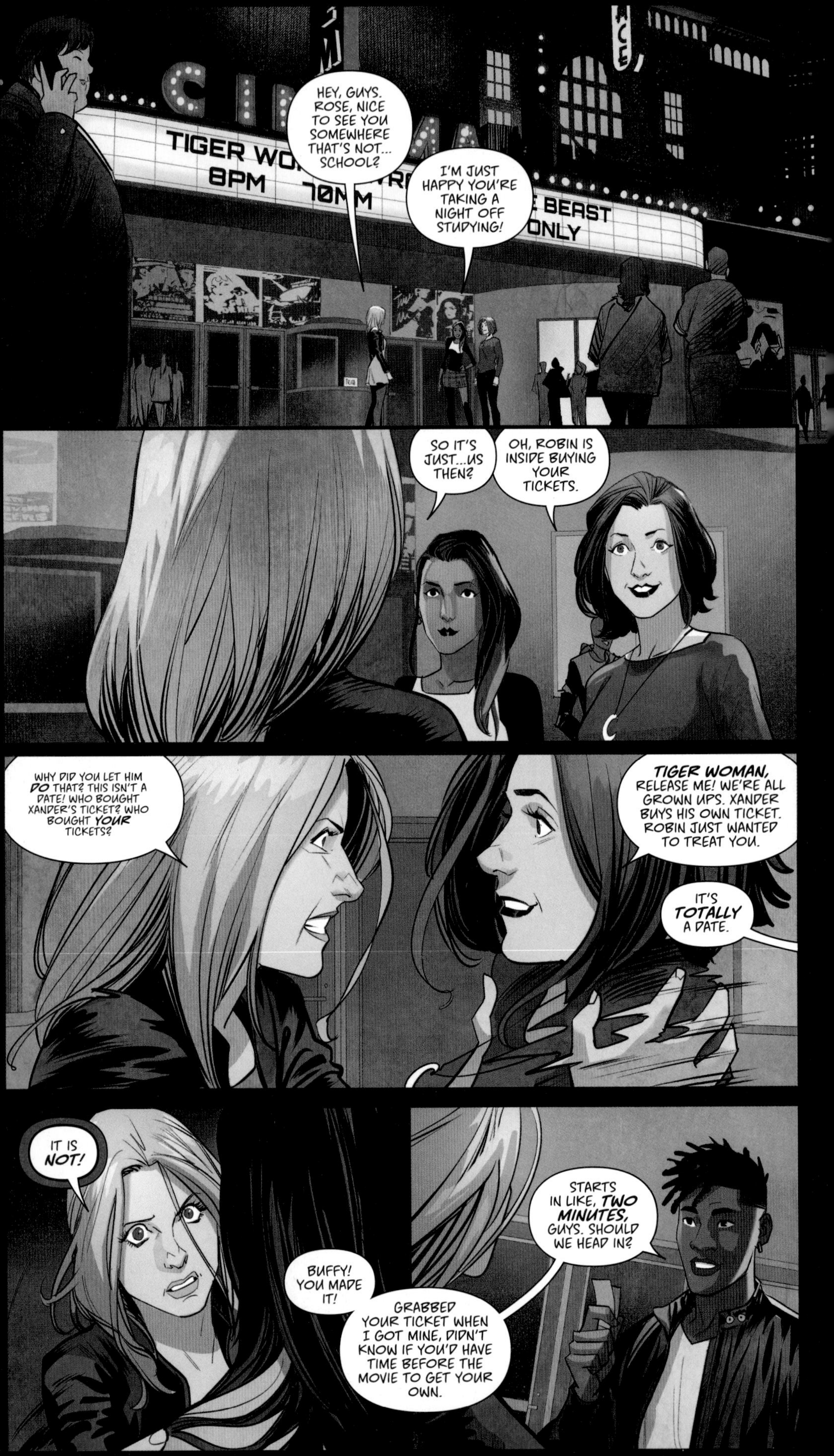
TIGER WO
8PM 70MM
BEAST
ONLY
HEY, GUYS. ROSE, NICE TO SEE YOU SOMEWHERE THAT'S NOT... SCHOOL?
I'M JUST HAPPY YOU'RE TAKING A NIGHT OFF STUDYING!
SO IT'S JUST...US THEN?
OH, ROBIN IS INSIDE BUYING YOUR TICKETS.
WHY DID YOU LET HIM DO THAT? THIS ISN'T A DATE! WHO BOUGHT XANDER'S TICKET? WHO BOUGHT YOUR TICKETS?
TIGER WOMAN, RELEASE ME! WE'RE ALL GROWN UPS. XANDER BUYS HIS OWN TICKET. ROBIN JUST WANTED TO TREAT YOU.
IT'S TOTALLY A DATE.
IT IS NOT!
BUFFY! YOU MADE IT!
GRABBED YOUR TICKET WHEN I GOT MINE, DIDN'T KNOW IF YOU'D HAVE TIME BEFORE THE MOVIE TO GET YOUR OWN.
STARTS IN LIKE, TWO MINUTES, GUYS. SHOULD WE HEAD IN?

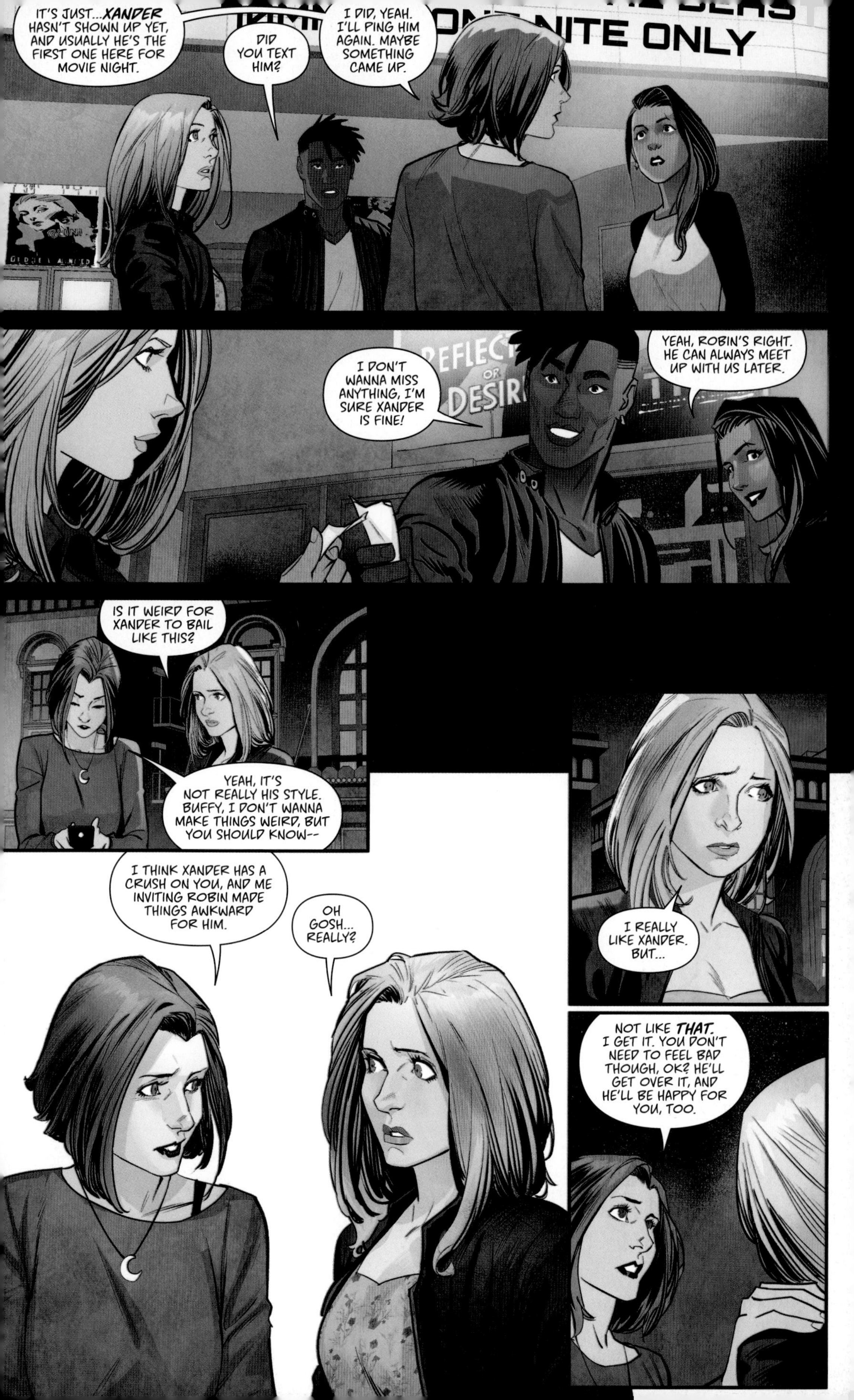
ONE NITE ONLY
IT'S JUST...XANDER HASN'T SHOWN UP YET, AND USUALLY HE'S THE FIRST ONE HERE FOR MOVIE NIGHT.
DID YOU TEXT HIM?
I DID, YEAH. I'LL PING HIM AGAIN. MAYBE SOMETHING CAME UP.
I DON'T WANNA MISS ANYTHING, I'M SURE XANDER IS FINE!
YEAH, ROBIN'S RIGHT. HE CAN ALWAYS MEET UP WITH US LATER.
IS IT WEIRD FOR XANDER TO BAIL LIKE THIS?
YEAH, IT'S NOT REALLY HIS STYLE. BUFFY, I DON'T WANNA MAKE THINGS WEIRD, BUT YOU SHOULD KNOW--
I THINK XANDER HAS A CRUSH ON YOU, AND ME INVITING ROBIN MADE THINGS AWKWARD FOR HIM.
OH GOSH... REALLY?
I REALLY LIKE XANDER. BUT...
NOT LIKE THAT. I GET IT. YOU DON'T NEED TO FEEL BAD THOUGH, OK? HE'LL GET OVER IT, AND HE'LL BE HAPPY FOR YOU, TOO.

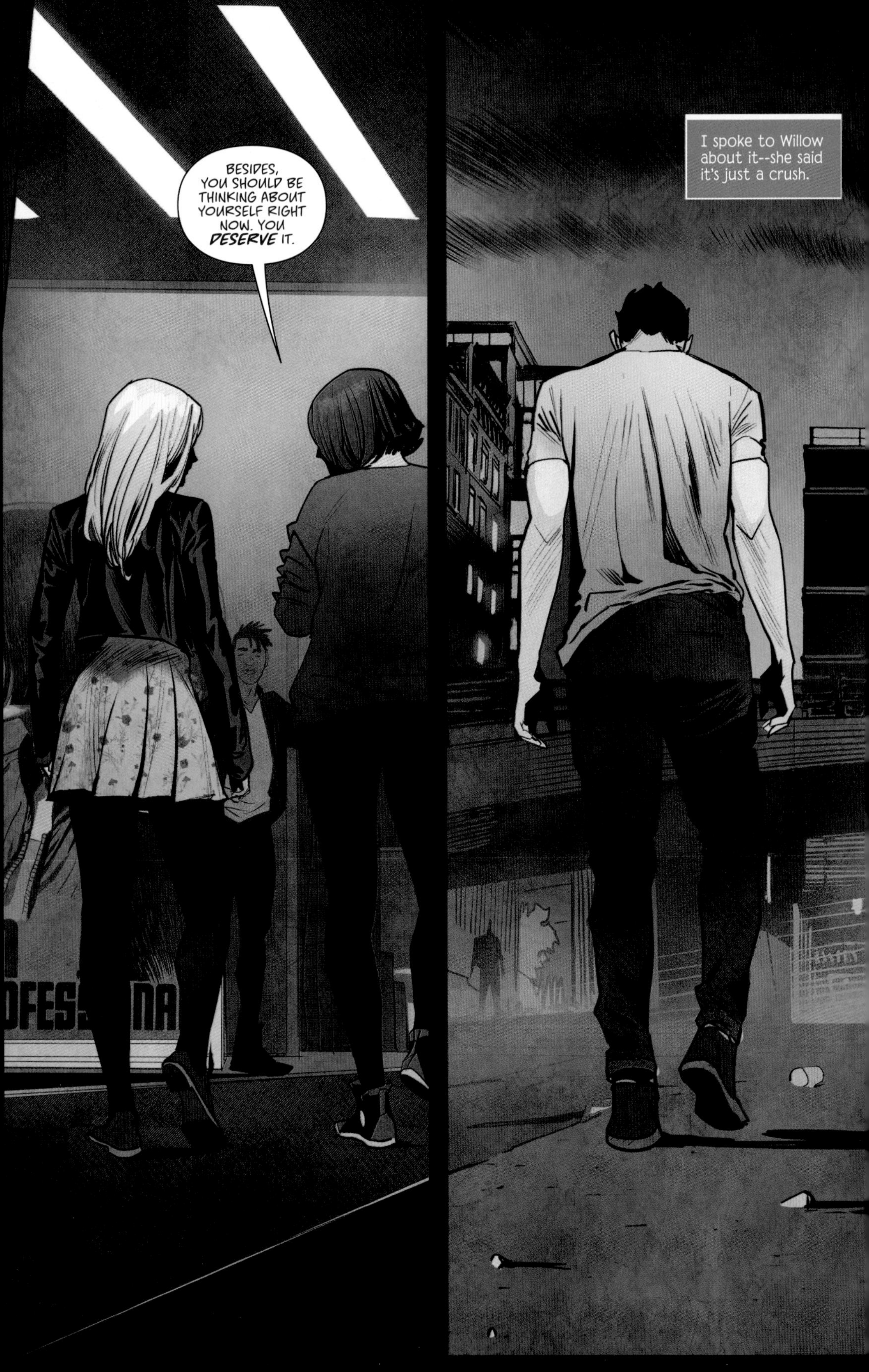
BESIDES, YOU SHOULD BE THINKING ABOUT YOURSELF RIGHT NOW. YOU DESERVE IT.
I spoke to Willow about it--she said it's just a crush.

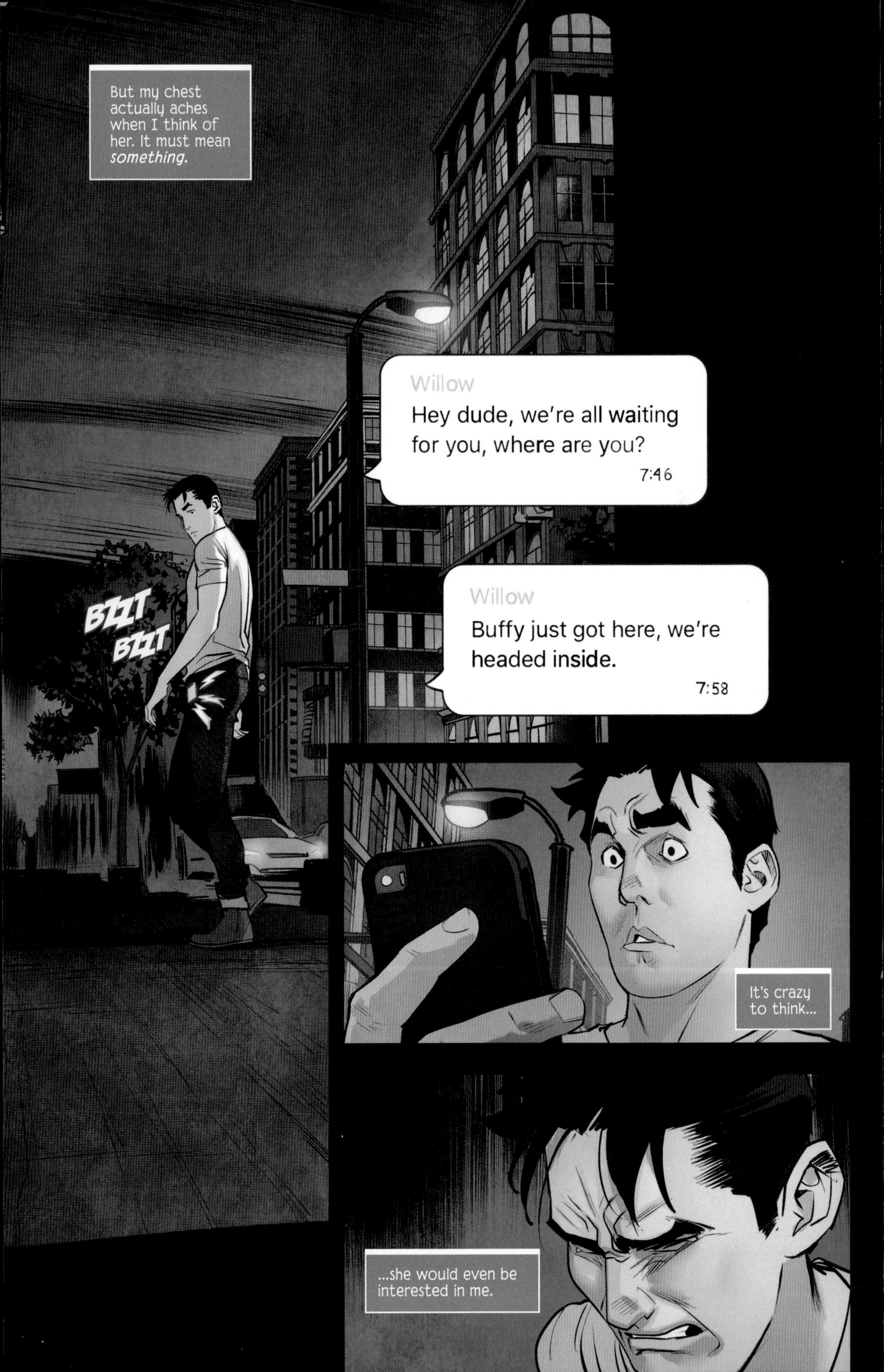
But my chest actually aches when I think of her. It must mean *something.*
Willow
Hey dude, we're all waiting for you, where are you?
7:46
Willow
Buffy just got here, we're headed inside.
7:58
BZZT
BZZT
It's crazy to think...
...she would even be interested in me.

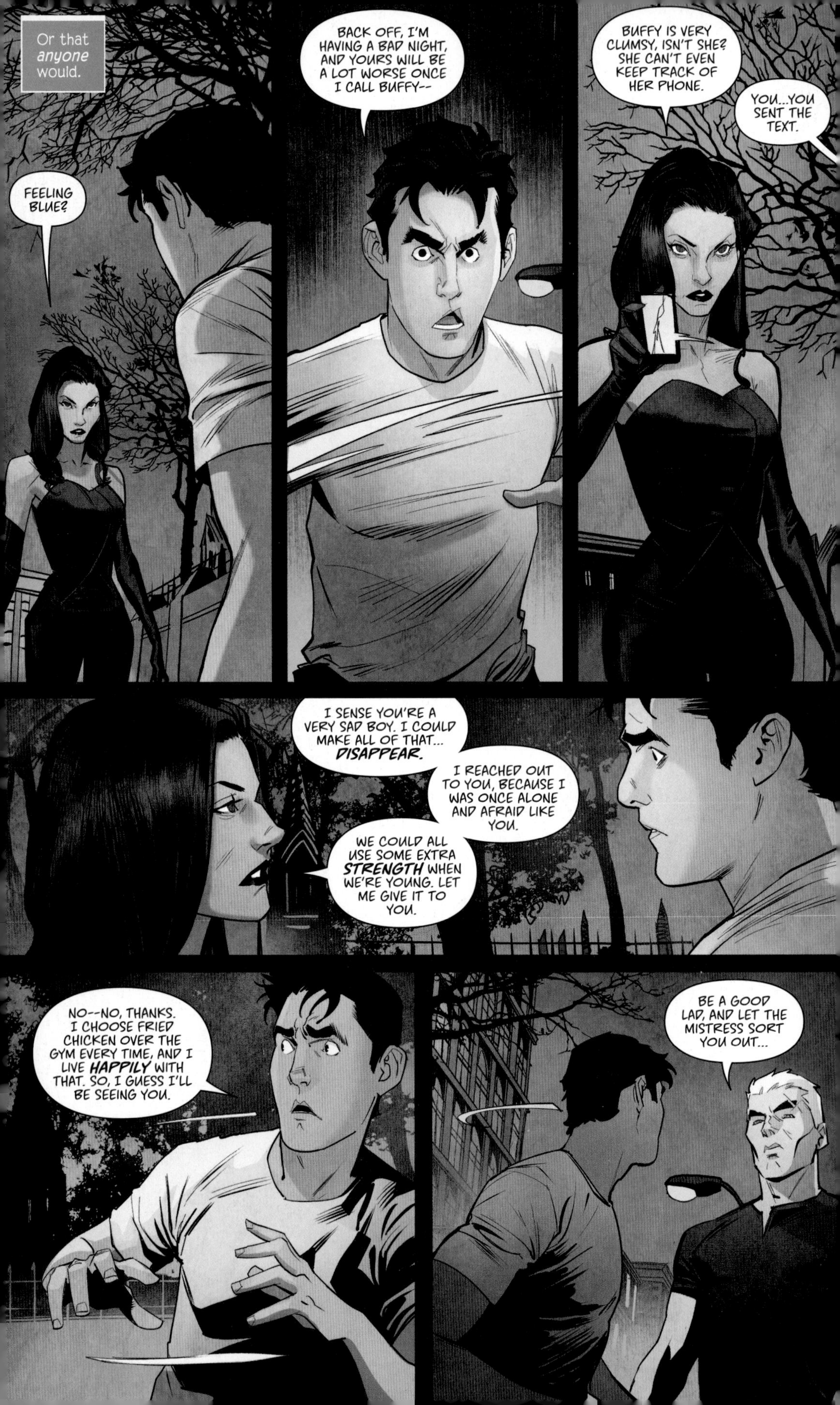
Or that *anyone* would.
FEELING BLUE?
BACK OFF, I'M HAVING A BAD NIGHT, AND YOURS WILL BE A LOT WORSE ONCE I CALL BUFFY--
BUFFY IS VERY CLUMSY, ISN'T SHE? SHE CAN'T EVEN KEEP TRACK OF HER PHONE.
YOU...YOU SENT THE TEXT.
I SENSE YOU'RE A VERY SAD BOY. I COULD MAKE ALL OF THAT... **DISAPPEAR.**
I REACHED OUT TO YOU, BECAUSE I WAS ONCE ALONE AND AFRAID LIKE YOU.
WE COULD ALL USE SOME EXTRA ***STRENGTH*** WHEN WE'RE YOUNG. LET ME GIVE IT TO YOU.
NO--NO, THANKS. I CHOOSE FRIED CHICKEN OVER THE GYM EVERY TIME, AND I LIVE ***HAPPILY*** WITH THAT. SO, I GUESS I'LL BE SEEING YOU.
BE A GOOD LAD, AND LET THE MISTRESS SORT YOU OUT...

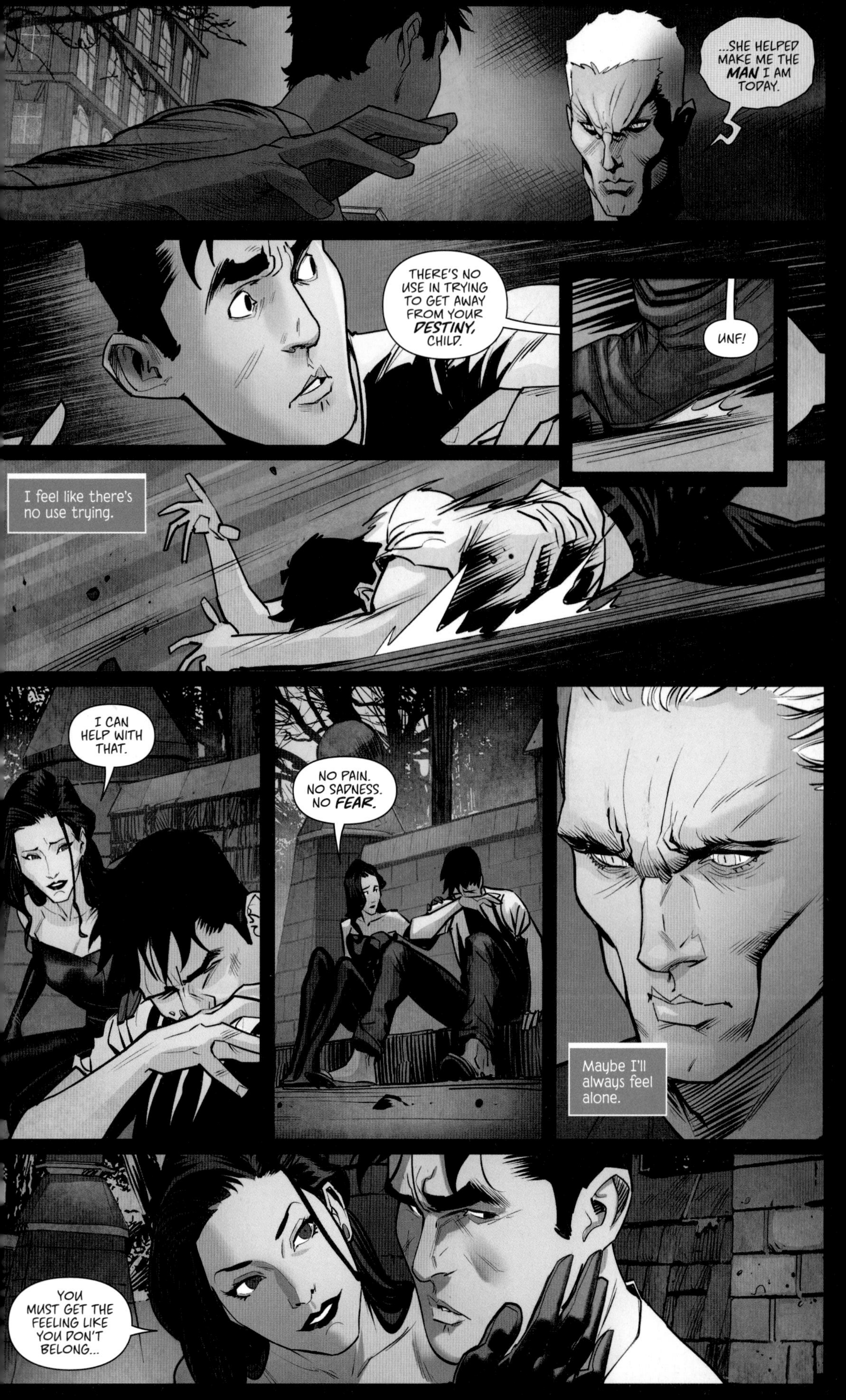
...SHE HELPED MAKE ME THE MAN I AM TODAY.
THERE'S NO USE IN TRYING TO GET AWAY FROM YOUR DESTINY, CHILD.
UNF!
I feel like there's no use trying.
I CAN HELP WITH THAT.
NO PAIN. NO SADNESS. NO FEAR.
Maybe I'll always feel alone.
YOU MUST GET THE FEELING LIKE YOU DON'T BELONG...

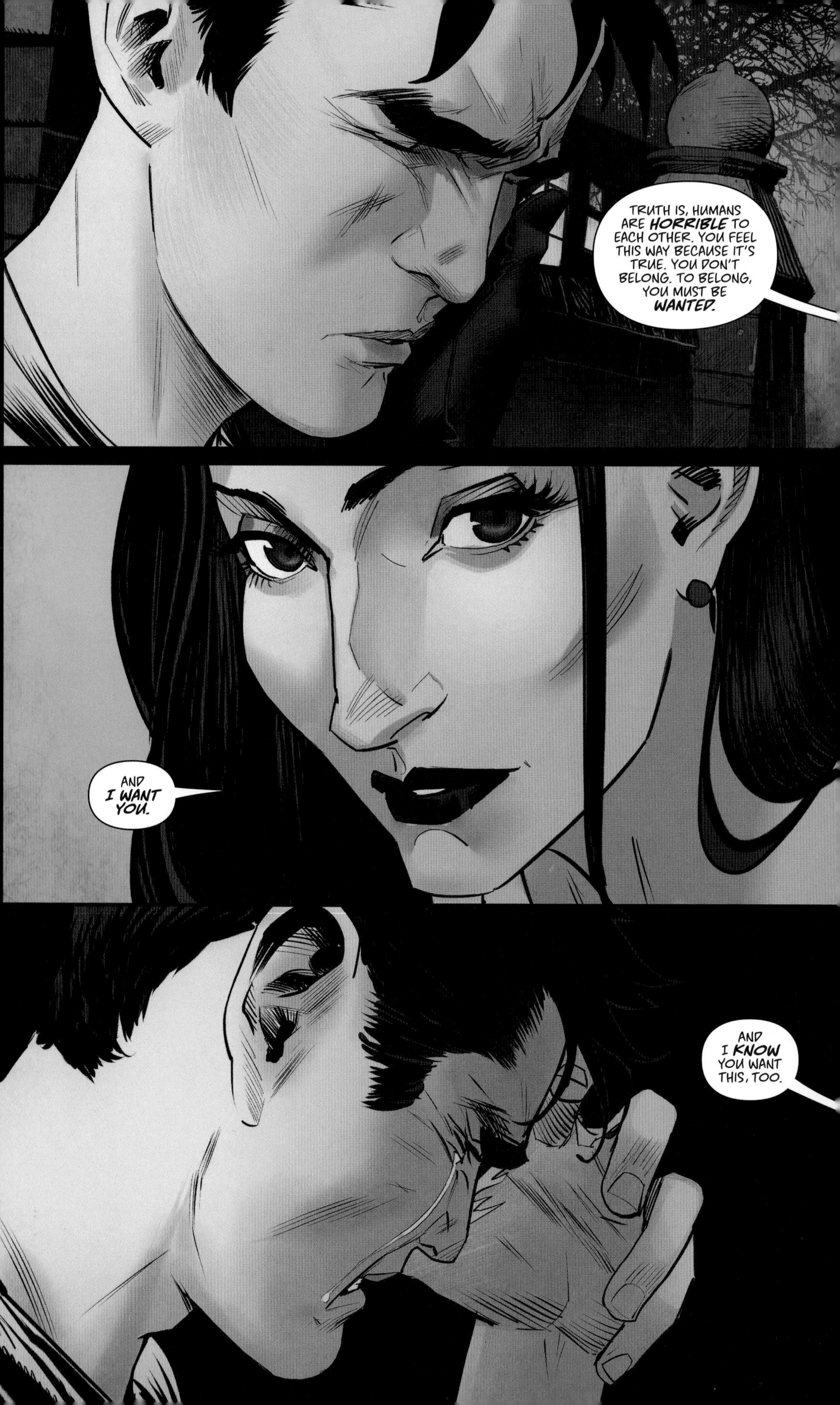
TRUTH IS, HUMANS ARE HORRIBLE TO EACH OTHER. YOU FEEL THIS WAY BECAUSE IT'S TRUE. YOU DON'T BELONG. TO BELONG, YOU MUST BE WANTED.
AND I WANT YOU.
AND I KNOW YOU WANT THIS, TOO.

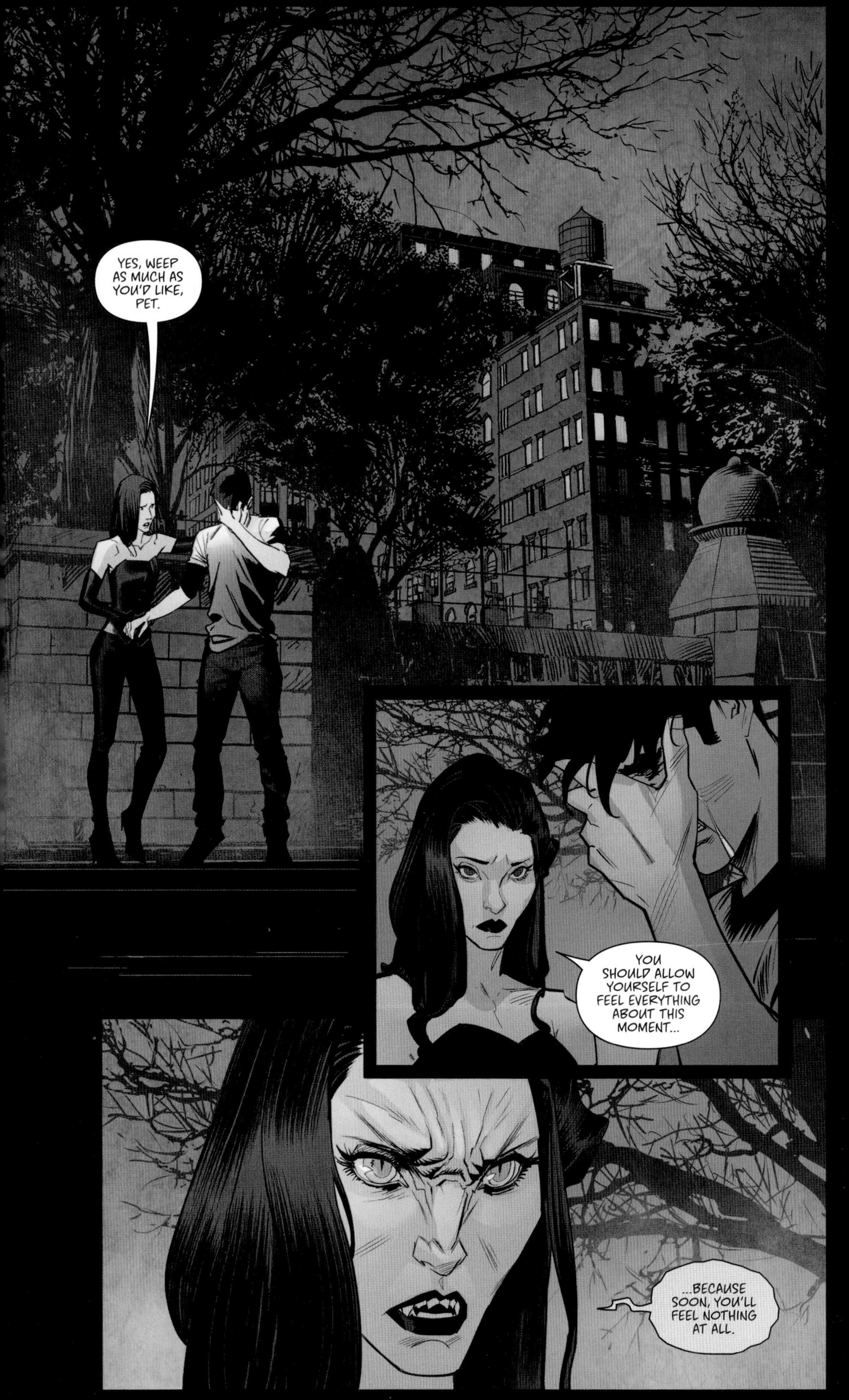
YES, WEEP AS MUCH AS YOU'D LIKE, PET.
YOU SHOULD ALLOW YOURSELF TO FEEL EVERYTHING ABOUT THIS MOMENT...
...BECAUSE SOON, YOU'LL FEEL NOTHING AT ALL.

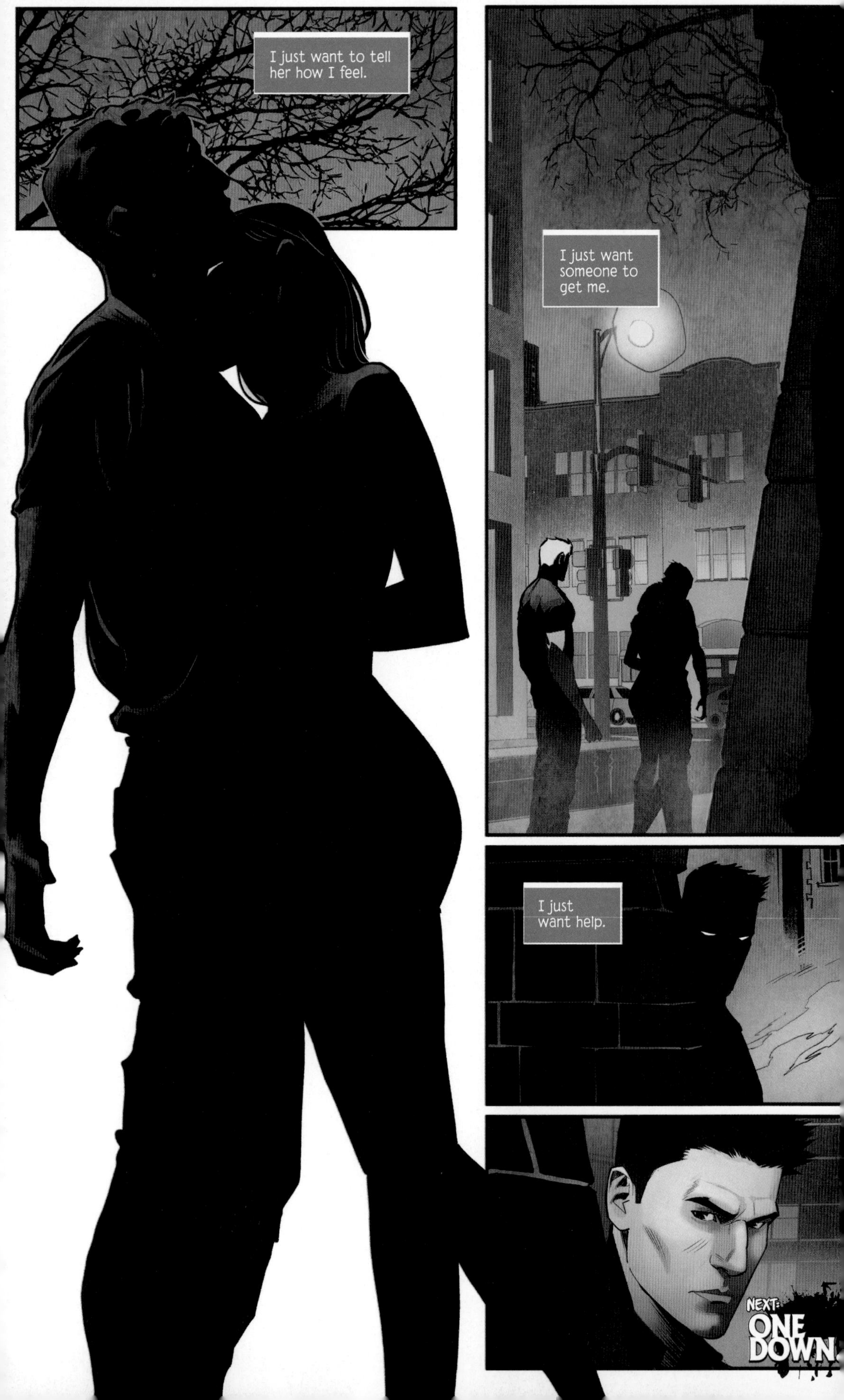
I just want to tell her how I feel.
I just want someone to get me.
I just want help.
NEXT:
ONE DOWN

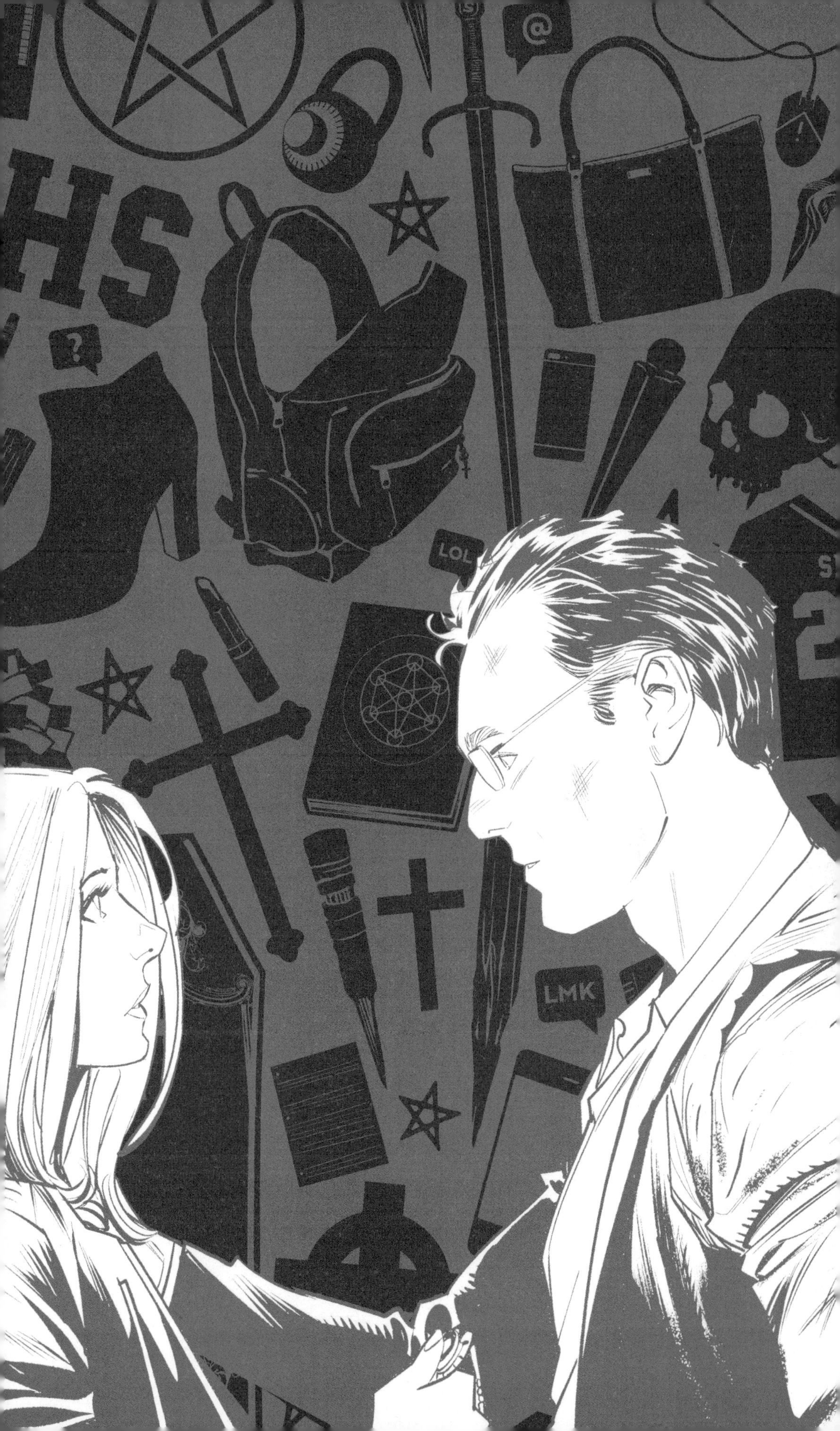
HS
LOL
LMK

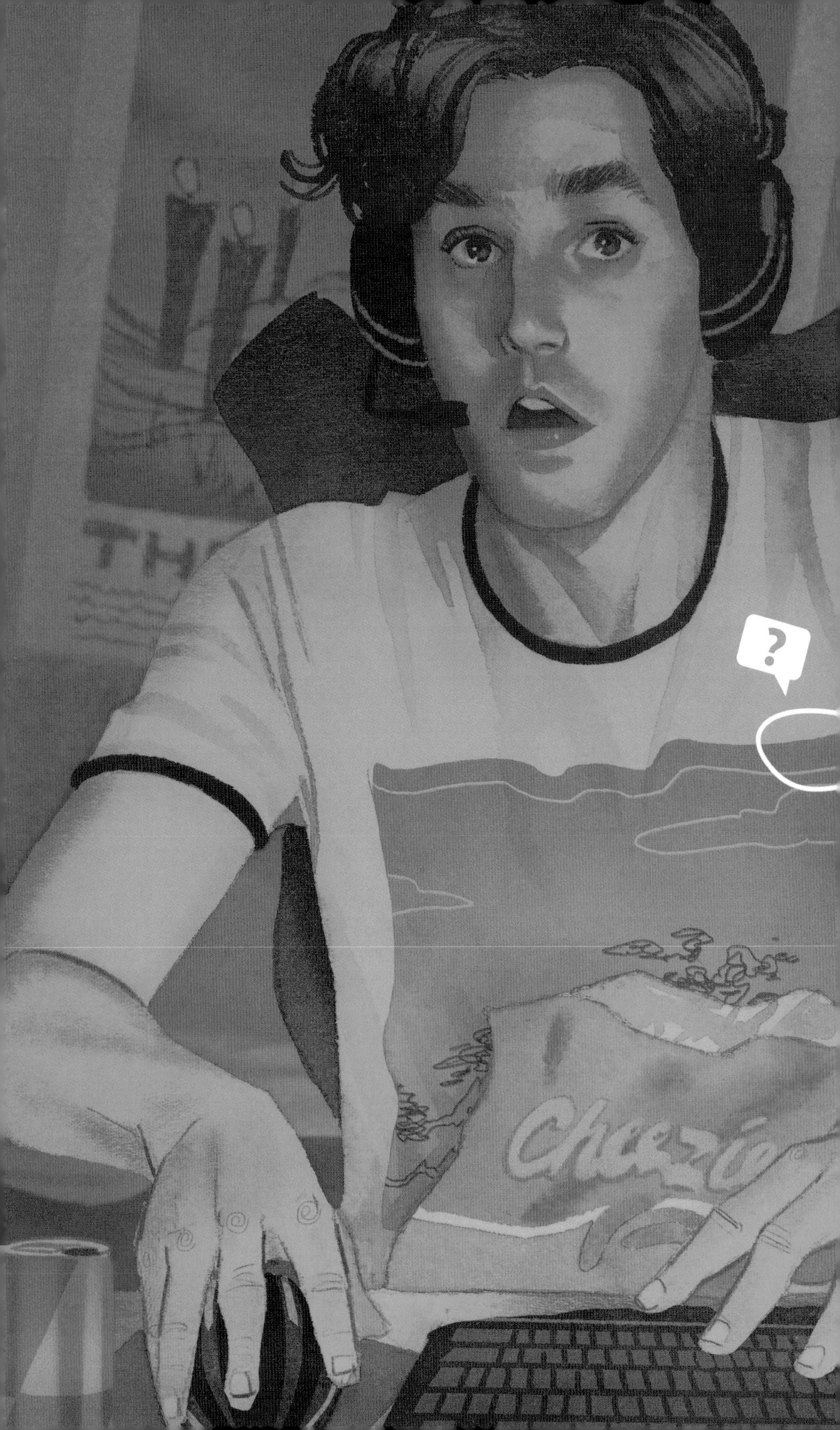
?

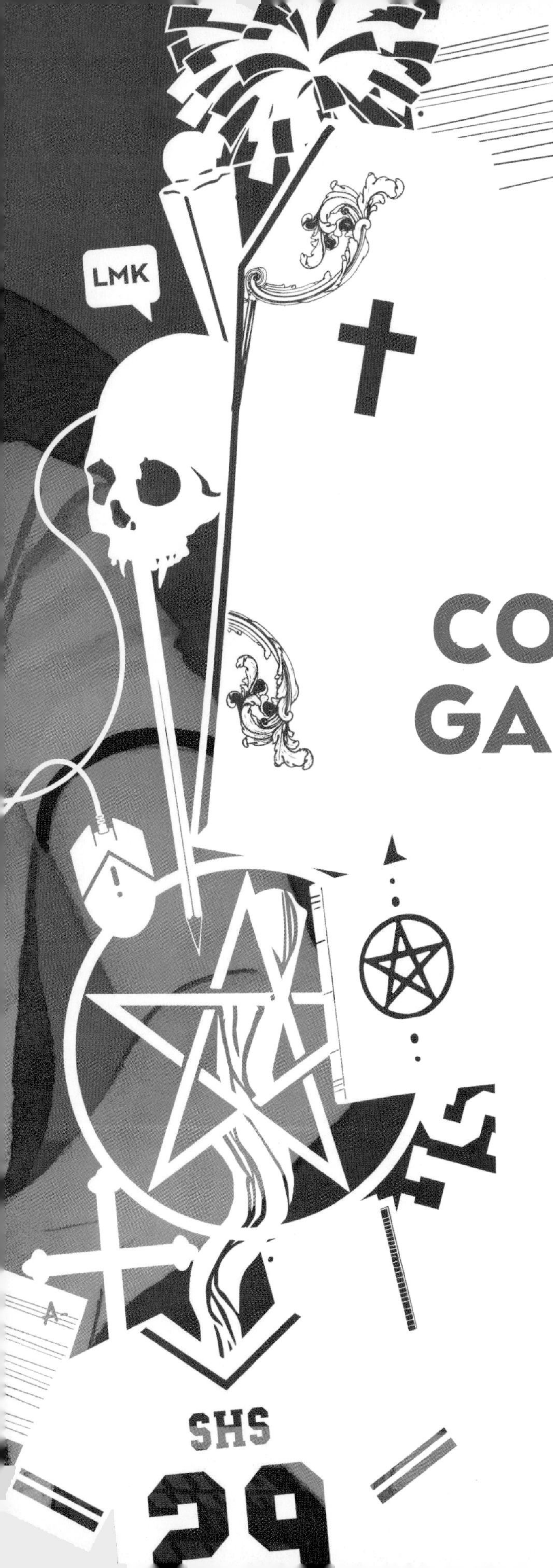
LMK
SHS

COVER GALLERY

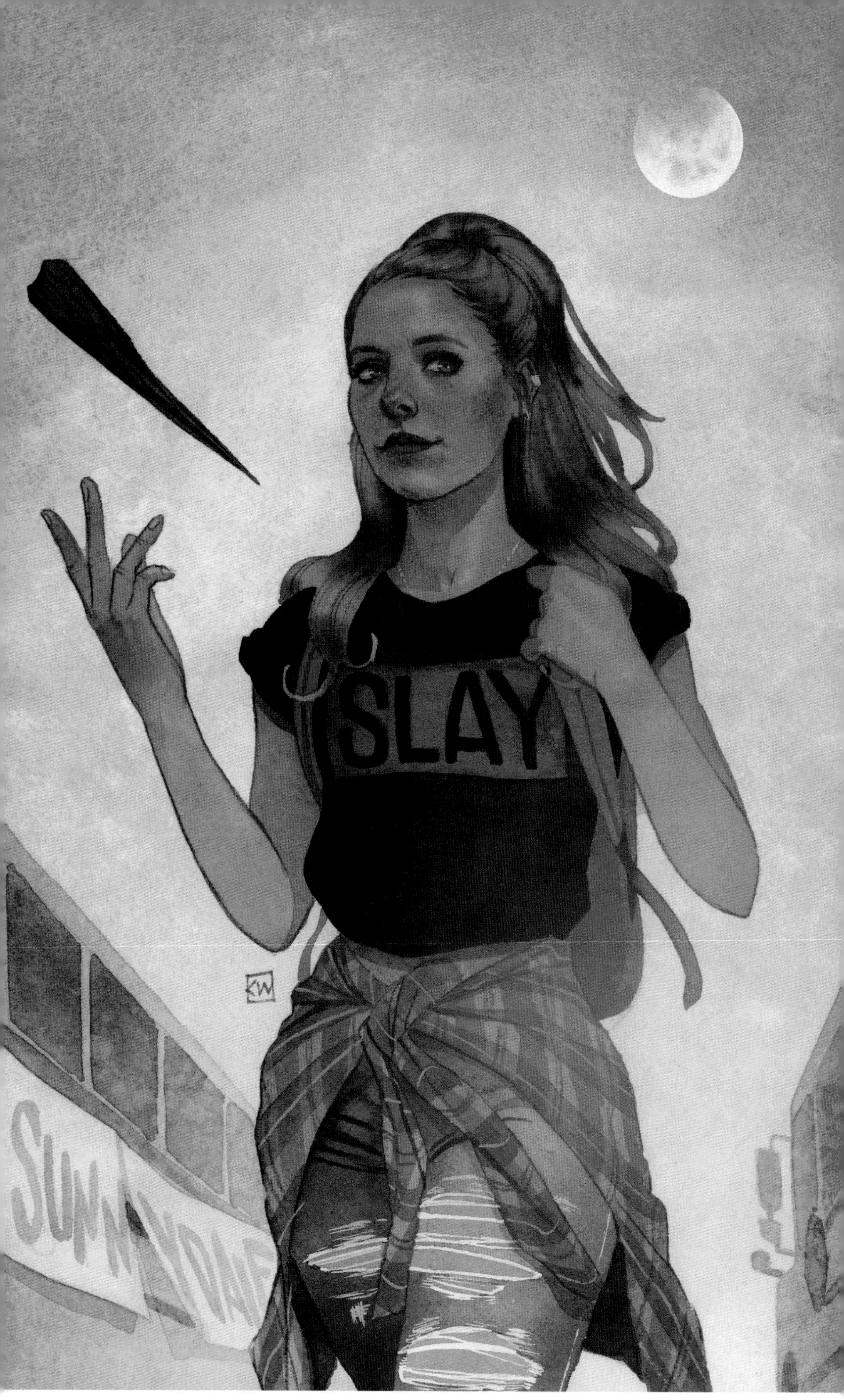
SLAY
KW
Issue One Spotlight Variant by **Kevin Wada**

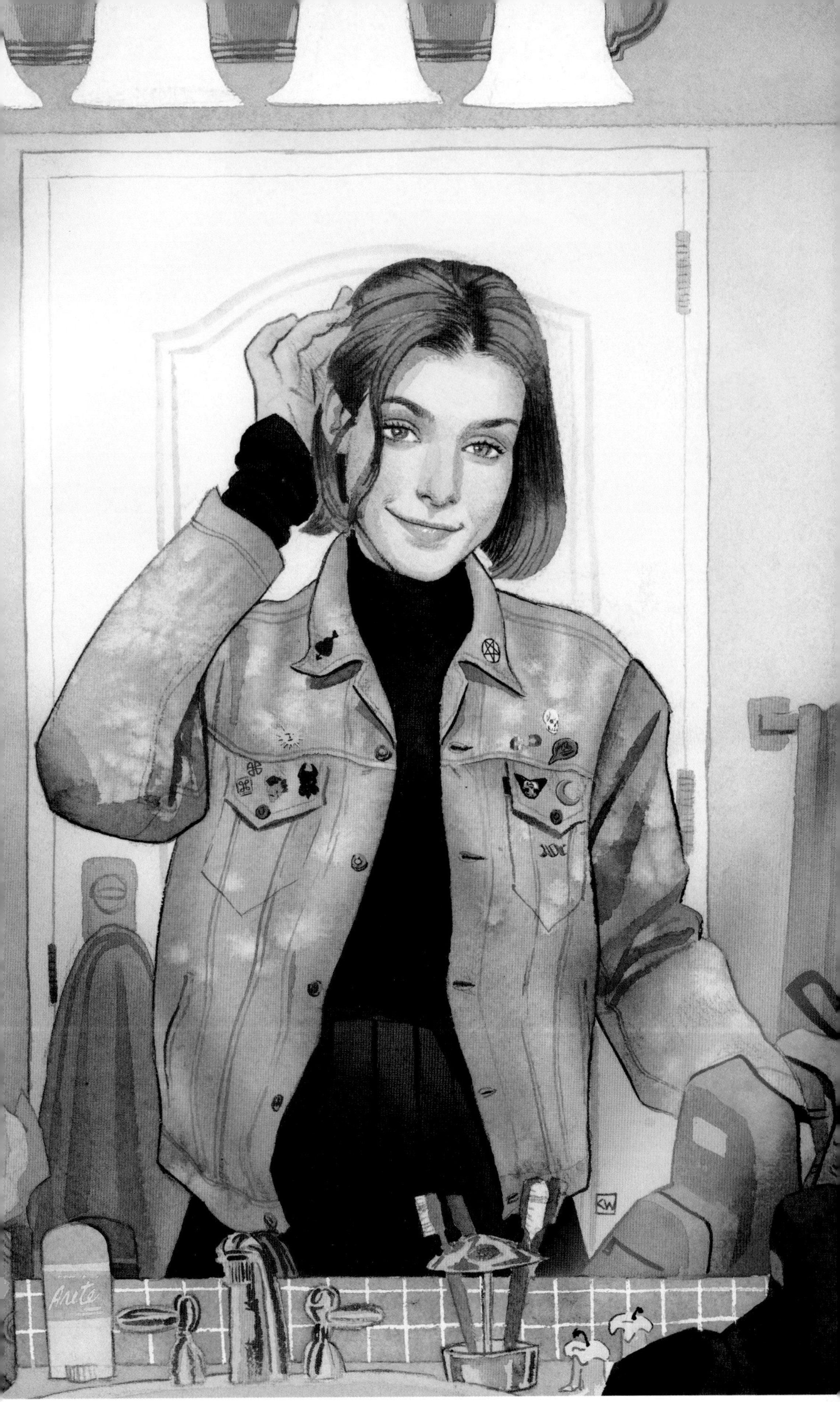

Issue Two Spotlight Variant by **Kevin Wada**

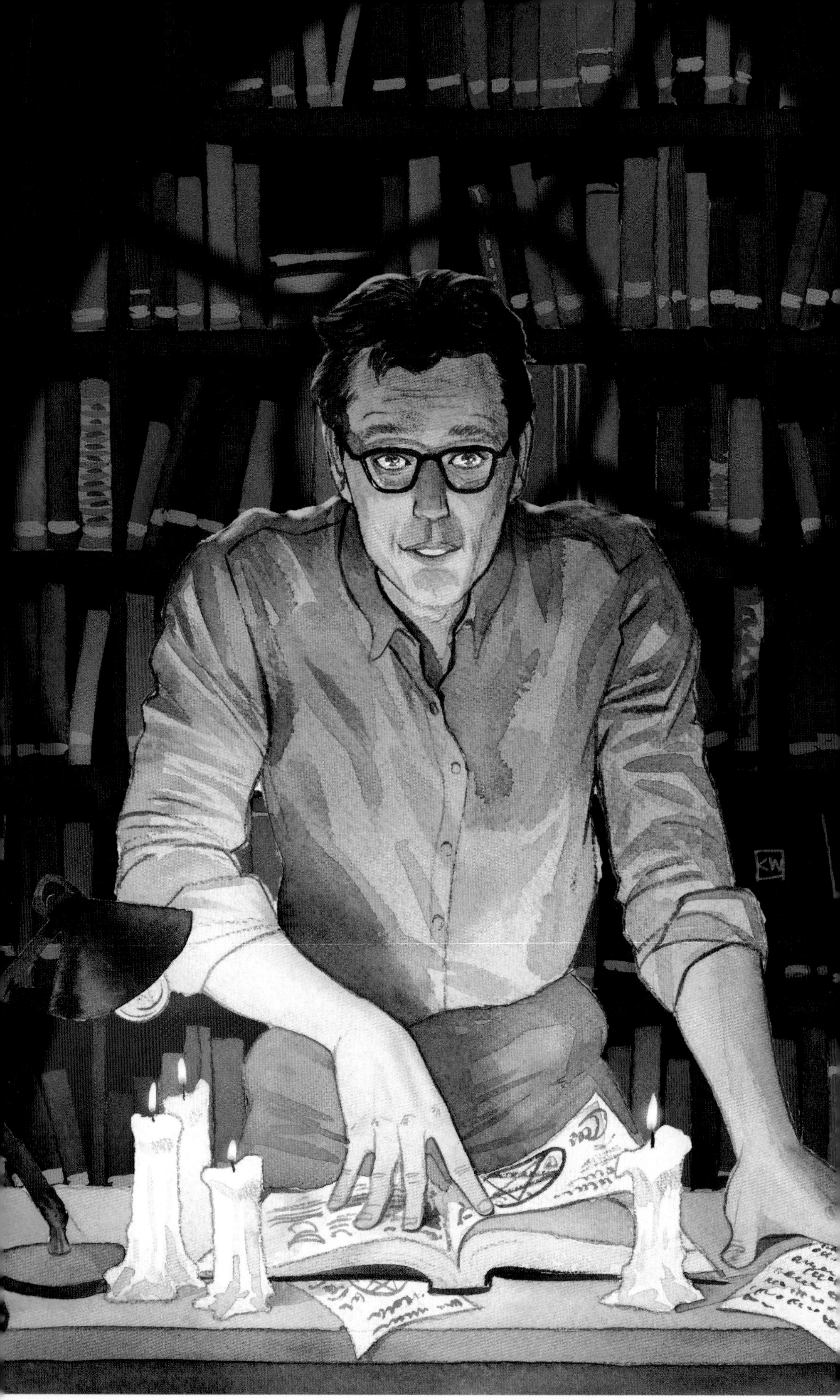
KW

Issue Three Spotlight Variant by **Kevin Wada**

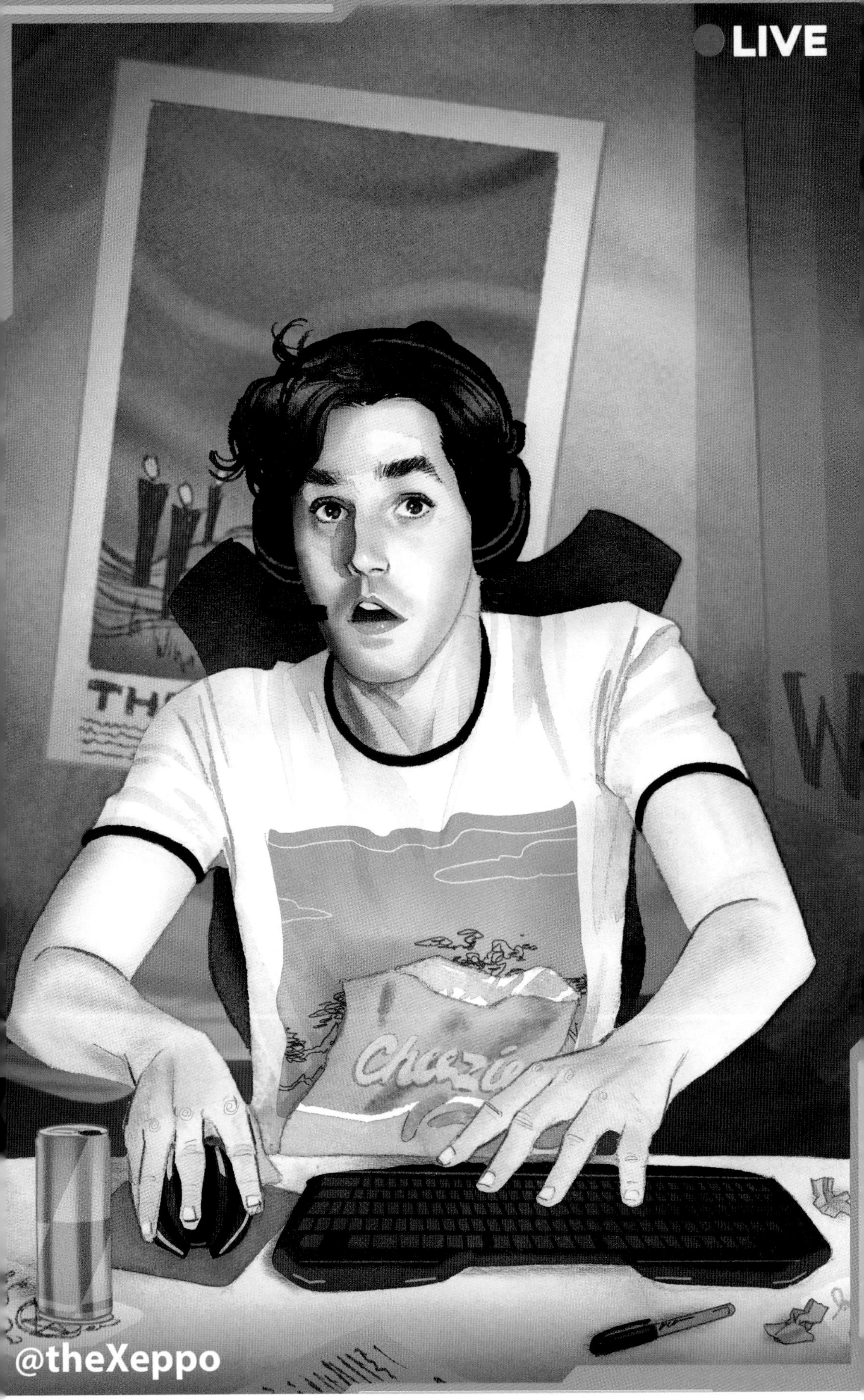
LIVE
@theXeppo
Cheezie

Issue Four Spotlight Variant by **Kevin Wada**

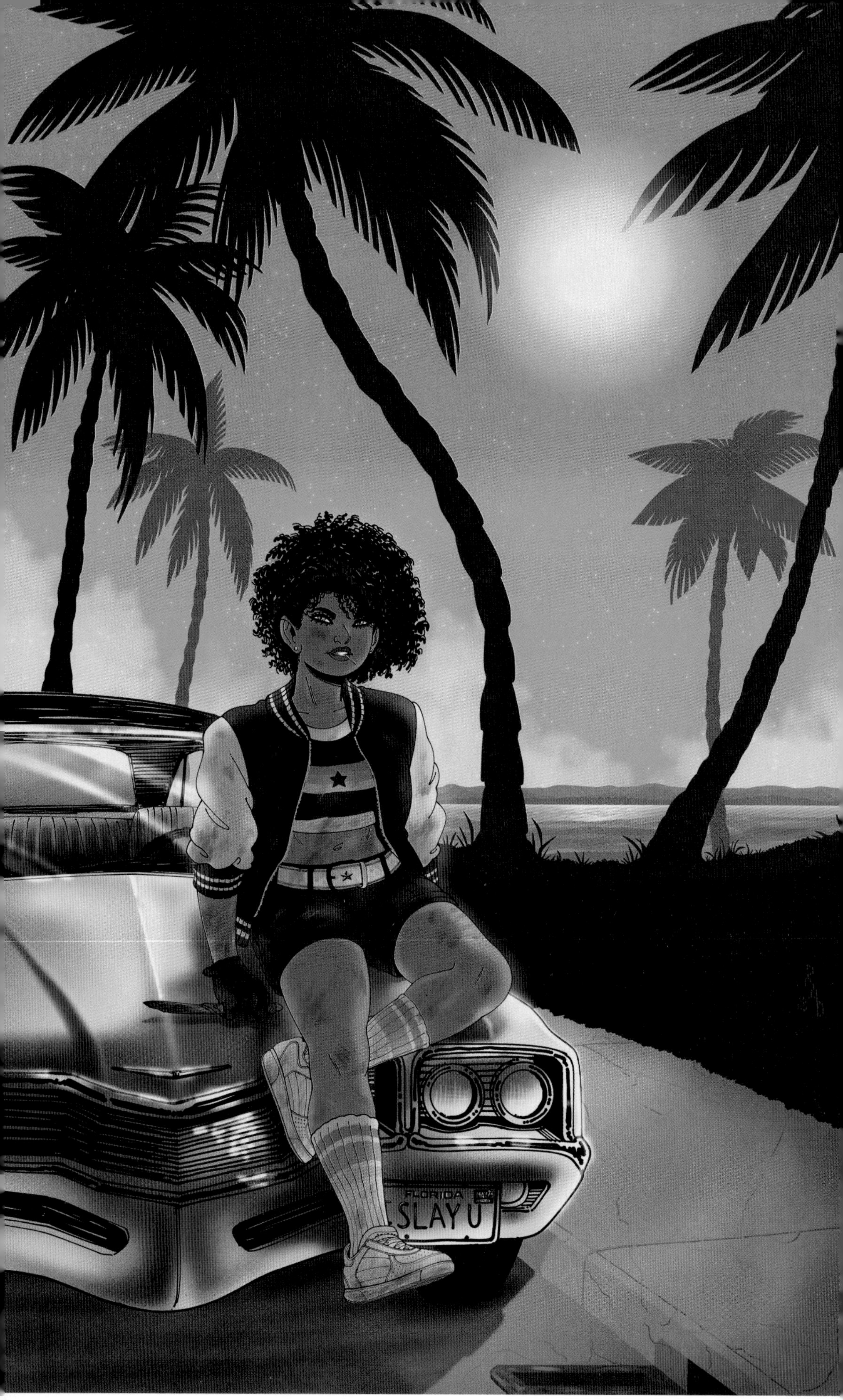
FLORIDA
SLAY U

Issue One Chosen One Variant by **Royal Dunlap**

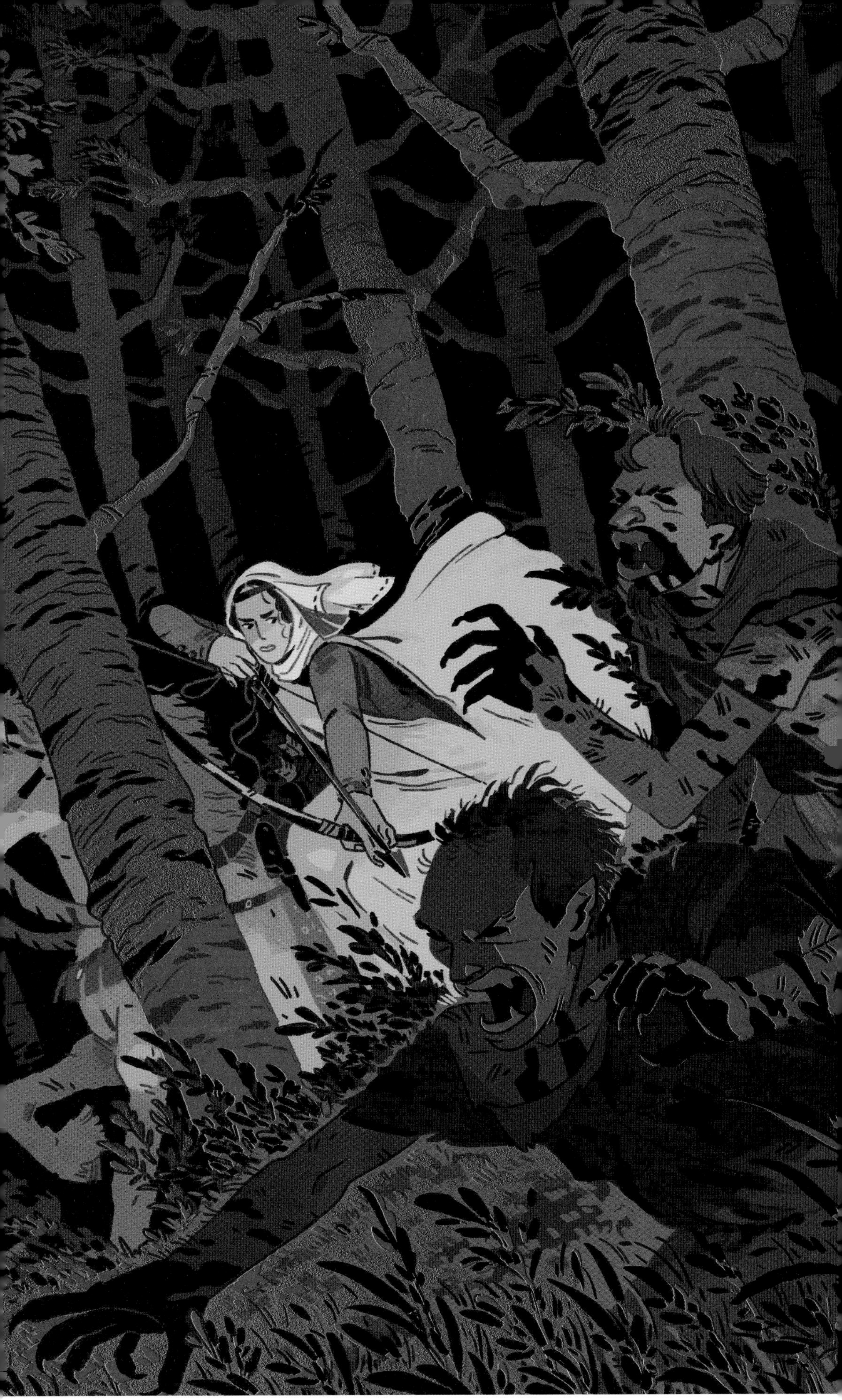

Issue Two Chosen One Variant by **Celia Lowenthal**

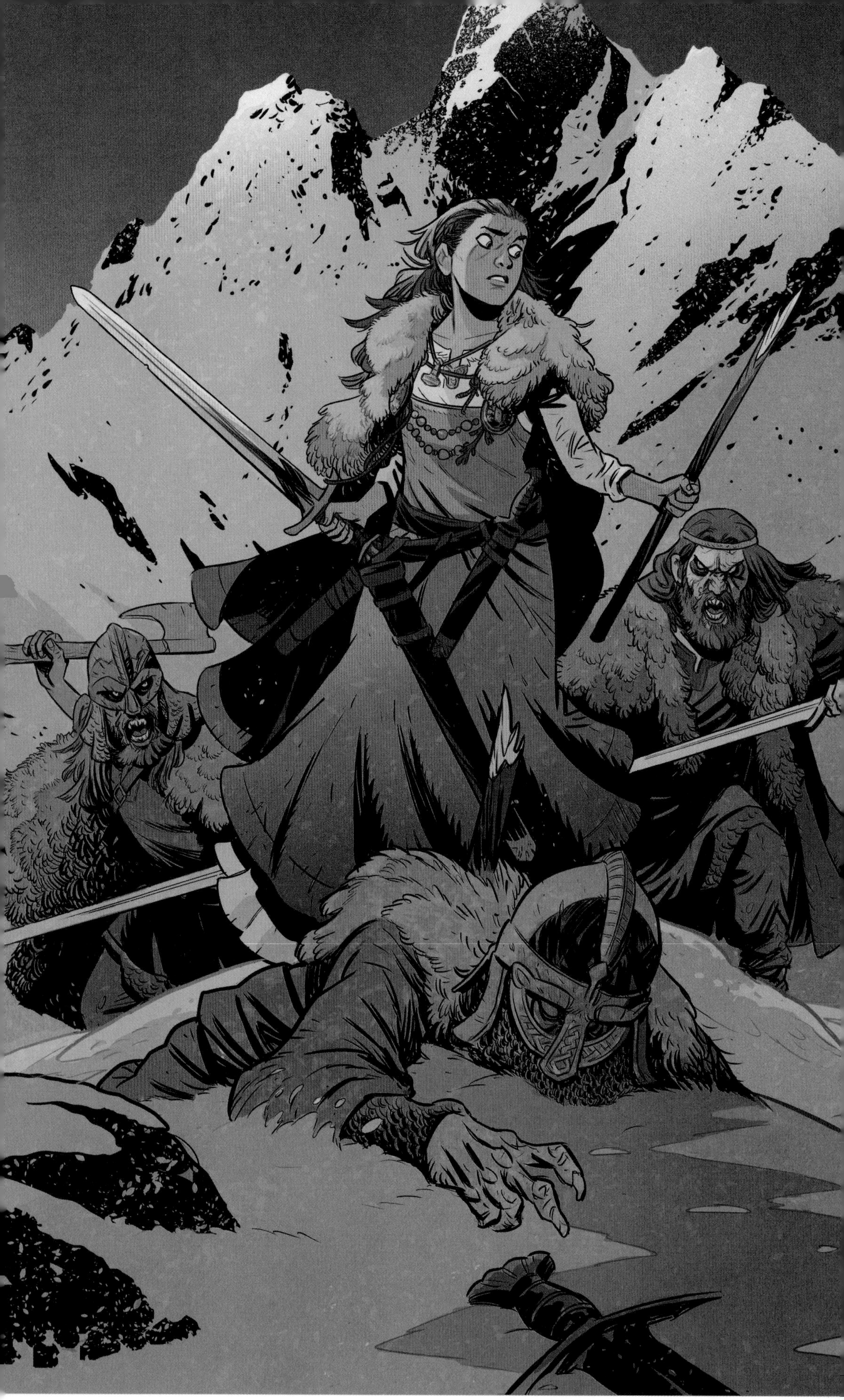

Issue Three Chosen One Variant by **Matt Smith**

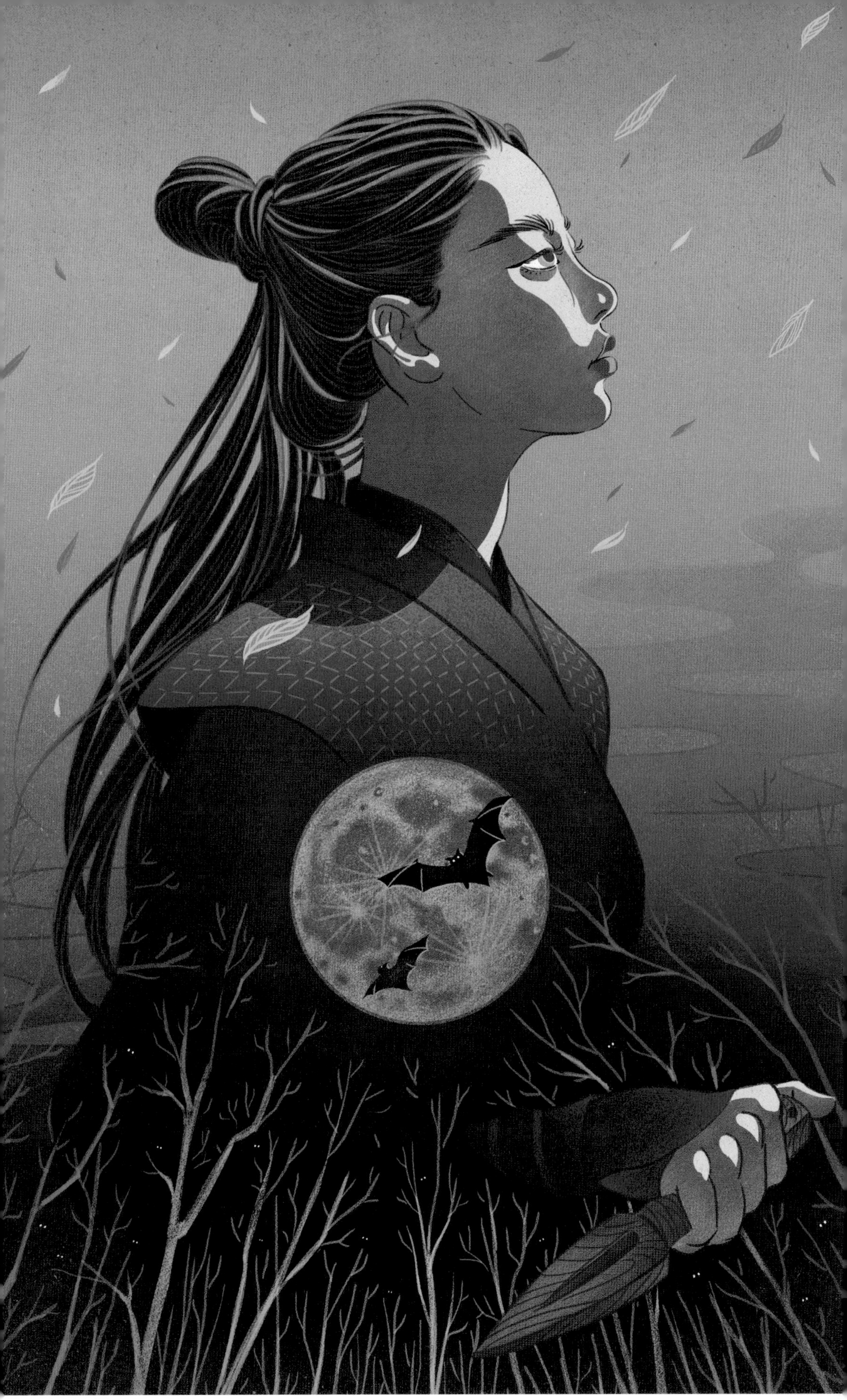

Issue Four Chosen One Variant by **FeiFei Ruan**

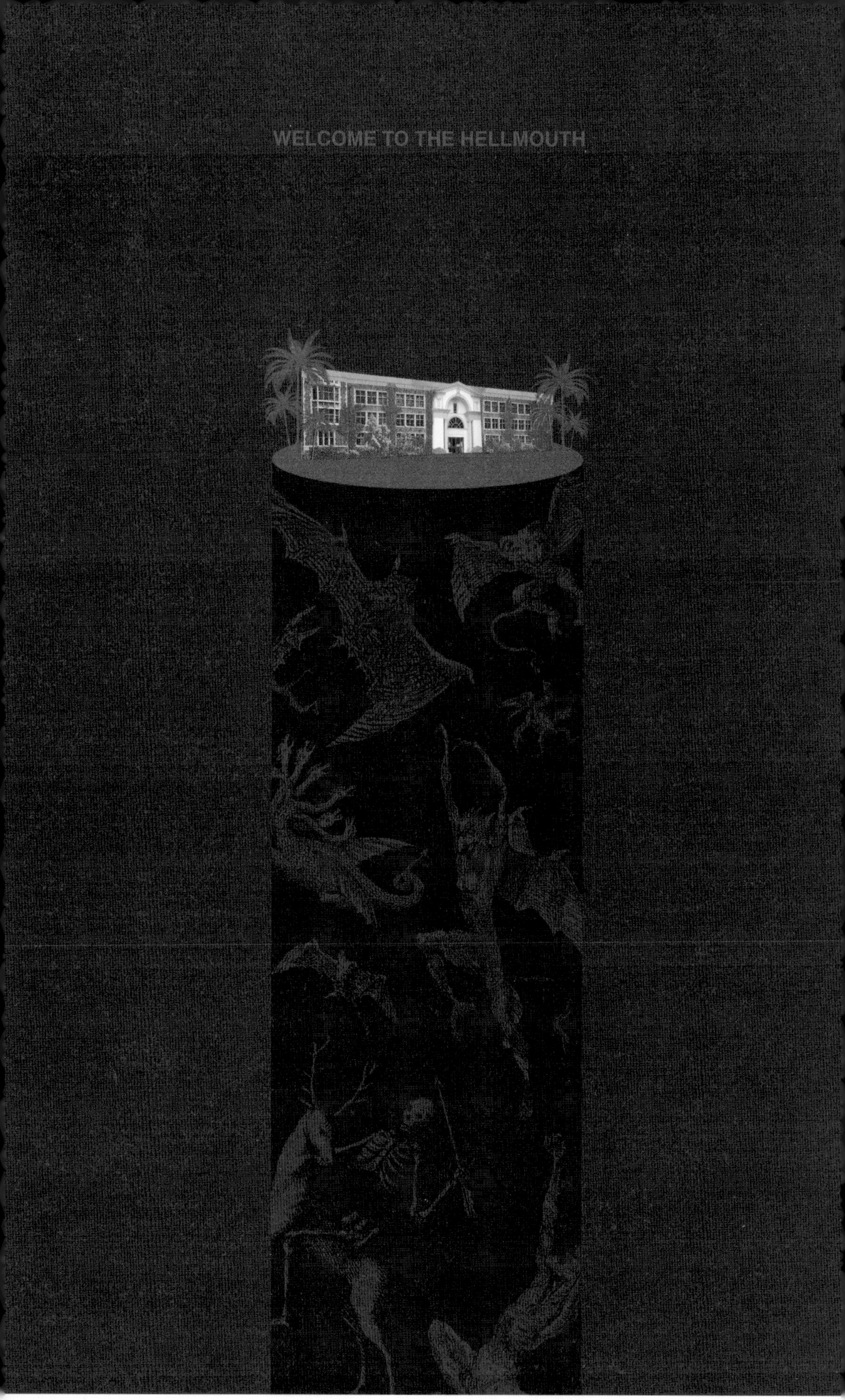
WELCOME TO THE HELLMOUTH

Issue One Episode Variant by **Becca Carey**

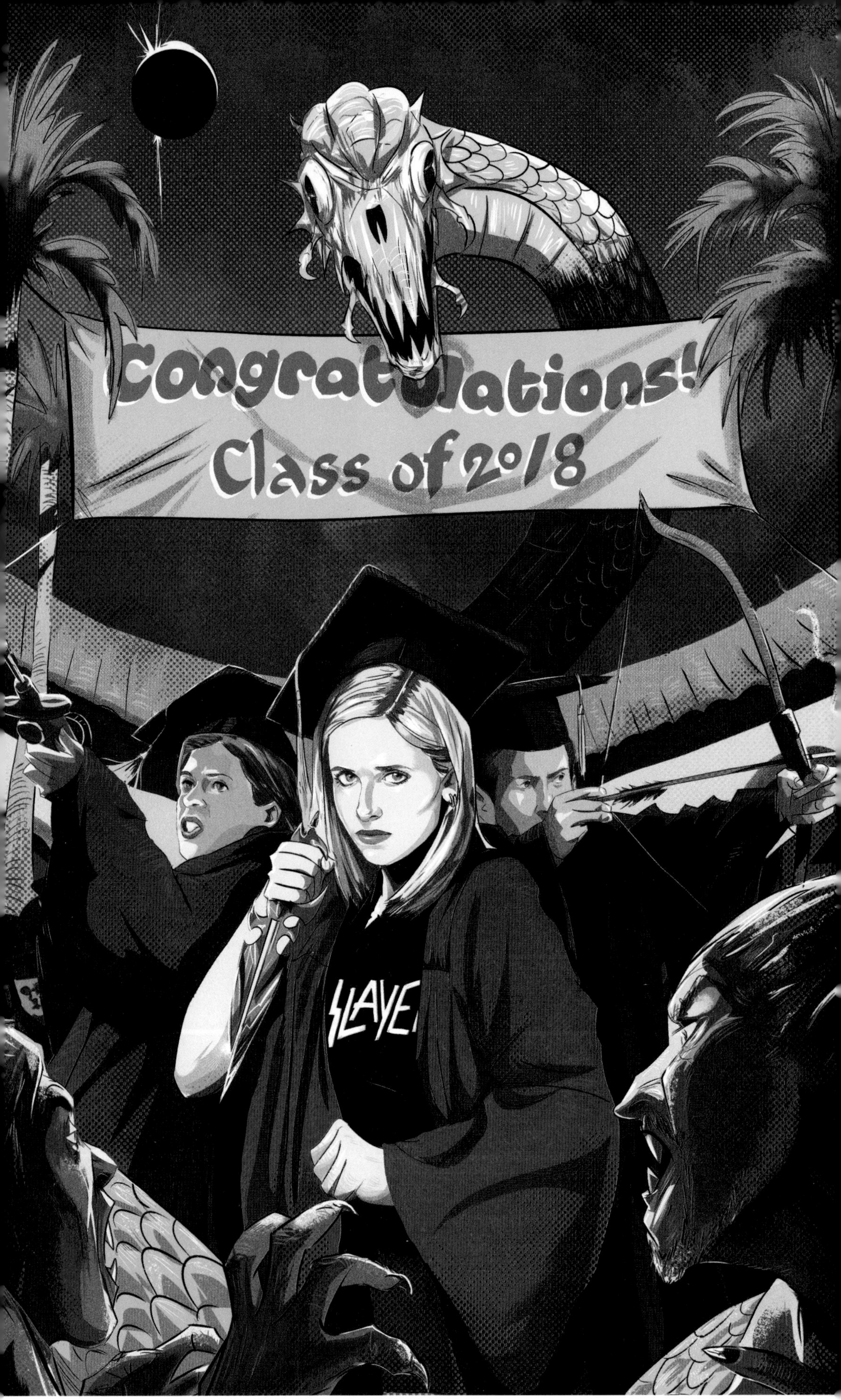
Congratulations!
Class of 2018
SLAYER

Issue Two Episode Variant by **Ryan Inzana**

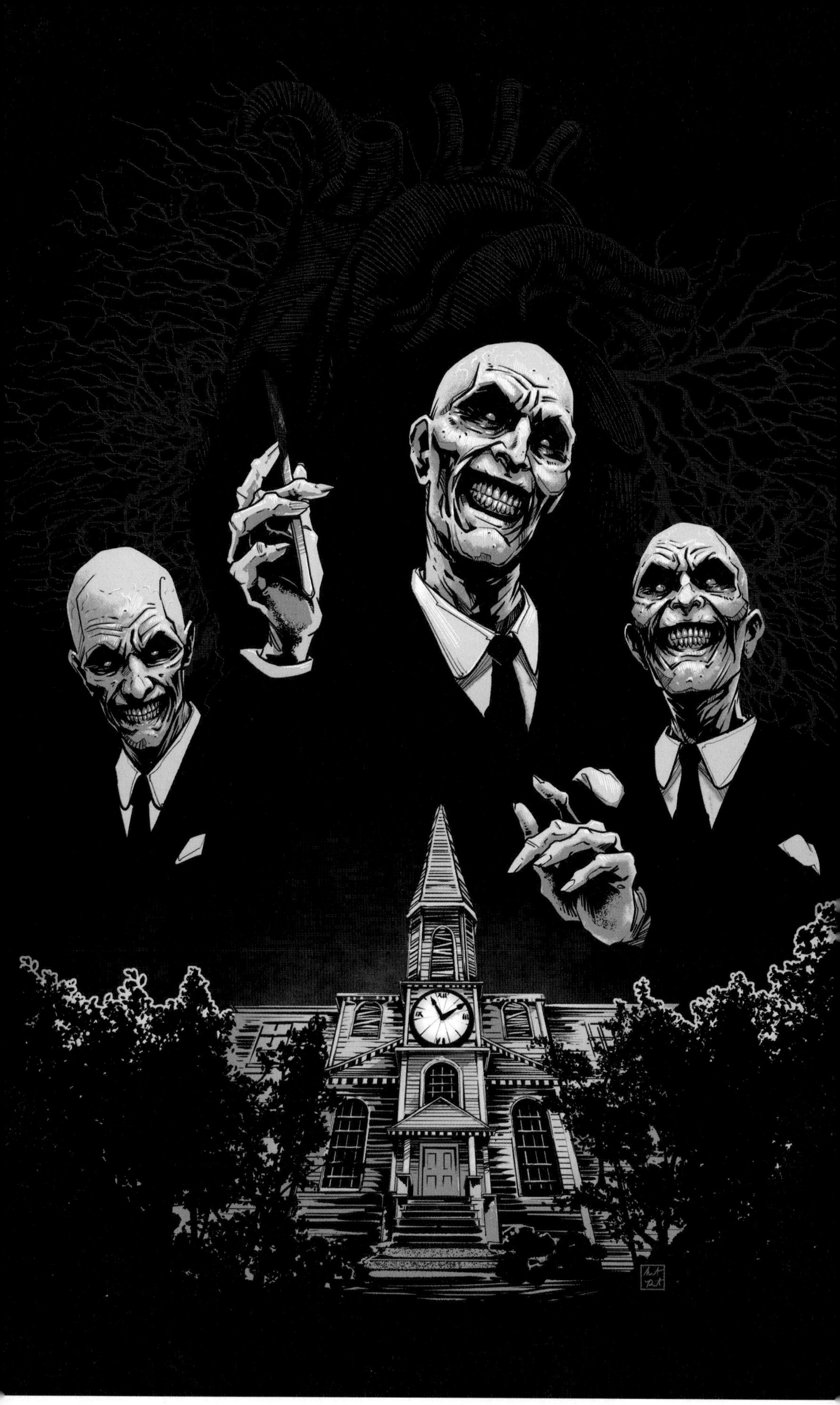

Issue Three Episode Variant by **Scott Buoncristiano**

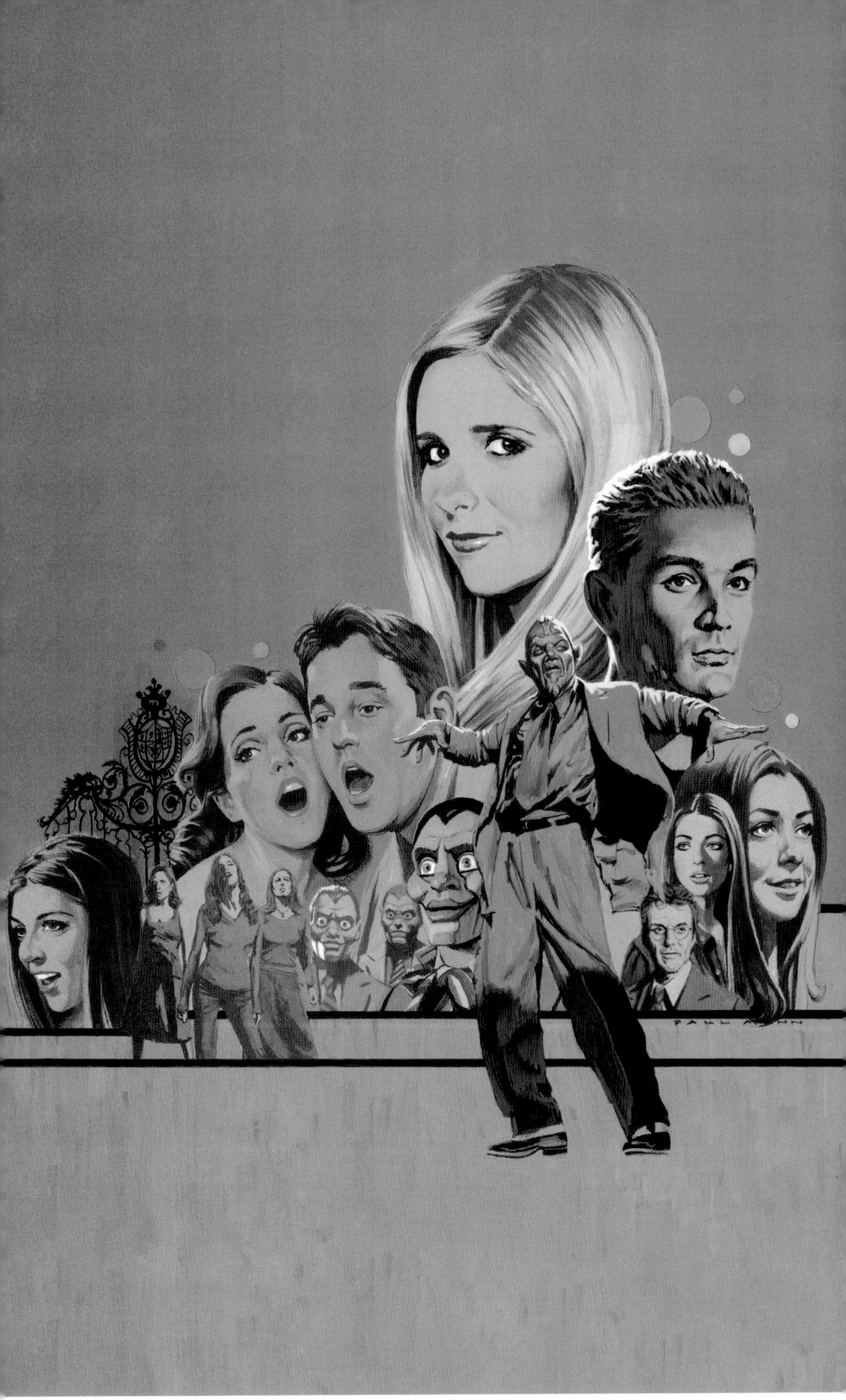
PAUL MANN

Issue Four Episode Variant by **Paul Mann**

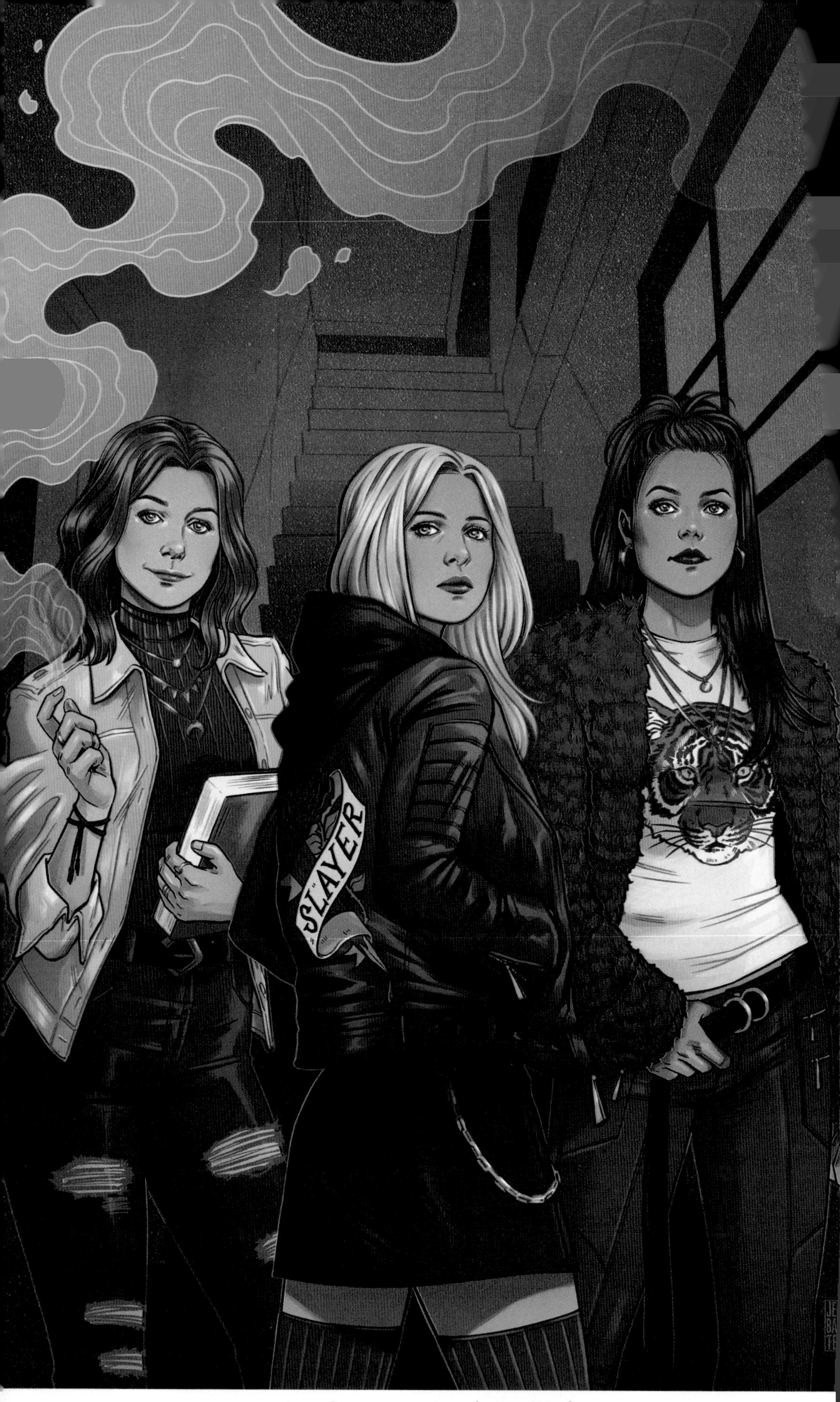
SLAYER
Issue One Incentive Cover by **Jen Bartel**

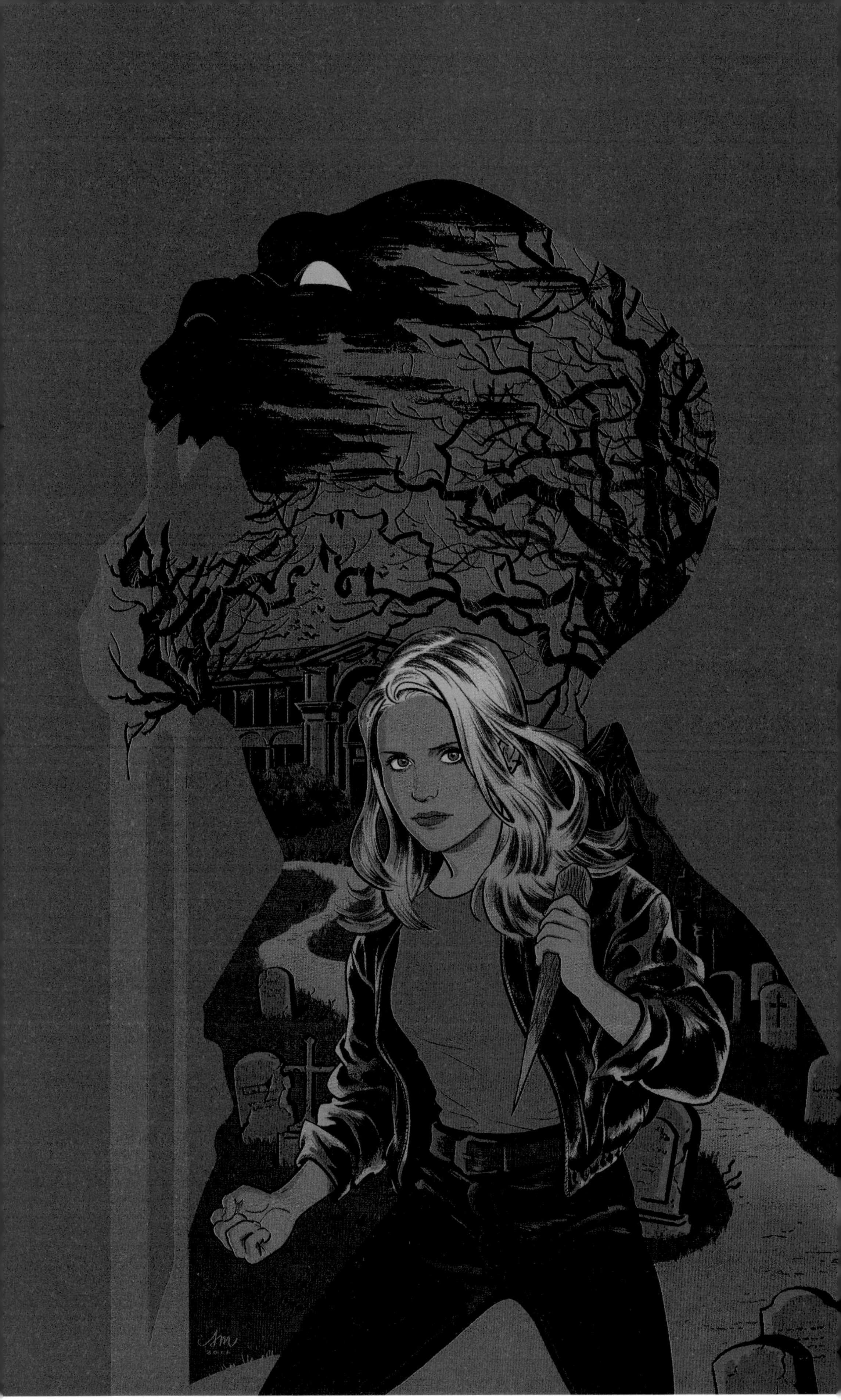

Issue Two Incentive Cover by **Audrey Mok**

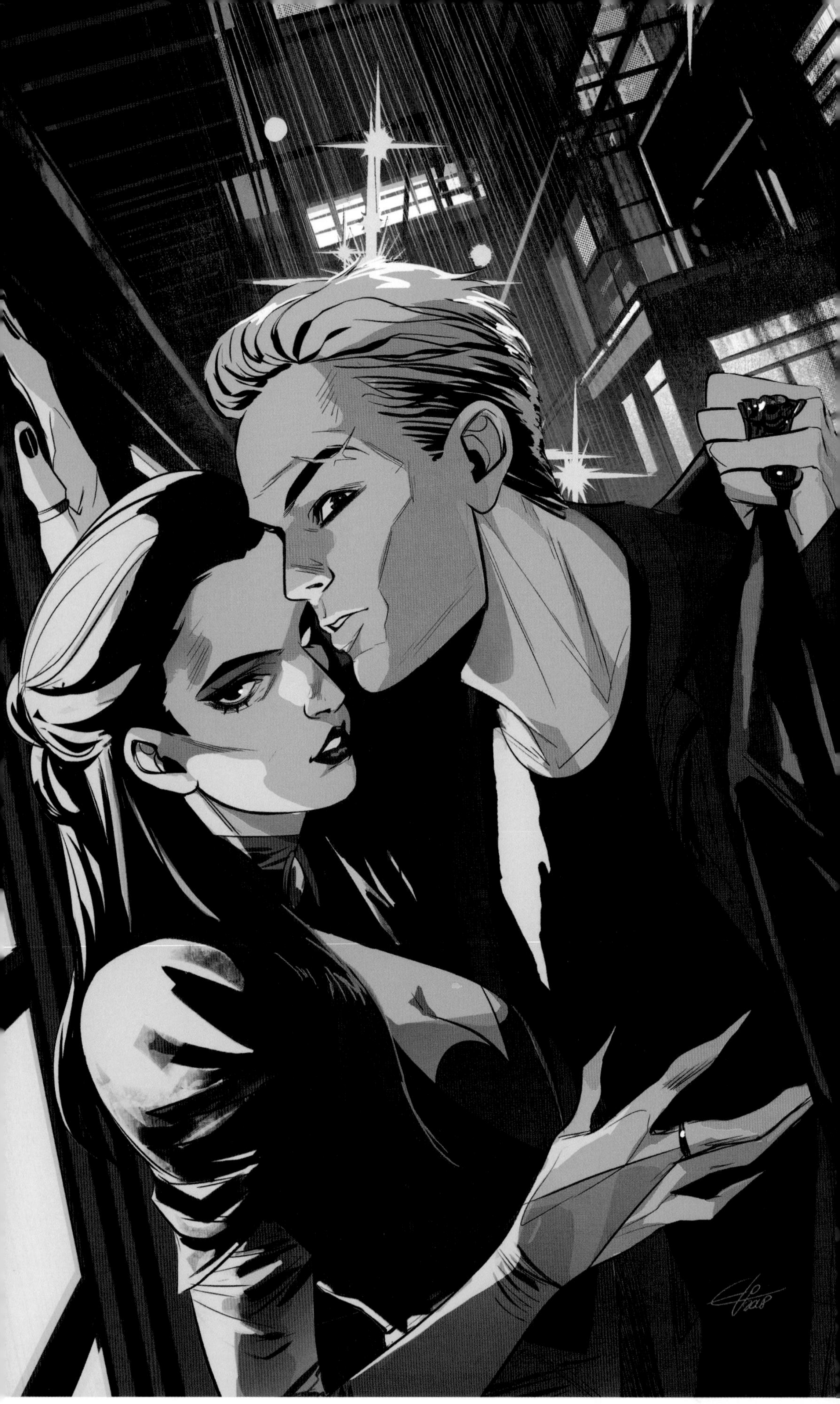

Issue Three Incentive Cover by **Eleonora Carlini** with colors by **Walter Baiamonte**

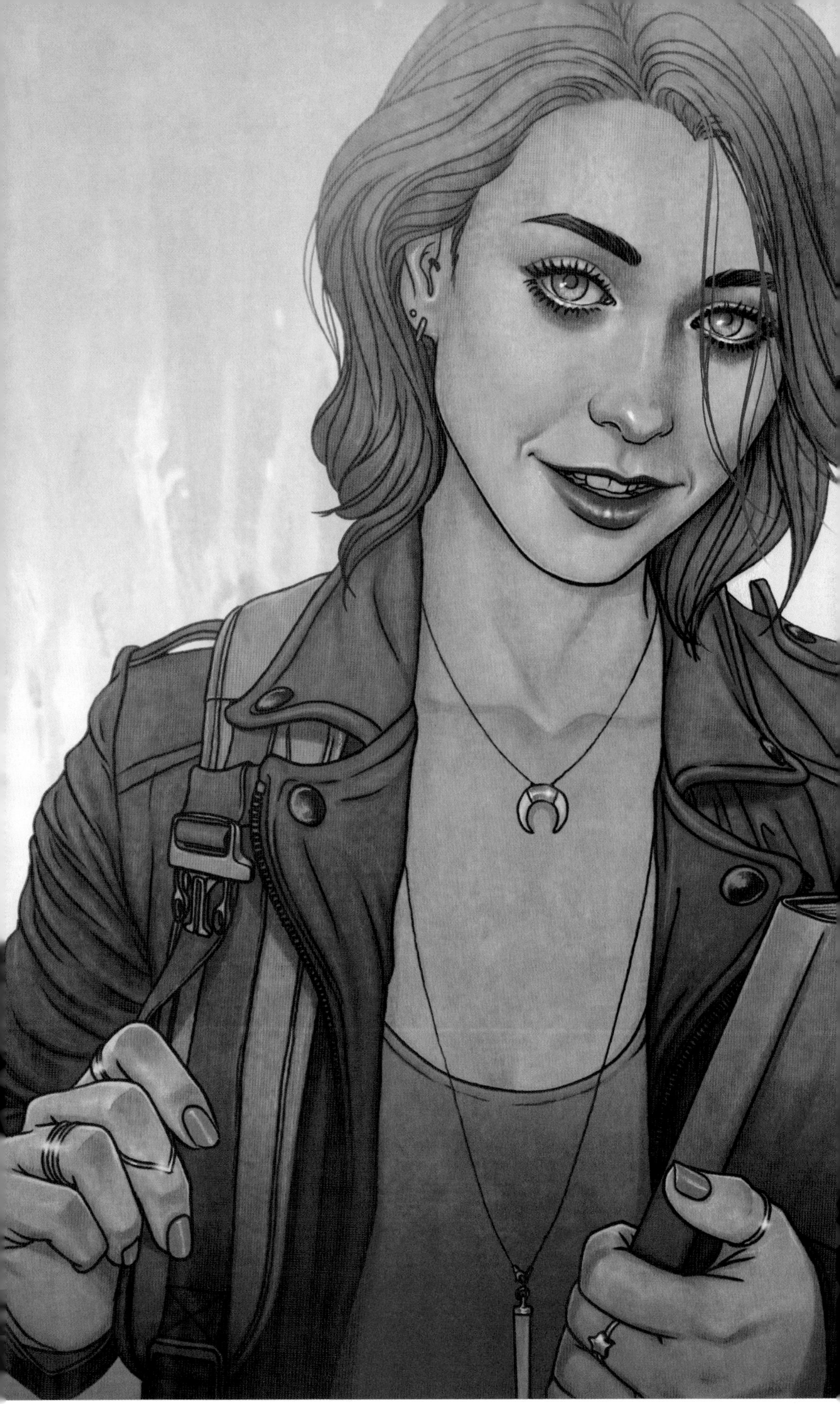

Issue Four Incentive Cover by **Jenny Frison**

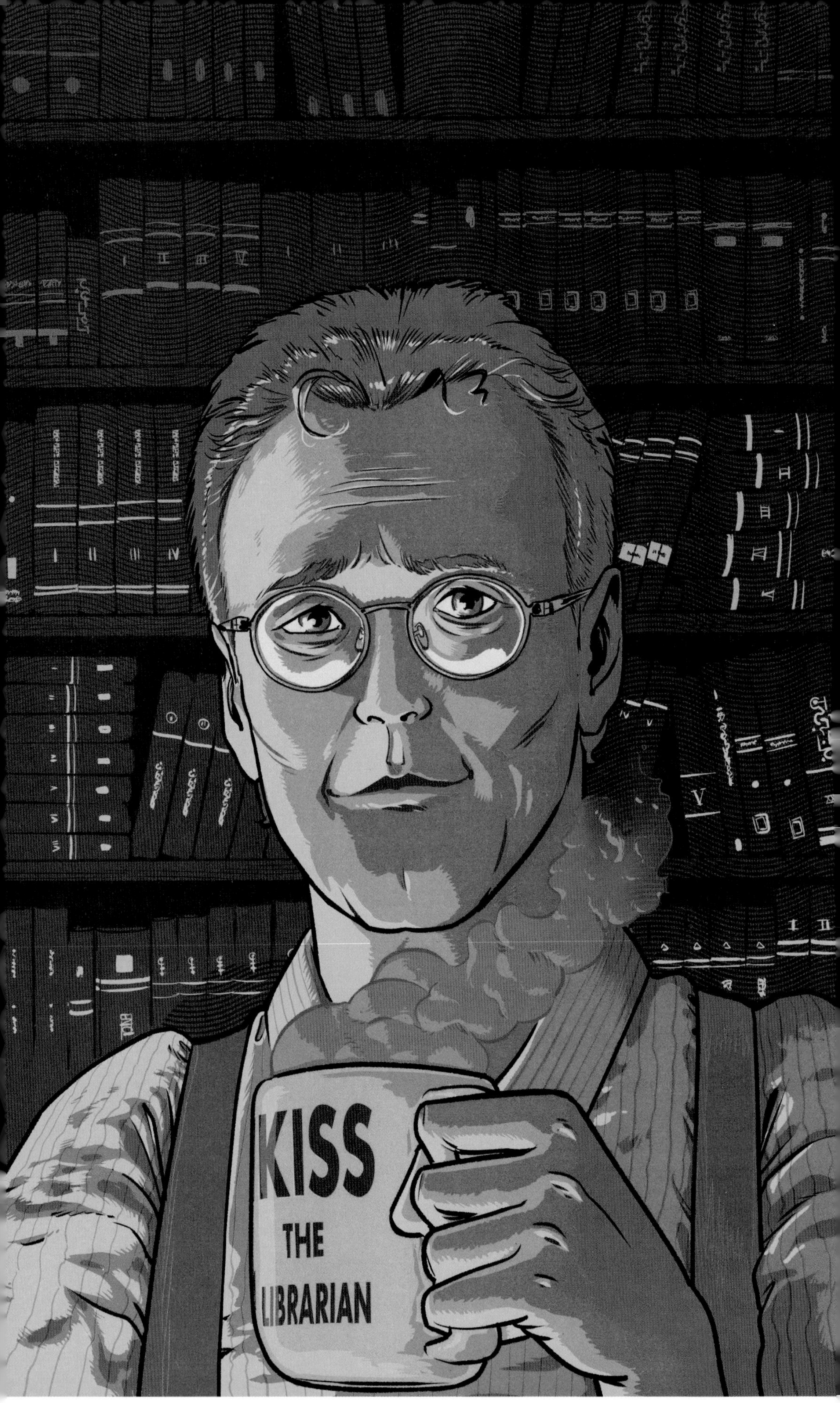
KISS
THE
LIBRARIAN

Issue One ALA 2019 Midwinter Variant by **George Schall**

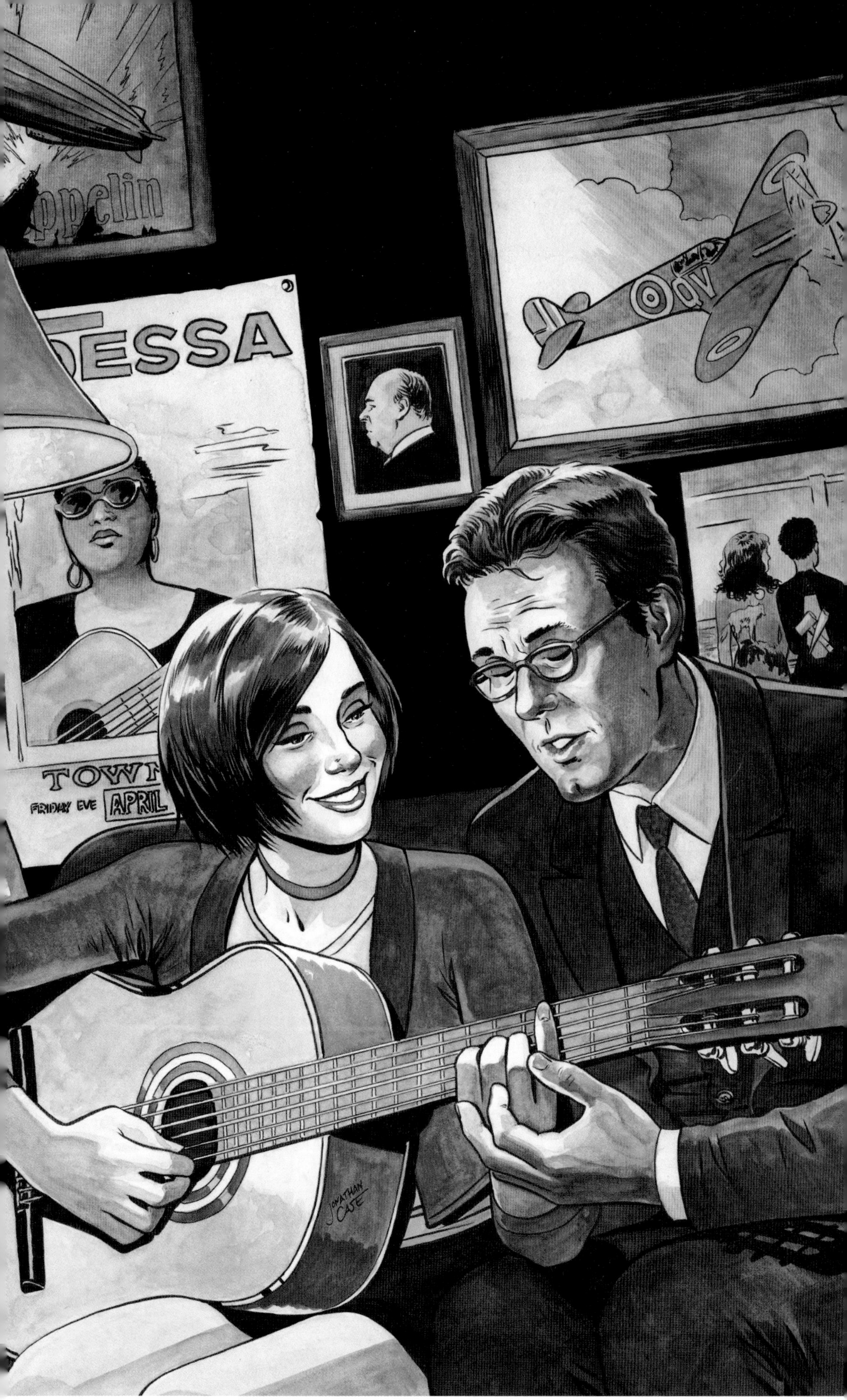
FRIDAY EVE
APRIL
JONATHAN CASE

Issue One ComicsPro 2019 Variant by **Jonathan Case**

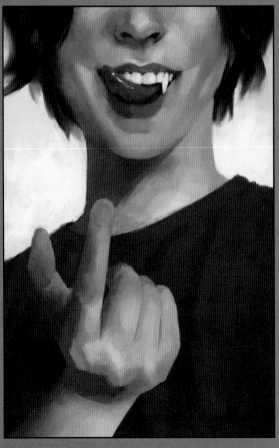

Issue One Choose Your Side Variants by **Miguel Mercado**

Issue One Rare Willow Choose Your Side Variants by **Kaiti Infante**

Issue Two Choose Your Side Variants by **Miguel Mercado**

Issue Three Choose Your Side Variants by **Kaiti Infante**

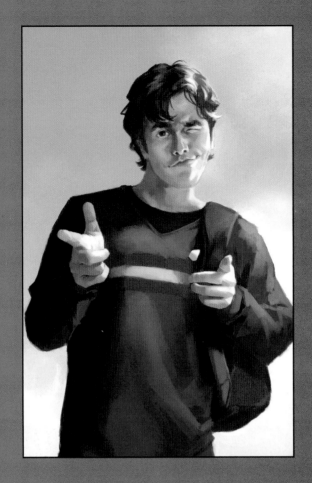

Issue Four Choose Your Side Variants by **Miguel Mercado**

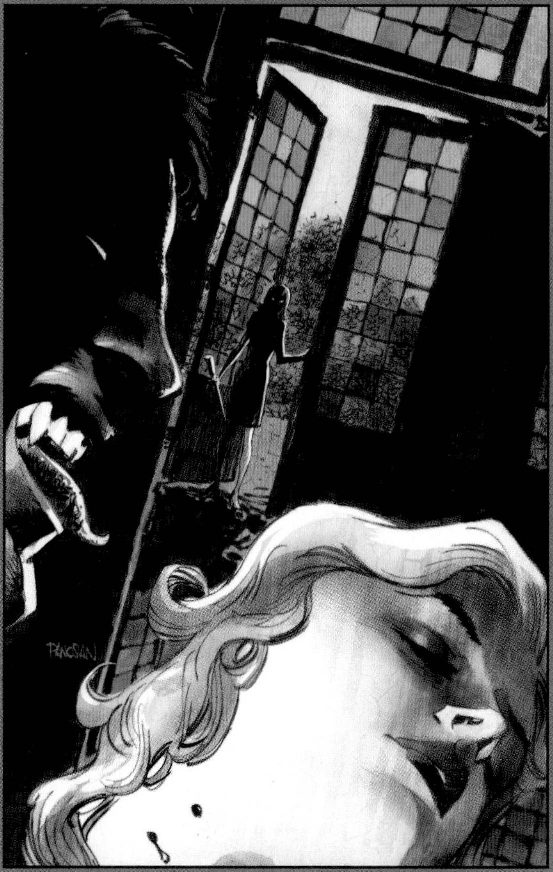
PANOSIAN

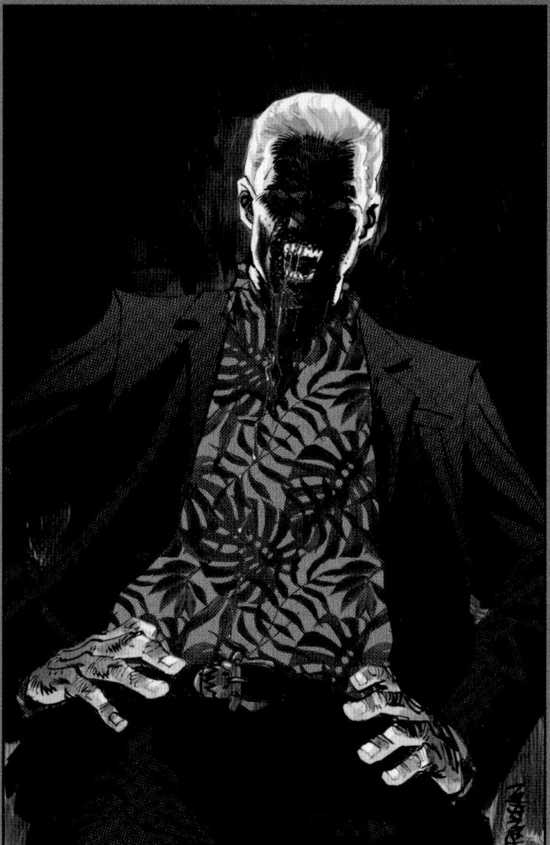
PANOSIAN

Issue One Ultra Rare Intermix Variants by **Dan Panosian**

DISCOVER
VISIONARY CREATORS

THE WOODS
JAMES TYNION IV • MICHAEL DIALYNAS
VOL. 1
THE ARROW

"The Spire is fantastic! My kind of genre free-for-all."
—BRIAN K. VAUGHAN (Saga)
THE SPIRE
SIMON SPURRIER
JEFF STOKELY
ANDRÉ MAY

MARK WAID • PETER KRAUSE
IRREDEEMABLE
AFTERWORD BY GRANT MORRISON

MARK WAID • JEAN DIAZ
INCORRUPTIBLE

MICHAEL ALAN NELSON
DAN MORA
GABRIEL CASSATA
HEXED
THE HARLOT & THE THIEF VOLUME ONE

ABNETT & CULBARD
WILD'S END
FIRST LIGHT
"IT'S REALLY GREAT!"
JEFF LEMIRE

BOOM! STUDIOS

AVAILABLE AT YOUR LOCAL COMICS SHOP AND BOOKSTORE

To find a comics shop in your area, visit www.comicshoplocator.com

WWW.**BOOM-STUDIOS**.COM

James Tynion IV

The Woods

Volume 1
ISBN: 978-1-60886-454-6 | $9.99 US
Volume 2
ISBN: 978-1-60886-495-9 | $14.99 US
Volume 3
ISBN: 978-1-60886-773-8 | $14.99 US

The Backstagers

Volume 1
ISBN: 978-1-60886-993-0 | $14.99 US

Simon Spurrier

Six-Gun Gorilla

ISBN: 978-1-60886-390-7 | $19.99 US

The Spire

ISBN: 978-1-60886-913-8 | $29.99 US

Weavers

ISBN: 978-1-60886-963-3 | $19.99 US

Mark Waid

Irredeemable

Volume 1
ISBN: 978-1-93450-690-5 | $16.99 US
Volume 2
ISBN: 978-1-60886-000-5 | $16.99 US

Incorruptible

Volume 1
ISBN: 978-1-60886-015-9 | $16.99 US
Volume 2
ISBN: 978-1-60886-028-9 | $16.99 US

Michael Alan Nelson

Hexed The Harlot & The Thief

Volume 1
ISBN: 978-1-60886-718-9 | $14.99 US
Volume 2
ISBN: 978-1-60886-816-2 | $14.99 US

Day Men

Volume 1
ISBN: 978-1-60886-393-8 | $9.99 US
Volume 2
ISBN: 978-1-60886-852-0 | $9.99 US

Dan Abnett

Wild's End

Volume 1: First Light
ISBN: 978-1-60886-735-6 | $19.99 US
Volume 2: The Enemy Within
ISBN: 978-1-60886-877-3 | $19.99 US

Hypernaturals

Volume 1
ISBN: 978-1-60886-298-6 | $16.99 US
Volume 2
ISBN: 978-1-60886-319-8 | $19.99 US

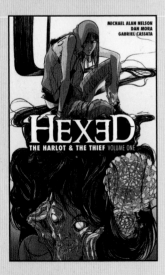

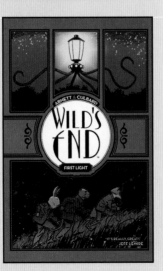